Katrin Antweiler

Memorialising the Holocaust in Human Rights Museums

Media and Cultural Memory/ Medien und kulturelle Erinnerung

Edited by
Astrid Erll · Ansgar Nünning

Volume 37

Katrin Antweiler

Memorialising the Holocaust in Human Rights Museums

DE GRUYTER

Die Publikation wurde gefördert durch die Stiftung Zeitlehren.

ISBN 978-3-11-162711-3
e-ISBN (PDF) 978-3-11-078804-4
e-ISBN (EPUB) 978-3-11-078821-1
ISSN 1613-8961

Library of Congress Control Number: 2022946810

Bibliographic information published by the Deutsche Nationalbibliothek
The Deutsche Nationalbibliothek lists this publication in the Deutsche Nationalbibliografie; detailed bibliographic data are available on the internet at http://dnb.dnb.de.

This volume is text- and page-identical with the hardback published in 2023.
Cover image: Canadian Museum for Human Rights, CMHR Ramps (Ramps_R4_6896_20191101_raw.jpg). Photo: Aaron Cohen/CMHR-MCDP

www.degruyter.com

Endorsement

Katrin Antweiler's book offers its readers a new set of concepts and empirical studies that deepen and challenge the established understandings about politics of Holocaust remembrance. Braiding together questions of public narrativization and historical emplotment of the Holocaust, the international human rights project and the imperative of contemporary museums to educate and raise awareness, *Memorialising the Holocaust in Human Rights Museums* shows with admirable deftness that museums, no less than prisons, clinics, or laboratories, are sites of discursive operations of power, discipline, and docile embodiment. While Antweiler skilfully navigates the empirical field of debates, exhibitions, installations, artefacts, and ideas found in three museums of Holocaust remembrance in Germany, Canada, and South Africa, she also needs to be credited with paying careful attention to *what is not seen*—to discursive inconsistencies and omissions she encountered during her fieldwork, to mnemonic myopias and exclusions, to tacit interests and agendas, as well as to power relations and structures of domination that remain hidden from view. In effect, the book masterfully critiques the presumed reparative effects of contemporary curatorial practices and acts of 'putting memory on display'—acts that Antweiler aptly dubs 'exhibitionary atonement'—and thus stipulates an important reflection about the political frameworks of visibility in relation to the broader narratives of redress for historical wrongdoing.

By meticulously demonstrating its central premise—that the way we remember the painful and difficult past is inseparable from the emergence of truth regimes, dominant norms, and citizen-subjects—the book casts into stark relief the key problem of global governmentality and global citizenship: that the notion of shared humanity and of the human as a universal rights holder is a politically contested and ethically suspect category. Drawing expertly on a wide spectrum of scholarly texts from memory and museum studies, governmentality theory, human rights museology, post-colonial debates, and critiques of neo-liberalism, *Memorialising the Holocaust in Human Rights Museums* presents the political and ethical implications of the imbrication of human rights with mnemonic discourses, museum displays, and educational programs with clarity, eloquence, and sophistication.

If indeed the provocative thesis at the heart of the book is correct—that museums' capacity to disseminate knowledge and to produce memory is inseparable from the social processes of subjectification—how do we respond to these interpellations into position of moral innocence, dutiful and compassionate citizenship, and 'norm entrepreneurship'? Equally critical of narratives of prog-

https://doi.org/10.1515/9783110788044-001

ress and tolerance, *Memorialising the Holocaust in Human Rights Museums* offers no easy answers; it does, however, outline for the reader a hypothetical project of a museum that is to come, and which the author intriguingly references as 'the Museum of Doubt'. She thus explores the potential of memory to fuel resistance, counter-action, and civic disobedience, and the museum as a space where one can, potentially, become receptive to what is confronting, uncomfortable, perhaps even unbearable, in history.

This book is a *tour de force* critique of the ways in which in today's world memory has been institutionalized, instrumentalized, and optimized to neo-liberal effects. Antweiler clearly demonstrates that memory has emerged as a key technique of power and governance. Anyone in doubt about how our dominant cultural patterns of remembrance and commemoration produce political rationalities, shape norms of conduct, and influence cultural policy, should reach for this brilliant and masterful text.

Acknowledgments

Four years after I started working on my PhD project, I am now looking at the result – my first book – something that, even though it was written by me, would have never been possible without the help of many people.

Firstly, I would like to say thank you to Professor Ansgar Nünning and Professor André Keet for providing guidance and feedback throughout this project and for their genuine encouragement and enthusiasm for my work. My thanks also go to the entire team at the International Graduate Centre for the Study of Culture in Giessen for providing generous financial assistance as well as many non-material opportunities to be a part of an academic community. I was lucky to be able to pursue my studies within such a supportive environment. The same applies to the International PhD Programme Literary and Cultural Studies, especially my colleagues at the IPP colloquium, to whom I am grateful for their stimulating questions and comments: you have been thinking with me and engaging in my project all these years, and for that I thank you. I would also like to thank the Humboldt Graduate School, the German Exchange Service (DAAD) and the Center for Holocaust Studies at the Leibniz Institute for Contemporary History in Munich for their additional support and funding.

I would also like to extend my special thanks to Professor Iris Därmann, without whom I might have never started this project in the first place and who bore with me the entire way, inviting me to her colloquium and taking the time to listen to my thoughts, even long after our supervisor-student relationship had ended. Moreover, I would like to thank the team at the Johannesburg Holocaust & Genocide Centre for hosting me twice and for being immensely kind and supportive both times. Similarly, I am grateful to the Rempel family in Winnipeg for their hospitality as well as to all the others who cannot be specifically named here but who helped me in various ways during my research trips. I would also like to express my gratitude to the other members of the Critical Thinking on Memory and Human Rights working group at the MSA, especially Magdalena Zolkos for her kindness and thoughtful advice, as well as Hanna Teichler and Professor Astrid Erll of the Frankfurt Memory Studies Platform, who engaged with my project at various stages and always provided such valuable feedback.

I am especially thankful to Thomas Foth: you inspired my academic journey in so many ways and enriched the ways in which I think about the issues raised in this project, yet we never seem to run out of topics to disagree on, for which I am even more grateful than for all the views we share. Both Thomas Foth and David Kowalski took the time to read the entire manuscript in its initial state and challenged me greatly with their ideas and questions, which was an immense help.

https://doi.org/10.1515/9783110788044-002

Thanks also to Andrea Kirchner and Maren Leifker, who were always willing to help me, even on quite a short notice, and also to David Jünger, for keeping me company throughout this project. Your interest in my study, your advice and the many moments when I knew you were thinking of me and my work helped me in myriad ways and made me feel less alone in this sometimes perplexing academic business. I would moreover like to thank Ada Whitaker for all her help editing this manuscript. You did an amazing job despite the stress I put you under. On a similar note, I would like to thank Rinus Kempf for helping me to overcome the horrors of formatting the bibliography. Thanks also go to Bernd Guth for making sure there are as few typographical errors as possible in this volume. And special thanks also go to Lydia J. White for the final language polishing.

I would also like to express my immense gratitude to Gabi and Wolfgang Mangold, who opened their home in Giessen to me and always made me feel welcome. I am in awe of the trust and support you were so willing to give me and am grateful for the evenings we spent simply watching the news together. Having you make fun of how early I go to bed often made my day. I could not have performed the strenuous commute between two cities without you – Tausend Dank. Special thanks furthermore go to my GCSC colleagues Riley Linebaugh, Eugenia Matz and Zoran Vuckovac, without whom my time in Giessen would have been less bright, filled with fewer, sometimes heated but always fruitful discussions, and certainly with less laughter.

And thank you also to all my friends and family who cannot be mentioned here due to space limitations. I am so very grateful for all the unconditional support you have given me through the years, for the many ears lent, the countless conversations over lentil soup at lunch time, and for helping me take breaks, recharge and not lose sight of other things that matter. I could not have done this without you.

Last but not least, I would like to express my deepest gratitude to Holger Wilcke. None of this would have been possible without you. You have travelled with me on this journey from day one, you have always stood by me and supported me in ways I could never have hoped for. Because you are my partner and the best imaginable father to our children, I was able to complete this book without ever having to feel guilty or worried in any way, as I knew you were with them and always there for us. Thank you.

This book is dedicated to Hedda, who has not only brought my life the utmost joy but who also gives me perspective and constantly reminds me of what is most important. It is also dedicated to Lasse, who was born only hours after I converted my dissertation, which would later become this book, into a final PDF document and who, in the most literal way, was always with me in the final months I spent finishing this project.

Contents

1 Of Memorialisation and Citizenship Ideals: Introduction to a Constellation of Contemporary Memory

Even as the events of the Holocaust recede into the past, new monuments to its memory are still being debated, commissioned and eventually inaugurated in various places in and outside of Europe. While a Holocaust memorial and learning centre is expected to open its doors in the British capital of London in 2025, the Dutch city of Amsterdam erected a new national Holocaust monument in September 2021. In the same month, the city of Frankfurt in Germany saw the dedication of a new memorial to the *Kindertransport*.[1] Another monument in memory of the victims of the 1941 Babyn Jar massacre was also erected in the Ukrainian capital of Kyiv in 2021, including a larger memorial centre yet to be opened at the site of the massacre itself (the realisation of which is uncertain at the time of writing due to the war that Russia launched against Ukraine in February 2022). More recent Holocaust memorials can be found across the Western Balkans, most of which were only commissioned in the past five to ten years, mainly in relation to EU membership prospects (Miloševic and Trošt 2021). Another area that has seen a recent upsurge in memorial sites is Canada, which inaugurated its first official National Holocaust Monument in September 2017 and, in 2021, announced the opening of a new Holocaust museum in Toronto. Not all of these sites and centres are state-sponsored. Many were initiated by local and global NGOs, sometimes in partnership with, sometimes in opposition to, government politics.

However, these concrete manifestations of Holocaust memory and their spread are only one indication of a trend that began at the dawn of the new millennium and which Daniel Levy and Natan Sznaider (2006) have described as the globalisation of Holocaust memory. Furthermore, it is related to the increased "standardisation of memory" (David 2017), evinced not only by a large number of similar-looking monuments – many of them even designed by the same artists – but also in the statements made on the occasion of their inauguration or on memorial days more generally. The speeches given by state representatives around such days frequently sound alike, even when the respective speakers are political

1 The term *Kindertransport* refers to the relocation of approximately ten thousand Jewish child refugees who fled from the Nazis. Between November 1938 and September 1939, these children were rescued from the German Reich and neighbouring countries threatened by Nazi occupation and brought to safer places, mostly to Great Britain.

https://doi.org/10.1515/9783110788044-003

opponents and have no other common ground but their repudiation of the horrendous crimes of the Holocaust. Forms of Holocaust memorialisation are thus gradually becoming a moral obligation for policies promoting human rights and peace across the globe. States, international organisations and NGOs are being urged to design and organise commemorative events as well as educational initiatives to be incorporated into national curricula, memorial museums and monuments. Global Holocaust education is seen as an important pedagogical tool for shaping future generations into "global citizens"[2] interested and invested in human rights issues and ready to support both developmental and humanitarian causes. (The extent to which such activism is welcome is, however, another issue) In a similar vein, a new category of museums is spreading across the globe: human rights museums (Carter and Orange 2012). These museums are often a combination of memorial museums and "idea museums" that focus on past wrongdoings – particularly often the Holocaust – and simultaneously on disseminating societal ideals such as tolerance and equality (Brown 2006; Carter 2017). In this specific constellation, according to one of the core claims that I will investigate in this book, the memory of the Holocaust serves as a template for how *not* to behave and thus goes beyond commemorating or acknowledging certain events, crimes or individuals.

For this reason, at the heart of my case-study-based research is a comparative analysis of representations of the Holocaust in human rights museums. My analyses seek to understand how, in this specific setting, looking at the past simultaneously gestures towards the future by positing historical literacy as something for every citizen-subject to aspire to attain and, furthermore, as the means necessary to create a more just world. It is due to the ability of Holocaust memory in its conflation with human rights discourse to delineate an ideal of citizenship that I suggest that certain forms of memory have become a means of government (in the Foucauldian sense).[3] That is to say: in certain constellations, public memory (indirectly) shapes citizens' conduct and thereby influences the ways in which they engage in society. The key aim of this book is to investigate this particular function of Holocaust memory while taking an innovative approach to memory studies that adds to a broader understanding of our times and political conditions.

In this context, my starting premise is that exhibitions and educational programmes about the Holocaust are increasingly being designed to foster the core

---

2 A detailed account of the concept and its relation to Holocaust memory will be provided in chapter 4 as well as chapter 8 of this book.

3 I use the term "government" in the Foucauldian sense. I will elaborate on the underlying analytical concept of governmentality in the first section of chapter 2.

values of liberal democracy and aim to create a sense of widely shared responsibility for society and for humanity at large. I will argue that the "lessons for humanity" to be drawn from the Holocaust are integral to the United Nations' endeavours to further global citizenship education. This is because, in contemporary democratic discourse, human beings are not only conceived of as the capital required to organise lives according to market rationale but also as active citizens who are empowered to claim their democratic rights just as much as they are expected to behave responsibly and in line with the laws and values of their societies (Cruikshank 1999; Brown 2015). In the broadest sense, this means that each and every one of us is in charge of harnessing and protecting liberal democracy's core values and achievements, which are generally associated with peace, tolerance and, above all, human rights. By turning to the Holocaust, every citizen-subject is at once reminded of the dangers of undemocratic behaviour and consequently called upon to stay alert and to protect, if necessary, the democratic order. At the crossroads of human rights education and representations of Holocaust history, we therefore find a synergetic interplay between the two fields that is producing not only a new corpus of knowledge about the past and its impact on the present and future but also ideals for democratic conduct. This is striking and invites further analysis when scrutinised from a perspective that is critical of today's neoliberal forms of government and its subjects. If we understand neoliberalism as a modality of governing concerned with shaping subjects to be individualised enterprises with an immense responsibility for the well-being of society, we need to pay further attention to the normative concept of citizenship mentioned above and how it is underscored by Holocaust memory. Thus, the main goal of the project outlined here is to shed light on the ability of Holocaust memory to shape, guide and thus govern modern subjects – an ability that, as I hope to demonstrate, has taken on global dimensions.

Even though the trend described has been growing since the beginning of the 2000s, efforts to re-establish peace across Europe gave way to a notion of "sharing history" as a means of harmonising the war-torn continent as early as in the immediate aftermath of the end of the Second World War (Judt 2006).[4] Attempts to generate shared memory subsequently shaped the idea that memories of the past, even – or especially – very painful ones like those of the Holocaust, have a bridging ability if they are understood as "shared" (Bevernage 2018, 73). This assumption eventually gave rise to the imperative of global memory, which operates on the level of recommendations rather than laws and which requires nation states and individuals alike to acknowledge the importance of sincerely facing

4 A more nuanced account of the evolution mentioned here can be found in chapter 3.

difficult pasts in order to "heal" (David 2020). Moreover, the "globalisation" and thus transformation of Holocaust memory into a universal warning sign has simultaneously fused with "the contemporary salience of human rights" (Moyn 2014, 87). The entanglement between Holocaust memory and the global human rights project[5] has resulted in the ongoing interdependence of these two discourses, meaning that the universalised memory of the Holocaust gives legitimacy to human rights politics, while the human rights issues of today are assigning immense, direct importance to Holocaust memory because of the lessons to be learned from it. Therefore, global, public Holocaust memory has come to rely on human rights discourse just as the human rights discourse in turn needs popular Holocaust memory in order to flourish. In its interconnectedness, this fused discourse aims to prevent future atrocities and bring closure to the past in order to achieve social harmony via shared narratives of the past that will eventually stimulate greater respect for human rights (Miloševic and Trošt 2021). In the following, I will refer to the fusion of these two discourses as the "Holocaust-human rights nexus".[6] As a result of this nexus, the Holocaust is frequently consulted as a case study of evil that vividly demonstrates the dangers of exclusivist thinking, the loss of citizenship and, ultimately, the expulsion of humans from the human collective – what is supposed to be humanity. What the Nazis and their collaborators did to the people whom they considered to be less than human is well known and has become a point of reference for the worst kinds of human rights abuses.

However, the risk and reality of not being respected as a human being and thus of being targeted by various forms of discrimination and physical violence are not something exclusively historical at which we look back in horror. It is the truth and lived experience for many people even today, because we live in a world that promises equal rights to all, although it is simultaneously being shaped by a political rationale that is based on inequality and violence (Mbembe 2017a). In this sense, the central paradox up for discussion here is that the seemingly aspirational version of democracy, for which many examples of global Hol-

5 By "the human rights project" I mean the conglomerate of various policies, programmes, institutions and actors fostering universal human rights, whether in parliament, within the United Nations or as an NGO. Moreover, I view all sorts of educational efforts cherishing the values of liberal democracy, from programmes in local schools to UNESCO's Global Citizenship Education, as part of this global project to which I will turn in more detail in chapters 4–8. My presuppositions about the political nature of human rights will be spelled out even earlier, in the second part of chapter 3.

6 This core presupposition will be played out in chapter 3.

ocaust memory education advocate,[7] is rooted in non-emancipatory practices, even though it formulates freedom and equality as its central tenets. What is more, references to or actively produced memories of the past help to set, and at the same time limit, political imagination and concepts of society. Therefore, my research is concerned not only with the lessons that Holocaust memory teaches at a superficial level – such as its inherent warnings about the dangers of hatred – but also with the less tangible impact of global memory politics on imaginaries of the present and the future. In this regard, I seek to inquire into whether and how, in correlation with human rights discourse, Holocaust memory might have become productive of the paradox described above. I suspect it has, because it promises to caution against the deadly consequences of hatred and prejudice while at the same time helping to maintain a world order that is premised on hierarchy and injustice, as it continuously suggests that liberal democracy is the best we can and should hope for.

Yet, it is not only the history and memory of the Holocaust that is woven into the fabric of the human rights project. More generally, as Joan W. Scott argues, we can see how "[a]lmost every day someone invokes the idea that history is the final arbiter of right and wrong, that if we can line up on 'the right side of history', our actions will achieve their ultimate legitimacy and a better future will be secured for all" (2020, 1). It is, of course, far from easy to agree on where the "right side of history" might be located and how we might position ourselves on it, let alone what a "better future" might look like on the societal level. This "right side of history" is often the subject of heated disputes, as vividly demonstrated by current anti-colonial movements and their demands for the decolonisation of cities and their infrastructure, as well as, for example, curricula and museums. But in the realm of the human rights project and its practices of memorialisation, there seems to be a consensus that condemning the Holocaust and relating this condemnation to human rights activism does indeed position us on the desired "right side of history".[8] This frequent linkage of the wish to be on the

7 I came up with the term "memory education" in an attempt to grasp the interdependence of public memory and education. More on this can be found in chapter 4.

8 I am, of course, aware of contestations of this consensus voiced foremost by members of the many old and new right-wing movements that are on the rise around the world. Nevertheless, even members of the German AfD party visit Holocaust memorial sites and demand to be allowed to lay flowers at memorial ceremonies – for whatever dubious reasons (Antweiler 2018). That is to say, despite ongoing disputes surrounding the consensus, there is a widely agreed upon and institutionalised public opinion in favour of Holocaust memory, as memory laws such as the prohibition of Holocaust denial, for example, show (Belavusau and Gliszczyńska-Grabias 2017).

"right side" with the turn to Holocaust memory is plain to see in the ever-increasing numbers of monuments and exhibitions dedicated to the history of the Holocaust noted above as well as the growth in visitor numbers at Holocaust-related memorial sites (in pre-pandemic times). Interestingly enough, it is tourists in particular who come to visit these memorial sites, often as a part of a new "dark tourism" trend (Bajohr et al. 2020; Martini and Buda 2020). In the early 1990s, Holocaust survivor and literary scholar Ruth Klüger made a related observation, which she polemically described as follows:

> If you are in the least interested in German literature, you'll want to travel to Weimar, Goethe's town, and once you are there, you feel obliged to trudge up the steep hill of nearby Buchenwald in a show of an awe and consternation. The camps are part of a worldwide museum culture of the Shoah, nowhere more evident than in Germany, where every sensitive citizen, not to mention every politician who wants to display his ethical credentials, feels the need to [...] have his picture taken. (Klüger 2001, 61)

Whereas the "worldwide museum culture" of the 1990s usually involved taking pictures in front of memorials to prove one's "ethical credentials", today's historical conscience is morally charged with an even greater duty than individual sensitivity: the responsibility to line up on "the right side of history" in the name of human rights. So, the trend observed by Klüger has intensified, and her comment about the "sensitive citizen" offers a premonition of the new ideal global citizen, whom I propose calling *the historically aware human rights activist*. In this vein, citizenship, or "the citizen" in its current formation, can be understood as follows:

> The citizen is an effect and an instrument of political power rather than simply a participant in politics. [...] [D]emocratic citizenship is less a solution to political problems than a strategy of government. [...] This is a manner of governing that relies not on institutions, organized violence or state power but on securing the voluntary compliance of citizens. (Cruikshank 1999, 5)

In accordance with this definition, I am postulating one aspect of citizenship that will be crucial throughout the analysis pursued in this book: that the formulation of citizenship and hence the construction of the citizen-subject is a highly political endeavour. Scrutinising normative concepts of citizenship can therefore provide important insights into current political rationale as well as its techniques of government – and I consider memory to be one of these techniques.

* * *

There is a rich body of literature concerned with the trend towards the universalisation of Holocaust memory as well as with the proliferation of the use of historical narratives within the human rights paradigm.[9] Many recent studies have focused on the problem of globalised Holocaust memory, drawing on concepts of collective and cultural memory.[10] From this starting point, investigations into recent trends in Holocaust memory culture and politics soon identified a correlation between the globalisation of the Holocaust and human rights, and, since the early 2000s, scholars from disciplines as diverse as cultural studies, history, sociology, literary studies and political science have sought to make sense of this increasing interlinkage of Holocaust memory and human rights. Approaches include a focus on how the memory of the Holocaust is being "Europeanised", which usually means attempts to find a unified European narrative of the Shoah, including clear-cut lessons to be learned from this history across the member states (e.g., Assmann and Novik 2007; Schmid 2008; Assmann 2012). Others go even further and look at how Holocaust memory is being "universalised" into a "prototype of evil" and thus transformed into a negative reference point across the world (e.g., Levy and Sznaider 2006, 2010; Sznaider 2008).

More generally speaking, most scholarly accounts focused on Holocaust memory since the transnational turn have concluded that there was a paradigm shift at the beginning of the twenty-first century. Aleida Assmann, for example, asserts that, "The year 2000 marks the starting point of a new era. In retrospect we may say today that with the beginning of the new millennium the Holocaust went global" (2010, 98). Assmann's chronicle of the development of Holocaust memory from something national to something transnational, or, more precisely, from something national to European to global, is in line with the findings made by other influential historians and memory scholars in the field, such as Tony Judt (2006), and Daniel Levy and Natan Sznaider, whose 2006 study on the globalisation of Holocaust memory and the emergence of "cosmopolitan memory cultures" is still instructive today. Theirs was one of the first efforts to think about Holocaust remembrance beyond Europe in a transnational context. In this as well as in their 2010 study, which they carry out against the backdrop of Ulrich Beck's theory of cosmopolitanism, Levy and Sznaider examine the ex-

---

9 The reason for keeping the literature review short at this stage is twofold: firstly, this book has been informed by different scholarly fields and debates which need to be spelled out in more detail than is possible in a literature review. Secondly, the entire third chapter of this book is consequently dedicated to the Holocaust-human rights nexus and therefore not only functions as a clarification of the most important presuppositions on which this project is based but also expands upon the literature review provided here.

10 The second chapter's sub-section "Memory and museum studies" is dedicated to the key concepts from the field of memory studies and will explain the different approaches in more depth.

tent to which collective Holocaust memory is being increasingly globalised, with a "cosmopolitan memory" emerging as a result. The development they attempt to grasp is mainly related to their observation that "memories of the Holocaust [...] have the potential to become the cultural foundation for global human rights politics" (Levy and Sznaider 2006, 4). They expand upon the theorisation of this trend in ten essays in their later book, *Human Rights and Memory* (2010), in which they use memory to open up broader perspectives on this entanglement by approaching constellations of human rights, looking at specific themes such as reconciliation and the function of human rights after 9/11.

While the importance of Holocaust memory for the rise of the international human rights project is increasingly being emphasised (Moyn 2014; Huyssen 2015), in the US, debates about the "Americanisation" of the Holocaust have been analogous to the ones on Europeanisation, attesting to an increase in attempts to develop shared narratives of the past and make it relatable for a US public. In 2011, Alvin Rosenfeld saw "the end of the Holocaust" in such developments, by which he meant that the universalisation of the Holocaust in memory culture and politics would eventually lead to a "diminution" (9) of its meaning. In the years that followed, more work was published on this supposed threat to the significance of Holocaust memory and often centred on issues of particular as opposed to universal perspectives on the Holocaust's complex history (Sznaider 2008; Uhl 2009; Schoder 2012). Since these seminal publications, a multitude of journal articles and book chapters have been devoted to the relationship between Holocaust memory and human rights, but few researchers have taken the genealogy of this interplay into consideration, and even fewer have attended to its wider political implications. One notable study is, for example, Bünyamin Werker's 2016 monograph, *Gedenkstättenpädagogik im Zeitalter der Globalisierung*, which sets human rights education and policy in relation to pedagogical work at Holocaust memorial sites. However, because it was produced in the field of education sciences, this volume primarily examines ongoing pedagogical programmes. Similarly, the work of sociologist Lea David (2017; 2018; 2020) also researches the relationship between memory and human rights regimes. David focuses in particular on memory politics in the former Yugoslavia and Israel, arguing against the idea that standardised forms of engaging with the past can mend divided societies or groups. A publication by Chiara De Cesari and Ann Rigney (2014) aims to create a synthesis of the two topics as well but is also largely limited to individual examples, instead of providing more thorough analysis.

One other strand of research into Holocaust memory and both the reasons for and effects of its universalisation is concentrated around issues of "competitive memory" as opposed to "multidirectional memory" (Rothberg 2009). Here, the question is whether different memories of different genocides or mass atrocities are in conflict because they repress each other or if, as Michael Rothberg posits, they eventually produce *more* memory. In emphasising the dialogical development of public memory, Rothberg, looking at the US context, argues against the widespread assumption that, if it becomes very prominent in a society, Holocaust memory might take space away from or even block the memories of other experiences of mass violence, first and foremost systemic racism and slavery. Throughout his book, he foregrounds incidents of "cross-referencing" and tries to "re-narrate the history of Holocaust memory in relationship to discourses on colonialism, slavery and decolonisation" (Rothberg 2021, personal communication). Genocide scholar A. Dirk Moses (2021a) has put forward similar considerations and criticised the strong emphasis on the Holocaust's uniqueness within memory culture in general and German memory culture in particular. His article on the "German catechism" provoked a number of responses from primarily Anglophone genocide scholars as well as in the *feuilleton* sections of leading German newspapers such as *Die Zeit*, *Süddeutsche Zeitung* and *Berliner Zeitung.*[11] By arguing in favour of relational instead of unidirectional memory, Rothberg's and Moses' assessments differ from those of Levy and Sznaider (2006), who primarily link the globalisation of Holocaust memory to developments within Western memory culture, which has ultimately been adopted as a global standard. We may therefore contend that there are two strands within the work on globalised Holocaust memory, one that is mostly concerned with analysing the ways in which the Shoah is deprived of content and meaning, while the other looks at the imperialist or "anti-liberal" (Moses 2021b) implications such universalised memory might have due to the fact that it only allows for one "right" interpretation of the Holocaust and its legacy (Goldberg 2015, Phillips Casteel 2019).

While the academic engagement with Holocaust memory outlined above is (with some exceptions of course) a phenomenon of the 1990s and even more so of the new millennium, universal human rights have been the subject of scholarly research since their institutionalisation in 1945 at the latest. However, it is only since the 2000s that they have increasingly come into focus.[12] Since then, there have been many studies of the history of human rights and their in-

11 This complex debate also moved onto social media, and many different scholars and practitioners have participated in it under the hashtag #CatechismDebate, and some seminal articles have been collected on the blog *New Fascism Syllabus*, while the heated German-speaking debate continues and has extended across various publications such as the aforementioned newspapers.

12 I will provide my attempt to grasp the increased interest in and relevance of human rights in chapter 3.

fluence on the development of international law in particular, with varying research focuses. The well-known essay "The Aporias of Human Rights" by Hannah Arendt (1955) presented an early critique of human rights and the politics involved, which was taken up and developed further by Giorgio Agamben (1995), among others. Both Arendt and later Agamben point to a paradox intrinsic to the political project of universal human rights, which relates to the political reality of those humans who are only seen as "bare life" and not as human beings who already enjoy the right to have rights (DeGooyer et al. 2017). In Arendt's text, written in the wake of the Second World War and the Holocaust, this primarily refers to stateless people, but it can easily be applied to twenty-first-century political realities, for example, those of refugees.[13]

In her attempt to grasp human rights in their historical evolution, Lynn Hunt (2007) presented a publication on the emergence of human rights in light of the French Revolution, which was widely read. In his study, *The Ambivalence of the Good*, historian Jan Eckel (2014) addresses human rights as a policy issue in international relations since the 1940s. Other contributions to the genesis of human rights and international law have been made by José Brunner and Daniel Stahl (2016) as well as by Ruti G. Teitel (2010, 2016). Teitel's work in particular has been significant in my research for the present volume as it shows how human rights and transitional justice have together transformed into a universal morality, which she analyses against the backdrop of a globalised world, starting from the premise that transitional justice is both a legal and political concept that is being increasingly depoliticised in that it is often treated as a moral value. Following on from this, mention should be made of the research on humanitarian interventions presented by Costas Douzinas (2000, 2013) Douzinas and Gearty (2014), Stephan Hopgood (2013), and Nicola Perugini and Neve Gordon (2015), who all critique human rights policies as a novel governmental technique of the global North that claims the ability to mitigate political issues of inequality and violence (such as the situation of refugees dying in the Mediterranean Sea while attempting to reach safety in Europe) by solely addressing them as a matter of the law, before which all humans are regarded as equal despite their obvious inequalities. Didier Fassin (2012) has added to this critical scholarship with his acclaimed book *Humanitarian Reason: A Moral History of the Present*, in which he explores the meaning and political function of humanitarianism as a particular form of governmentality, one that relies on the employment of "moral sentiments in contemporary politics" (2012, 1).

13 I will discuss this issue in more detail in the second section of chapter 3, as it is key to my overall analysis.

Historian and lawyer Samuel Moyn, who specialises in the recent history of human rights (2010; 2014; 2018), has expanded on this work by adding his own interest in memory politics. He has shown how social human rights in particular have led to the depoliticisation of decolonial struggles for more human rights, thereby pointing to the overall contrived nature of shared narratives about universal human rights. Unlike other historiographies, Moyn and, like him, linguist Andreas Huyssen (2003; 2010; 2011) situate the breakthrough of human rights and their moral imperatives in the late 1970s, and Huyssen draws a direct parallel to the rise of memory in this context. Following on from their findings, both Moyn and Huyssen raise the question of what rights have to do with cultural memory and why the current narrative about the history of human rights has taken the Holocaust as its point of departure, even though it played no relevant role whatsoever in the 1940s, for example, in the context of the newly founded United Nations. Moyn in particular argues that history has been instrumentalised in this context, which distinguishes his work from that of political scientist Wendy Brown (2001; 2006), who takes up a governmentality approach. Brown (2001) studies "politics out of history" and identifies a development that she calls the moralisation of politics. This refers to a tendency that seeks to explain and resolve political issues, such as conflicts between nation states, in terms of moral parameters, rather than recognising them as outcomes of power mechanisms and (nation state) interests. Following on from these analyses, Brown has also examined tolerance as a particular dimension of contemporary governmentality (a dimension Foucault could not have foreseen when he developed the concept). Both works raise the question of the discursive entanglements between tolerance, human rights and historical politics, and are therefore highly relevant to this project.

Even though I have referred above to a number of publications that consider Holocaust memory and human rights in their interconnectedness, there has still only been limited systematic or detailed exploration of the wider political implications of this nexus to date. Samuel Moyn (2014), Andreas Huyssen (2011), and Levy and Sznaider (2006; 2010) have offered explanations, but none of them thoroughly capture how these discourses came to be fused nor the extent to which this interlinkage has been accepted. However, the impact of the Holocaust-human rights nexus on global politics needs more in-depth analysis, especially with regard to decolonial critique, and the research that I have conducted for this book is only one step in this direction. One of the key aims of this book is thus to trace and subsequently give an account of more of the components in the Holocaust-human rights nexus, with a particular focus on the conditions which brought it into being.

As outlined above, since the dawn of the new millennium, a remarkable amount of work has been produced that addresses the universalisation of Holocaust memory. Many studies have been intended as a critique of these developments and have linked them to other notable changes of the time, such as the end of the Cold War, as it is commonly called (Shubin 2015), or the rise of human rights as a global ideology.[14] However, none of these efforts seem to have grasped the full extent, be it geographical or political, of this continuing globalisation of Holocaust memory. This study intends not to close a gap or fill a void but to genuinely add to the already rich but nonetheless incomplete scholarly debate by considering the very political character of public memory that is potentiated even more by its entwinement with the human rights project.

In an interview about the remits of memory studies, Andreas Huyssen (2018) explains that the study of memory "emerged as of the 1980s/90s in reaction to the loss of twentieth-century futuristic utopias". As a result, he identifies a "privileging of the past over the future", which might lead to a fixation on past events instead of "thinking about the future today" (2018). However, during my research for this volume, I have come to the conclusion that, in certain constellations, memory might actually be more about the future than it is about the past. The main aim of this book is therefore to unravel references to the history of the Holocaust which, in their intersection with human rights, have come to function as a future politics that shapes aspirations (for ourselves as much as for others) and marks the limits of our horizons of hope. Furthermore, what distinguishes my work from the research that has already been conducted around the Holocaust-human rights nexus is my focus on how the Holocaust has been memorialised in regard to the norms of citizenship that it produces: I surmise that memorialising the Holocaust in order to safeguard a better future has become a core obligation for the democratic citizen of the twenty-first century. I am therefore asking about the ways in which this new citizenship ideal can be regarded as a means of government. Ultimately, considering the important role played by the memory of the Holocaust as a moral discourse in the context of global governmentality[15] can improve upon the widespread assessment of memory as something either "good', "used appropriately" or "morally credible", or, the opposite of that, as something that is "manipulated", "highjacked" or "utilised" in the wrong way and for the wrong reasons. That is to say: the theoretical perspective of my research project – a perspective which relates it to decolonial thinking

14 I will introduce both trends in more detail in chapter 3.

15 I will explain the particularities of global governmentality in the last section of the subchapter entitled "Studies of governmentality".

as much as to Foucault's work on governmental techniques – allows us to think of memory not as something that is primarily instrumentalised by, say, the state or lobbyists, but that is instead conditioned by certain regimes of truth and that has, as I will demonstrate, its own function in the production of political rationale. In order to be able to approach the research topic outlined here holistically, the following questions will guide me through my analysis:

1. How is the Holocaust-human rights nexus narrated by institutions of memory?
2. In what sense does this nexus impact formulations of global citizenship?
3. How can the values of citizenship that are derived from the Holocaust-human rights nexus be understood in the light of global governmentality?
4. Can Holocaust memory preserve its notion of disobedience despite its universalisation in the human rights project?

Thus, my book answers interrelated questions that look at how the Holocaust-human rights nexus materialises within museums as well as the ways in which it impacts and is impacted by the ideal of global citizenship. I will then seek to answer the question of how this nexus can be regarded as a technique of global governmentality.

The perspective that my work puts forward is one that not only challenges conventional affirmative positions about human rights as our "last utopia" (Moyn 2010) but also contests the conviction that memorialising the Holocaust and learning lessons from it will automatically elevate us to become better (because we are less prejudiced) human beings. Shirli Gilbert has recently stated that "the assumption that Holocaust education can help eradicate racism and promote tolerance is a naive one" (2019, 372). In agreement with this claim, I propose a critical reading of the Holocaust-human rights nexus that goes beyond Gilbert's analysis: that is, we do not automatically stand on "the right side of history", nor do we assume some other superior position simply because we acknowledge the horrors of the Holocaust. Instead, we risk slipping into new modes of hierarchical and exclusionist thinking if we assume that such a morally "loftier" stance makes it possible to claim that the current (neo)liberal democratic political order is the most we can (and should) hope for. This volume therefore examines the global mnemonic strategy by which the Holocaust memory and Holocaust education have been judged to be especially valuable because of the "lessons for humanity" they provide. These clear-cut lessons have little in common with the once proclaimed ability of Holocaust memory to deeply unsettle and thus transform key assumptions about our world order. Moreover, it is in this vein that my project scrutinises the global trend towards turning to the history of the Holocaust for reassurance that we are standing on the right side of history instead of reintroducing doubt into the practices of memorialisation. But the notion of doubt, of the unknown, will not just be referenced due to its scarcity but, as my last research question suggests, will also be scrutinised in terms of its continuing potential to resist some of the trends that I will identify as hegemonial.

* * *

As the title of this book suggests, I have chosen museums and, more precisely, human rights museums as sites for my investigation. In looking at these museums, I would like to probe contemporary global Holocaust memory politics by specifically focussing on the narrative that each museum conveys about the history of the Holocaust in relation to universal human rights. My research fuses the features of a conceptual volume that predominantly operates within the realm of theory with those of an empirical study. In one sense, I have proceeded as Mieke Bal suggests in *The Practice of Cultural Analysis* and made my analysis a "cohabitation of theoretical reflection and reading in which the 'object' from subject matter becomes subject, participating in the construction of theoretical views" (1999, 13). Whereas I had first planned my study to be a historical, or rather, archaeological study of the Holocaust-human rights nexus, I soon became fascinated with the contemporaneity of narratives that are rooted in (or fixated on) the past, although they are equally oriented towards the future and hence inseparable from the "now". I felt compelled to dare to do what Bal, referencing Spivak, had identified as the starting point of cultural analysis: an analysis that "involves 'saying no to what you inhabit' [...], thus impelling the analyst to reflect both on the 'no' and on the habitat; the self and the present" (1999, 12).

This book opens with a rather extensive chapter on theoretical perspectives (chapter 2), which paves the way for the specific analysis pursued here. I will not only introduce the theoretical and methodological frameworks on which I rely but will also move beyond merely describing them towards developing my own research strategy and corresponding methodology: a decolonial study of public memory from the perspective of global governmentality (chapter 2, section 4). The first subchapter presents an account of Foucauldian studies of governmentality. It is followed by another theoretical subchapter dedicated to decolonial theory, which will "brush" hegemonic knowledge production "against the grain"[16] and furthermore provide important considerations about studies

16 I am borrowing the image of "brush[ing] history against the grain" from Walter Benjamin, who closed the seventh deliberation (*These*) in his famous essay *On the Concept of History* by referring to the need to "brush history against the grain" (2002).

of global governmentality, thereby dispelling a common misunderstanding that identifies the origins of anti-colonial thought in poststructuralism (Terri-Anne and Wynne-Hughes 2020). Then, operating on the micro level, I will map out the field of memory and museum studies in relation to the theoretical insights gained in the previous two chapters. The synthesis in the last section of chapter 2 deserves special mention because it not only introduces the analytical framework for my specific investigation but more generally puts forward a novel, innovative research strategy for the field of memory studies. This will provide us with an analytical tool that will enable us to more comprehensively grasp the relationship between memory politics and the politics of citizenship as well as their impact on coloniality[17] (and vice versa). While both governmentality and decolonial approaches to aspects of world order challenge the many binaries on which conventional analyses of global politics are premised, the decolonial lens invites us to envisage the world differently, in terms of an interconnected space discursively constituted by actors who exist contemporaneously with each other. And since the "contemporary political lexicon" of democracy, human rights and tolerance reflects the naturalisation of Eurocentric imaginaries (Sharma 2019, para 4), it is imperative to challenge the formation of these popular imaginaries and their associated normative connotations. As asserted above, imaginaries of the world(s)[18] we live in are closely related to Holocaust memory at the crossroads of the human rights projects. Thus, probing the political imaginaries of democracy and human rights is key to my analysis, not least because it is concerned with programmes for global citizenship as well as a standardised set of values and mnemonic frameworks.

After having prepared the ground for my research, the chapter on theory is followed by a shorter chapter which clarifies a few important presuppositions regarding the Holocaust-human rights nexus that undergirds the present volume (chapter 3). This chapter will, in a sense, expand upon the literature review provided above and seeks to untangle Holocaust memory and the human rights project for a moment in order to better understand the historical and political conditions that produced this nexus. The brief elaborations in chapter 3 are followed by five analytical chapters (chapters 4, 5, 6, 7 and 8). Chapter 4, about

---

17 The term "coloniality" and its implications will be explained in detail in the sub-chapter "Colonial conditions and decolonial critique".

18 I prefer to use the plural of "world" primarily because I have learned from the decolonial critics whom I reference that one way in which coloniality constantly re-establishes itself is by using concepts such as "world", "modernity" and "history" in the singular. However, there are a multitude of worlds and histories on this planet that need to be acknowledged and recognised if we want to genuinely understand its workings and help to make it more equal and just.

global Holocaust education endeavours in relation to human rights museology, sets the stage for the three rather descriptive case study chapters. This section already scrutinises the role of this specific museum format and connects it to ideas of conflating Holocaust education with global citizenship education. The findings presented in chapter 4 have led me to introduce the term *memory education*, which seeks to grasp precisely this merging of (global) educational programmes with practices of memorialisation. This introduction of the players in the field of global Holocaust education as well as the assessment of the importance of their work for human rights museology and vice versa is then followed by the three case studies at the heart of this book: the Memorium Nuremberg Trials in Nuremberg, Germany, with its special emphasis on the rule of law (chapter 5); the Canadian Museum for Human Rights in Winnipeg, Canada, a museum with the goal of establishing a global human rights culture (chapter 6); and, finally, the Johannesburg Holocaust & Genocide Centre in Johannesburg, South Africa (chapter 7), which aims to safeguard democracy. Since my overall analysis is supposed to be a comparative study, I have applied an identical research design in all three cases.[19] However, the three museums are not only interesting due to their similarities but also due to their differences; each case study chapter therefore focuses on both the unique features of the museums and on the aspects that they have in common. My special focus on museums stems from the premise that cultural institutions in general and museums in particular disseminate not only knowledge but also political rationalities. Museum spaces, as Tony Bennett rightly claims,[20] are not neutral but instead always suggest a certain moral obligation and a concept of citizenship that is conveyed within the museums themselves and also in additional educational material.

The insights from chapter 4 will enter into dialogue with the empirical findings collected at the three museums to inform the comprehensive interpretative chapter which follows the case studies (chapter 8). This chapter will not only bring together the different material from each museum but, more importantly, will also make tangible the claim that memory is a means of government. Therefore, the eighth chapter is the key analytical section of this book, which will testify to the utility of the governmentality approach to memory and, moreover, establish a totally new perspective on the Holocaust-human rights nexus, which is what makes this research bold and unique at the same time. My endeavour to probe current Holocaust memory politics in light of their tendency to become

---

19 I will provide a detailed account of my research design in chapter 2 as well as at the end of chapter 4.

20 I will expand upon my understanding of museums as sites of government in the third subsection of chapter 2.

politics of citizenship as well as to open up new possible perspectives on the world(s) eventually culminates in chapter 9. The final section of the book should be viewed as a thought experiment rather than a strictly analytical contribution to the overall project, as it seeks to bring into conversation with each other some of the previously marginalised narratives and perspectives which brushing hegemonic knowledge against the grain laid open – to emphasise their agency and utopian potential.

2 Theorising a Constellation of Contemporary Memory: Governmentality, Coloniality and Public Memorialisation

This book is informed by three main theoretical frameworks that could each, if presented thoroughly, fill an entire book (which they, of course, already do). However, my main aim is not to recapitulate or reconceptualise existing theory but to utilise different theoretical trends for my empirical research. As mentioned in the introduction, this project brings together different theoretical and methodological approaches from the field of cultural studies (in the broadest sense) and synthesises them into a methodology which is best suited to answer my research questions. To use Michel Foucault's famous metaphor of the toolbox, this chapter therefore serves to explain why I have chosen a screwdriver, and which specific one at that; what kind of a hammer I have picked in addition to the occasional saw and scraper; and to describe the specific function of each tool. Of course, my choice of tools was not accidental. Though most cultural studies scholars do have their own preferences, they are informed less by some clear-cut methodological canon than by the fact that they have proven – at least in my case – to be most helpful in the (impossible) project of making sense of the worlds we live in.

Furthermore, there is a reciprocity I have come to identify in my work: the theoretical approaches I choose generate the questions I ask and shape the point of view from which I look at the objects of my investigation. But at the same time, the subject matter of the study itself requires that I consider certain theories that cannot be ignored if my findings are to be taken seriously. To be more precise, this book is centred around three case studies of museums that are located on three different continents: Europe (Central), Africa (South) and America (North). Two of the three societies in which the museums are situated have been historically shaped by settler colonialism[1] (South Africa and Canada) and one by the European liberal tradition – which cannot be understood without making reference to colonialism either – in particular by the history and aftermath of National Socialism (Germany). It was therefore out of the question for me to attempt to analyse each societal context without taking into consideration postcolonial and decolonial theory as well as insights from Holocaust studies that specifically focus on Germany as a post-Nazi society (Adorno 1997).

1 For an account of the concept "settler colonialism", please see, for example, Veracini 2011.

https://doi.org/10.1515/9783110788044-004

What is more, bringing together memory studies methodology and global governmentality was a choice I made in the midst of collecting my empirical material. After engaging with different cultural studies strands, such as cultural analysis and narratology, this specific coupling all of a sudden enabled me to take a perspective from which I felt I could best grasp my research topic in all its complexity. The scholarly work I rely on and that I turn to for instruction but also in order to challenge what I thought I knew ranges from the mainstream cultural studies canon to lesser-known works by scholars from the global South and others explicitly seeking to challenge the coloniality of knowledge.[2] I deliberately looked for ideas and sources, for theory which I could quote that has been produced by anyone but *white cis men*,[3] who still dominate academia and its production of knowledge today. I did this to educate myself and to disturb hegemonic assumptions about expertise and (academic) authority because, as Olivia Rutazibwa argues, "privileged research agendas shape academic career paths; and, increasingly, careers in 'the real world' shape academic disciplines. In this context, the marginalisation of critical decolonial perspectives in research and in practice becomes mutually reinforcing" (Rutazibwa 2019, 66). In this understanding, the approach I will map out in the following becomes more than a theoretical framework, instead presenting a research strategy that aims to contribute to the pluralisation of knowledge production and consumption – of my own and also the reader's. Effectively understanding and facilitating epistemic diversity in the sense of a decolonial research strategy, however, entails certain efforts: "(1) the need to de-mythologize, pertaining to issues of ontology; (2) the need to de-silence, which more explicitly relates to epistemology; and (3) the need to anticolonially de-colonize, addressing both the tangible, material and the normative of knowledge production/cultivation" (Rutazibwa 2018, para 6). For me, this means continuously, though often implicitly, considering how I understand the world and the power relations that shape it (including a critical awareness of why I think of "the world" in the singular and not the plural). Furthermore, it means not only including scholarship from the global South to expand my otherwise Eurocentric bibliography but also engaging with assessments of the worlds that practise "epistemic disobedience" – in other words,

2 I will elaborate upon the concepts of coloniality and decoloniality in chapter 2.

3 The prefix "cis" is short for cisgender and has come to be used in the same way as "trans", though meaning exactly the opposite. Cisgendered people accept the gender presumed for them from birth and are therefore either men or women, as those are the two sexes accepted within the binary order of the heterosexual matrix. The prefix "cis" was therefore primarily introduced to avoid the use of terms such as "normal" or even "biological", which in turn deem transgender abnormal.

worlds that sever themselves from the phantasm that makes the "knowing subject" appear to be entirely neutral and not affected at all by "geo-political configurations" and instead continuously make visible the construction of knowledge (Mignolo 2009, 160 – 161). Overall, it is a very "limited pool" from which we draw in our attempts to understand the world (Rutazibwa 2018, para 4), which is why I am trying to explicitly consider the implications of this kind of limitation. But being mindful of the many asymmetries that structure the worlds we live in, including of course academia itself, and reflecting on them in academic work is far from easy. This is due to restraints within academia but also due to my own situatedness (Haraway 1988), which can blind me to certain perspectives or make it difficult for me (read: I might be too frightened, sluggish, arrogant...) to resist casting my European experience and knowledge as universal.

To be clear: my research design is by no means situated "outside of" Western expectations, canons or knowledge paradigms. Rather, I intend to make them visible throughout my work and emphasise the ongoing need for self-reflexive perspectives, keeping in mind Sara Ahmed's challenge to not "get over it, if you are not over it" (2013, para 28). In this vein, I will do my best to remain true to the ideal of my research strategy and hope to do justice to each of the approaches I have chosen in the following explications and to make my choices comprehensible.

Studies of governmentality

As stated in the introduction, I would like to advance the use of Michel Foucault's concept of governmentality in memory research. This analytical perspective allows us to grasp the political implications of the Holocaust-human rights nexus but is also fruitful for other subjects of investigation related to memory. In a similar vein, Tony Bennett has developed a persuasive position that suggests that museums function as sites of government because, as he claims, "going to the museum [...] is an exercise in civics" (1995, 102). But how are such exercises in civic education related to techniques of government and how can my central claim – that memory is a means of government – be understood theoretically? The following will briefly recap what can be understood by governmentality, how it applies to the global context and what it is that studies of governmentality look at.

The term *governmentality* was developed by Foucault between 1978 and 1979 in a series of lectures he gave at the College de France. He attempted to develop a "genealogy of the modern state", which he called "the history of governmentality" (Foucault 2007). Especially in the first lecture series, entitled "Security, Territory, Population", Foucault traced how the "art" of government has changed in Europe since the sixteenth century. In those lectures he developed a framework that takes into account all conceptualisations of power that govern human conduct – in other words, the ensemble of powers which circulate within and are utilised by society to control a population. This perspective not only allows us to think differently about the relationship between power and the subject; rather, what makes Foucault's account of government different from other understandings of power and how it is exercised is his focus on calculated freedoms instead of rules. For Foucault, government is "not a matter of imposing laws on men, but rather of disposing things, that is to say, to employ tactics rather than laws, and if need be, to use the laws themselves as tactics" (2009, 95). This means that the Foucauldian notion of governmentality refers to a political discourse that is largely nonlegal and therefore only occasionally enforceable. Foucault understands it to mean the assemblage of all the techniques that are used to regulate a population using various instruments that formulate and give direction to how we behave. This governmental rationale circulates – to a great extent as a popular discourse – in and amongst schools, churches, civic associations, museums and, of course, other institutions of memory as well. In the most simplified way, we can say that governmentality is an analytical concept that attempts to grasp the interdependence of government and rationality. Or, put differently, it captures the mode of governing through reason instead of repression. However simple it might sound here, this is a complex perspective on "the art of government", which I will map out in more detail in the following three subsections.

The history of governmentality

Through Foucault's concept of governmentality, we can begin to examine a new art of government, an exercise of power that developed in close relation to liberal thought, whose core aim is the "conduct of conduct" (Foucault 2000, 341; 2008, 186). According to Walters, governmentality is a "[f]ramework for analysis that begins with the observation that governance is a very widespread phenomenon, in no way confined to the sphere of the state, but something that goes on whenever individuals and groups seek to shape their own conduct or the conduct of others (e.g., within families, workplaces, schools, etc.)" (2012, 11). However, many of Foucault's deliberations were intended "to generate a novel perspective on the state" (Foucault 2008, 2–3, 76–78), a perspective that understands government in a "nominalistic" way, one that does not focus primarily on the state, understood as something made up of multiple institutions.

Instead, the analytical perspective of governmentality tries to "grasp its [the state's] history and existence at the level of the specific arts, practices and techniques that have combined in different ways and at different times to make something called 'the state' thinkable and meaningful in the first place, and viable as a framework for conducting human behaviour" (Dean 2006, 10). Studies of governmentality therefore try to diagnose specific formations of thinking, objectives, interventions and programmes as well as breakdowns and oppositions to these configurations (Dean 2010).

With the concept of governmentality, Foucault analysed a new way of governing that began to form in Europe in the sixteenth century and was linked to the institutionalisation of specific disciplines, tactics, technologies and regimes of truth, and that included in its broadest sense the governing of the self, families and the state (Dean 2010). Foucault argued that the "modern (Western) state is the result of a complex linkage between 'political' and 'pastoral power'" (Bröckling et al. 2010, 3). Political power, closely related to the early modern *raison d'état* (reason of state) and "police sciences", and later to (neo) liberal rationalities, derived from Greek and Roman ideas of the polis based on law, universality, the public etc. Pastoral power emerged from the "Christian religious conception centred upon the comprehensive guidance of the individual" (Bröckling et al. 2010, 3) and developed techniques of guidance that later extended into societies and became gradually secularised, particularly through resistance to religious leadership during the Reformation and Counter-Reformation. Foucault demonstrated that these "pastoral techniques eventually produced forms of subjectivation from which the modern state and capitalist society could in turn develop" (Bröckling et al. 2010, 3) and which constituted a revolutionary break with the concept of safeguarding and multiplying the power of the prince as the overriding goal of sovereign power: "'Political reason' represents an autonomous rationality derived neither from the theological-cosmological principles nor from the person of the prince. At the same time, the earlier goals of happiness, salvation, and well-being are now secularized and re-articulated in the framework of the 'political' problematic of the state" (Bröckling et al. 2010, 3). Foucault defined this new "art of governing" as

> a sort of complex of means and things. The things government must be concerned about [...] are men [sic!] in their relationships, bonds, and complex involvements with things like wealth, resources, means of subsistence, and, of course, the territory with its borders, qualities, climate, dryness, fertility, and so on. "Things" are men in their relationships with things like customs, habits, ways of acting and thinking. Finally, they are men in their relationships with things like accidents, misfortunes, famine epidemics and death. (Foucault 2009, 96)

Government defined in this way is concerned with "common welfare and salvation for all" and is about managing the human conduct of all members of the population. The "'conduct of conduct' therefore includes both the individual and the whole population and uses a wide range of technologies of power: law, discipline and apparatuses of security" (Foucault 2007, 108). In this vein, I will demonstrate that public memory, in certain constellations, has come to function as one of the many means to guide, and thus govern, human conduct. Public memory, understood in this sense, serves as a technology of the self, aimed at activating citizens to govern themselves.

Liberal governmentality was perceived by Foucault as a specific art of government that was different to those that preceded it. For him, it was a manifestly new rationale for deploying power in Western societies because it was concerned with population as a new target, and it discovered the economy as a novel reality. Government, as it developed from the end of the eighteenth century, transformed into a distinctive activity that utilised the knowledge and techniques developed in the humanities and political economy. The specificity of liberal forms of government is that they "replace external regulation by inner production" (Bröckling et al. 2010, 5). Liberalism "organizes the conditions under which individuals can make use of their freedoms", or, in other words, freedom is not contrary to liberal governmentality but is rather one of its tactical starting points for action. To make use of freedom as a mechanism of liberal governmentality means comprehending the governed autonomous actors able to act and reason in numerous ways that are often unpredictable for the authorities. Thus, to govern is to influence the field of possible action and involves reinforcing and modelling energies in both individuals and the population as a whole that otherwise seem to be unproductive or even self-destructive (Miller and Rose 2009; Rose 2005; Rose and Miller 1992). Therefore, liberal government

> is any more or less calculated activity, undertaken by a multiplicity of authorities and agencies, employing a variety of techniques and forms of knowledge, that seeks to shape conduct by working through the desires, aspirations, interests and beliefs of various actors, for definite but shifting ends and with diverse sets of relatively unpredictable consequences, effects and outcomes. (Dean 2010, 18)

According to Foucault, this form of governing "incites, it induces, it seduces, it makes easier or more difficult; it releases or contrives, makes more probable or less [...] but it is always a way of acting upon one or more acting subjects by virtue of their acting or being capable of action. A set of actions upon other actions" (2000, 341).

Scrutinising formations of public memory in accordance with this understanding of an art of government makes it possible to see such reactions in a new light as emotions and affects that are deliberately produced by memories of past atrocities (Witcomb 2013; Rausch 2022). Such affects, as I will show in the analytical part of this book, aim to emotionally bind the individual to the project of (neo)liberal democracy and therefore enhance both its willingness to conform to democracy's laws and values, and also its motivation to become actively involved in safeguarding the system itself. The idea of self-government and of the autonomous individual who is able to control and regulate their own conduct emerged in the seventeenth century and later merged with liberal governmentality. From then on, liberal governmentality embraced the idea of individuals problematising their own conduct; it thus becomes clear that governmentality is not just about exercising authority over others but also implies the expectation that individuals will govern themselves. This is the ethical dimension of governmentality: the action carried out by the self on the self (Rose 1993, 2005; Rose and Miller 1992). Thus, government does not merely imply power relations and an external authority but additionally raises questions about identity and the self. Embedded within the idea of government are considerations about how to indirectly guide human conduct towards specific ends. This means that, instead of regulating behaviours by imposing laws, governments began to incentivise certain behaviours and de-incentivise others. Thus, governing increasingly became about influencing the context and environment in which individuals act, thereby making certain outcomes more probable than others. Governing oneself and others is always based on particular regimes of truth that regulate beliefs about life, existence and what human nature is, and these regimes of truth include scientific and scholarly discourses such as medicine, psychology, education, demography etc. in their attempts to rule over individuals, communities or populations. The focus of any analysis of governmentality is therefore "the interrelations between regimes of self-government and technologies of controlling and shaping the conduct of individuals and collectives" (Bröckling et al. 2010, 13), paying special attention to political rationality. Rationality is understood as a form of thinking about how things are and how they ought to be. Political rationality and expertise are intertwined and are part of state formations; they can be found in all the domains of those state formations as well as in what is known as civil society.

According to critical theorists Jürgen Habermas and Axel Honneth, the emergence of a modern public sphere in the eighteenth century was facilitated by the separation of state and civil society. It was not until this separation occurred that opposition to state policies could be developed and resistance to the state could emerge. But according to Foucault (2004a), the idea of civil society emerged within – that is, as a feature of – liberalism. Civil society is neither an ideological construct nor a natural given that repels the government or opposes the state. Rather, civil society is a "transactional reality" at the interface between political power and the governing of populations. Foucault points to the work done by the proponents of the Scottish Enlightenment, who saw civil society as something that could counterbalance the cold, impersonal economic market. It was in civil societies that citizens would be able to develop philanthropic initiatives aimed at softening the consequences of the economic forces at play in the markets. Civil society therefore provides grounds for problematisation and for the development of a set of innovative techniques of government; it is both an object and an end of government, and it is predominantly in this space that the politics of memory flourish, even where they are implemented as laws.

The art of government transformed again with the rise of neoliberal rationality (Brown 2015). The term *neoliberalism* as such is controversial because, as many critics argue, the "term lumps together too many things to merit a single identity; it is reductive, sacrificing attention to internal complexities and geo-historical specificity" (Hall 2011a, 206). Despite these justified objections, I agree with Stuart Hall, who says that "naming neo-liberalism is politically necessary to give the resistance to its onward march content, focus and a cutting edge" (2011a, 206). Forms of neoliberal governmental rationale call for revised efforts to "understand how societies and populations may be ruled intensively, yet indirectly, how states and other institutions may themselves be brought into being and [...] combined in the practices of states and citizens" (Brown 2015, 116).

Neoliberal economists began deploring the huge bureaucratic apparatus required to manage the welfare state (Friedman 2011). No longer was the state to accompany the citizen "from cradle to grave" (Thatcher 1980; qtd. in Eccleshall 2002, 242–244). The state was now to maintain the infrastructure of law and order, and people were to promote individual and national well-being by taking responsibility and being enterprising. This reconceptualisation of the role of the state was based on the rationale that it had grown too large and that it was undertaking projects that would be better accomplished by the private sector. The neoliberal model was based on the idea of free, entrepreneurial, self-governing individuals, with the state having no right to prescribe how these individuals manage their property. While these are indeed important aspects of the multiple effects of neoliberalism, it is more than a mere cluster of economic policies. Neoliberalism must be understood as a political rationality that "both organizes [...] policies and reaches beyond the market" (Brown 2003, 2); neoliberalism is "undoing the demos" (Brown 2015) and radically transforming liberal democracies by submitting every dimension of our existence to an economic rationality, including the political sphere – and, as a part of that, public memory.

Neoliberalism is moreover a "constructivist project" because it is organised through laws and other regulations: it is the institutionalisation of a rationality that directs and protects the economy. The individual is conceived of as *homo oe-*

conomicus, the one who organises all areas of life according to this market rationality; individuals become entrepreneurs of themselves, organising life according to the model of the firm (Rose 2005). They are conceptualised in terms of human capital and, like any other kind of capital, "are constrained by markets in both inputs and outputs to comport themselves in ways that will outperform the competition and to align themselves with good assessments about where those markets may be going" (Brown 2015, 109). Human beings, understood as human capital, are responsible for themselves and at the same time become dispensable assets, because the neoliberal state grants no guarantees for the life of the individual. In classical liberalism, *homo politicus* was based on the idea of freedom, which was understood as the minimum necessary for self-rule and participation in liberal democracy for the common good. Under neoliberalism, freedom is "linked with a normatively diminished conception of the person. The concept of the person as a 'rational decider' is [...] independent of the idea of the moral person who determines their will through an insight into what is in the equal interests of all those affected [...]" (Habermas 2001, 94). In the simplest terms: another aspect of the neoliberal project and its subject, which is closely linked to the human being as capital but less obviously concerned with the market, is the citizen-subject who engages in the well-being of society. From this analytical perspective, any seemingly non-political act – charity, for example, or morally motivated volunteer work in the realm of civil society – is linked to power relations and is therefore political.

The analysis of governmental modes therefore focuses on specific aspects and particular practices that have, in different ways and at different times, combined into a mode of government that does not force its subjects to obey but instead governs their freedom to act by deliberately shaping the desired state of their bodies and souls. To grasp these various efforts and means, Foucault (1986), and scholars who draw upon Foucault's ideas like Ulrich Bröckling (2007) and Nikolas Rose (2000), use the term "the techniques of the self". By this expression, Foucault meant modes of governing that work especially in and through the manifold practices to which individuals subscribe. These can include mindfulness and practising healthy lifestyles to maximise resilience but also various forms of engagement in programmes like lifelong learning or, as explained above, activities in the realm of civil society. The constellation of civil society, educational institutions and international government bodies is most interesting for my analysis because it produces the "global citizen" who is supposed to establish and engage in a global civil society.

The following subchapter will thus look more closely at the relationship between internationally institutionalised educational programmes and the subject. This relationship represents a complex interplay between different forms of power in which various techniques of government constitute possible subject positions and influence individual ideas about life and lifestyles through technologies of the self. In other words, subjects emerge at the intersections of different lines of power. It is precisely the "productiveness" of power – which, according to my hypothesis, brings about new, historically literate subjects – in which I am most interested and that helps us to understand the correlation between memory politics and the politics of citizenship. As Brown has pointed out, current neoliberal governmentality "dissimulates its politics through seemingly apolitical rubrics" (2006, 142) such as benevolence and tolerance. These rubrics, as will become apparent in my case studies, are part and parcel of the bodies of knowledge disseminated within human rights museology and very much rely on representations of the past.

Techniques of the self and the politics of (global) citizenship

Education and programmes of empowerment are important features of the various techniques of government that exist in contemporary democratic societies. Expanding on Foucault's ideas, Wendy Brown explains that "neoliberalism carries a social analysis that, when deployed as a form of governmentality, reaches from the soul of the citizen-subject to education policy to practices of empire" (2003, 39). As one of the many results of neoliberal reason, today's democratic societies rely on a concept of citizenship that distinguishes between "subjects" and "citizens". In *The Will to Empower*, Barbara Cruikshank persuasively argues that individuals in a democracy are transformed into "self-governing citizens" by what she calls "technologies of citizenship" (1999, 19). Hence, citizens are "made" by discourses in a certain way and are allowed to "participate in politics, to act in their collective interest, desires and goals. Whereas subjects behave themselves because an external force exerts power over them, citizens have power to act for themselves; they are their own master" (Cruikshank 1999, 19). From this point of view, democratic rationality desires an active citizen because such a citizen does not burden the state by being dependent on welfare – or even the health care system. That is its basic logic. What is more, subjects and citizens alike are constantly being urged by various actors, institutions and programmes to become more engaged in society, either to empower themselves (something usually demanded of subjects) or to empower others (mainly a task assigned to citizens). As explained above, this technique of government does not force its subjects to obey but instead governs their freedom to act by deliberately shaping the desired state of their bodies and souls. In this regard, Cruikshank has shown that "democratic citizenship is less a solution to political problems than a strategy of government [...]. This is a manner of governing that relies not on institutions, organised violence or state power but on securing the voluntary compliance of citizens" (Cruikshank 1999, 4).

This way, politics of citizenship create a hierarchy amongst the members of society, which is composed of *citizens* on the one hand and *subjects* on the other. Those who are regarded as mere subjects are often the target of more repressive policies that attempt to coerce them into *bettering themselves*, which means activating themselves to become productive members of society or, in other words: citizens. This assessment is even more pertinent in the light of neoliberalism, because here the state takes even less responsibility for the well-being of its population, as market rationale has come to be the governing power. This means that neoliberal democratic rationality targets not only the economy but all spheres of politics and the everyday lives of governmental subjects. It promotes the individual's capacity for self-care and, if possible, to voluntarily care for others as well. But all citizens are simultaneously required to measure the benefits and drawbacks of their actions, which is supposed to have a consistently positive impact on "growth rates" (Brown 2015, 17). Unlike older forms of governmental rationality,

> [...] neoliberalism normatively constructs and interpellates individuals as entrepreneurial actors in every sphere of life. It figures individuals as rational, calculating creatures whose moral autonomy is measured by their capacity for "self-care" – the ability to provide for their own needs and service their own ambitions. In making the individual fully responsible for her- or himself, neoliberalism equates moral responsibility with rational action; it erases the discrepancy between economic and moral behaviour by configuring morality entirely as a matter of rational deliberation about costs, benefits and consequences. (Brown 2003, 42)

This observation is particularly interesting with regard to the techniques of the self that are disseminated via memory politics. Although the forms of memorialisation on which my analysis will focus are posited as being solely morally motivated, they still have to conform to the economic terms of neoliberal reason. In this sense, any unwanted behaviour such as racist violence amongst members of a society is not only (or even not at all) targeted for being morally and politically wrong but also (or primarily) due to its *unproductiveness*. I will return to this aspect later on in my analysis, but for I now, I would like to turn to the global scale of governmental rationale.

Governmentality in the global context

As explained above, governmentality, according to Foucault, is a very specific rationality through which different forms of power are exercised. Thus, there is not one but several ways of studying governmentality. Many studies of governmentality confine themselves to the global North and remain within the borders of nation states. Whilst the emphasis on the global North is a result of Foucault's own focus, who, however critically, primarily focused on "the West" and thus developed his theoretical perspectives by paying special attention to formulations of power and government within Western societies, especially France, the focus on the nation state might seem more surprising (Cook 2018). Given that research on governmentality tries to decentralise the state and thus investigate "power beyond the state", studies of governmentality should not generally fixate on the infrastructure of nation states (Larner and Walters 2004, 1). As Dean argues in regard to Foucault's own focus on the domestic sphere, "his analysis of the emergence of these domestic arts of government is at least implicitly framed within a narrative about the European state system which has for its symbol the international order if not inaugurated at least consolidated by the Peace of Westphalia of 1648" (2004, 43). This might provide an entry point into less nationally oriented studies and for applying governmentality to the "international order". Nevertheless, there have been few investigations of governmentality to date addressing social or economic spaces that exceed the framework of the nation state, one notable exception being a collection edited by Wendy Larner and William Walters (2004), which attests to the utility of the critical perspective of governmentality for understanding government in broader settings. Beyond this, only a few journal articles and even fewer monographs have been published that explicitly focus on global aspects of governmentality, which include studies on the role played by the World Bank, publications on politics related to climate change as well as some inquiries into global security mechanisms (e.g., Neumann and Sending 2007; Kiersey 2008; de Larrinaga and Doucet 2011; Joseph 2012). Many of these were written in the first decade of the new millennium, when the topic of globalisation was still popular amongst social scientists. Today we tend to take globalisation as a given, and with this, interest in global governmentality has decreased. What makes it nonetheless appealing to me with regard to a multilayered international realm is not so much how it might help us to understand processes of globalisation but the way that it conceptualises power as something "dispersed", thus calling for an investigation of "specific configurations of power" that does not view states or supranational organisations as the centre of power but instead as one of many features of government (Larner and Walters 2004, 4). Even though it has been argued that Foucault had only liberal democratic societies in mind when he conceptualised governmentality (Fraser 1981), making it difficult to apply this lens globally as many areas of the world do not classify as liberal democracies (Joseph 2009), his insights are nevertheless powerful for analyses of global order(s). As Dean explains:

> If a "global governmentality" is today propounded by multiple agencies (for example, WTO, IMF, OECD), it operates through both the existing arts of domestic government within nation states and as an attempted extension and generalization of them across the planet. It thus seeks to move from a liberal art of government to a liberal planetary nomos or world order. (Dean 2006, 53)

He therefore suggests that global governmentality is a useful perspective for shedding light on the many modes of universalising Euro-modern traditions of thought and customs, which seek to establish a common "nomos" across the world. Building on this assessment, works on colonial governmentality (Rabinow 1989; Scott 1995; Kalpagam 2000; Willaert 2013) have shown how colonial rule is not only exercised by force using repressive mechanisms and economic power, but that modes of indirect rule closely linked to infrastructures of knowledge and expertise are similarly important (Scott 1995).[4] Other important aspects of colonial governmentality have, of course, always been economic structures, financial policy and their influential tools, for example, debt. But since this realm is less directly connected to the overall topic of the present book, I will not consider it further here.

Related to these insights, theorising a present-day global episteme such as the Holocaust-human rights nexus from the perspective of governmentality can help us to understand tactics that aim to develop processes in line with neoliberal governmental rationale and gives weight to otherwise overlooked practices. These seldom-theorised practices include, for example, global exchange programmes (for students as well as volunteers), global expert training (especially in the field of education) and related means such as assigning responsibility to local experts who have received training to foster democratic structures within their respective societies (Antweiler 2022). For the human rights project, the training of local experts is key, and the entire field of international "development" would not work without the idea of exporting knowledge – predominantly from the global North to the South (Andreotti 2014). To some degree, the same can be said about Holocaust memory and even more so about Holocaust education. Programmes launched by UNESCO, the UN and the IHRA function precisely

4 The second and the fourth subsection of chapter 2 will follow up on the aspect of theorising colonial governmentality.

in this way: to expand knowledge about the Holocaust and help teachers to educate themselves about its history, but similarly to pin down the broader lessons to be learned from it and stimulate the universalisation of its memory. In this way, as I will show, these programmes not only provide historical content but also present the desired responses to their teachings, which purportedly strengthen democratic consciousness. While I do not wish to pass judgement on whether this is good or bad, the detailed theoretical discussions in this chapter clearly expose the highly political nature of such endeavours. From a decolonial perspective in particular, to which I will turn in the following section, an inherent tendency becomes visible by which local practitioners and their societies become the addressees of globally inspired memorialisation practices. Such memory practices are often endorsed by historical pedagogy and seem to suggest that these local, non-Western societies do not yet understand the core values of democracy well enough and instead require educational intervention in the form of studying the Holocaust. For this reason, the critical perspective of governmentality outlined here can be very fruitful when attempting to understand the power dynamics of global practices of memorialisation.

Colonial conditions and decolonial critique

"Decolonisation" has become a buzz word in the academic landscape and popular culture alike. It could be understood as "taking away the colonial", but what does "colonial" mean? What is revealed when we look at contemporary conditions, which suggest that coloniality has not yet drawn to an end? In this chapter I will primarily focus on the second question, that is, on the assumption that the colonial has persisted despite the end of formal colonialism, and I will begin by introducing some key theories on this paradox. I will discuss them in regard to the study carried out for this book, beginning by looking at knowledge production, as both forms of memorialisation and mnemonic practices are built on certain bodies of knowledge about the past. Moreover, I will look at how histories are recalled and what techniques are relied upon to do so. Then I will link the decolonial critique of hegemonic epistemologies to conceptions of who is or may become "human", as this is the central category in *human rights* as well as *humanity*. Finally, I will relate these insights to the problem of a single temporality, which also impacts dominant conceptions of *memory*. I hope to demonstrate that, even though some aspects of decolonial critique may sound unrelated to the study of the Holocaust-human rights nexus, they not only enrich my analysis but also make it more relevant in terms of my overarching research strategy.[5]

I have decided to use the term (and concept) "decolonial" instead of "postcolonial" because, first of all, "postcolonial" suggests, at least on the semantic level, an "after" to colonialism. This is true if we think of colonialism in its formal definition as a "policy or practice of acquiring full or partial political control over another country, occupying it with settlers, and exploiting it economically" (Cox 2017). This definition, however, obscures the key aspects of decolonial theory as I understand it. That is to say, the crucial critique of decolonial engagement points not only to the injustices of historical imperial conquest and rule – and hence to something that is *past* – but to *ongoing* colonial conditions. These have been shaped by a multitude of historical colonial endeavours, the earliest of which date back to the conquest of the Americas in the fifteenth century (Castro Varela and Dhawan 2015). Still, what colonial conquest and rule involved was different in different regions of the world and during the different periods of colonialism (Lorenzo 2010).[6] Despite the distinctiveness of the different colonial contexts, contemporary anti-colonial scholars and activists have, as is common in other scholarly fields too, identified their "classics" that make up something like a canon – essential literature if one wants to engage further with decolonial critique.[7] The thinkers referenced include Aimé Césaire, Frantz Fanon, Edward Said and W. E. B. Du Bois, as well as bell hooks and Sylvia Wynter – to name just a few. They all seek to unveil the close relationship between Western philosophy and European imperialism and colonial conquest, an entanglement that is still being denied or written off as irrelevant by scholars from this Western tradition.

Even though they reference some shared "classics", decolonial and postcolonial theory are diverse in terms of their geographic locations as well as in the

5 For a detailed account of postcolonial and decolonial theories see, for example, Ania Loomba (2015); Boaventura de Sousa Santos (2008); and Nikita Dhawan and Maria do Mar Castro Varela (2015).

6 In chapters 6 and 7 on the Canadian and the South African contexts and their respective museums, I will briefly elaborate on the specific forms of colonialism to which the conquered Indigenous people were subjected and how these impact the present.

7 It is not without regret that I must point out that, in all three conceptual chapters of this volume, the pioneers to whom scholars from each respective field refer as thought leaders or founders of the discipline are all cis men. This is of course due to heterosexist power relations that deny the voices and ideas of LGBTQI+ equal access to and importance within academic discourse. However, I sincerely hope that one day it will be possible to write a book such as this one without having to quote a majority of (white) men when reflecting on theoretical backgrounds and methodology.

sense that there are disciplinary differences with various trajectories (Bhambra 2014). However, it is also important to note one common trope: what the different theoretical trends driven by an anti-colonial ethos share – similar maybe to gender and queer studies and unlike academic fields such as memory studies – is that postcolonial and decolonial thought was explicitly developed as a form of resistance (Loomba 2015, 10): resistance both to political conditions in general and to particular paradigms within academia, primarily the many asymmetrical power structures that are mirrored in academic knowledge production. Moreover, it should be noted that this critical engagement started long before the "postmodern" turn in the West, for example, at the Bandung Conference of 1955 (and two years later in Paris), which for the first time in history assembled theorists, soldiers of anti-colonial resistance forces and representatives of twenty-nine countries, representing 54 % of the world's population, who had successfully fought against colonialism and came together to discuss the future of decolonialisation.

Modernity, coloniality and the global colonial matrix of power

Key focal points of decolonial theory are the epistemic locations of power, their deconstruction and the exploration of epistemologies and ontologies that debunk the Eurocentric tradition of thought in order to challenge its dominant conceptual frameworks. These are built on the foundation of "historical narratives and historiographical traditions emanating from Europe" (Bhambra 2014, 115) and still impact our understanding of the world(s) today. But by widening the scope from one singular and universal modernity (the existence of which is suggested by Western discourse) to multiple historical sites and temporalities, other, more pluriversal imaginaries of the world(s) we live in becomes possible. In this regard, Fernanda F. Bragato and Lewis R. Gordon use the term "Euro-modernity" in order to capture the constructedness of "modernity" and to point to modernity's complement, which is "coloniality":

> There was a transition from Euro-modern colonialism to global coloniality. […] Coloniality persists not only in global political, social, and economic relations, but also in many ways in which one constructs and adheres to knowledge. […] Drawing from a decolonial perspective, Euro-modernity is a global phenomenon whose underlying grammar is coloniality. (Bragato and Gordon 2018, 4–5)

Even though coloniality is (re)produced by multiple means and in all areas of society as well as throughout the global political order, the sphere of knowledge production is especially relevant as it spans all aspects of "social relations" and thereby impacts all political imaginaries (Quijano 2007). The observation put forward by Bragato and Gordon aligns with the assessment of a "global colonial matrix of power" and one of its most important pillars, the coloniality of knowledge.[8] These corresponding insights have been further expanded upon by decolonial thinkers such as Anibal Quijano, Arturo Escobar, Ramón Grosfugel, Catherine Welsh, Walter Mignolo and Santiago Castro-Gómez, who all belong to the modernity/coloniality school of thought, based in Latin America. Their core assumption is that "there is no modernity without coloniality, that coloniality is constitutive of modernity" (Mignolo 2007, 162). Drawing from this, many other scholars, for example, Achille Mbembe and Biodun Jeyifo, seek to advance this understanding and make it fruitful for discussions of postmodernism as well. This is because "[m]odernity (with the Enlightenment and Industrial Revolution, i.e., epistemic and technological (re)discoveries) and Coloniality (with Enslavement and Colonialism, i.e., genocide, epistemicide and ecocide) are hardly ever brought to us as sides of the same coin" (Rutazibwa 2018).

Accordingly, any analysis of the "modern" world needs to be conducted in the light of not only European history in the metropolis but also another important part of European history (Chakrabarty 2000), namely colonialism, as there would be no universal human rights without the Enlightenment but also no Industrial Revolution without slavery. Whilst a particular mode of thought was established in Europe during the eighteenth and nineteenth centuries which then became the theoretical basis upon which "Western civilization viewed its relationship to other societies and peoples" (Bhambra 2007, 34), the industrialisation of the modes of production simultaneously consolidated the myth of a distinctly new and *modern* form of society. This narrative is the foundation of the illusion that the Western world is something entirely different from and superior to all other societies. Colonial conquest was premised on this theoretical foundation of the "modern" world to the same extent as its growing wealth and industrial "progress" relied on enslaving the conquered. Such an understanding of "modernity" as something inseparable from "coloniality" is not only relevant in retrospect but continues to be equally decisive in the present, because even though formal political colonialism has been defeated, "this specific colonial structure of power produced the specific forms of social discrimination which later were

8 Lewis R. Gordon problematizes the use of "knowledge" in the singular because it "already situates the question in a framework that is alien to precolonial times, for the disparate modes of producing knowledge and notions of knowledge were so many that knowledges would be a more appropriate designation. Unification was a function of various stages of imperial realignment, where local reflections shifted their attention to centers elsewhere to the point of concentric collapse" (Gordon 2011, 95).

codified as 'racial', 'ethnic', 'anthropological' or 'national', according to the times, agents, and populations involved" (Quijano 2007, 168). Similar to Bragato and Gordon, Quijano emphasises the ongoing impact of coloniality that derived from colonialism and that remains very powerful. As he explains:

> in spite of the fact that political colonialism has been eliminated, the relationship between the European, also called "Western" culture, and the others, continues to be one of colonial domination. It is not only a matter of the subordination of the other cultures to the European, [...] we have also to do with a colonization of the other cultures [...]. This relationship consists, in the first place, of a colonization of the imagination of the dominated; that is, it acts in the interior of that imagination, in a sense, it is a part of it. (Quijano 2007, 169)

This means that Western European-derived ways of being, believing, knowing and doing were imposed on Indigenous conquered people who were, by various means, forced to acculturate to them. In due course, these ways of being were implicitly or explicitly normalised into a standard, a norm, whilst other ways of being, knowing, and doing still continue to be implicitly or explicitly presented as less worthy or less advanced. Edward Said furthermore suggests that "the actual geographical possession of land is what empire in the final analysis is all about" (1994, 93), adding yet another important dimension to an understanding of colonial conditions and their various current-day repercussions.

To capture the multilayered power relations described above, Anibal Quijano coined the aforementioned expression, *the colonial matrix of power*, which seeks to capture ongoing systems of oppression and will be employed in this study to complicate the analysis of the global governmentality perspective. Even though this might sound like a primarily academic activity, it is important to keep in mind that decolonisation is not simply a metaphor or a mere theoretical exercise, and thus is not something to be relegated to the academic sphere. Decolonisation has always been about genuinely and comprehensively questioning the colonial "eco-system" (Ramose 2001; Kasibe 2020) and the need that Frantz Fanon emphasised to completely call "in question of the colonial situation" (2001, 28). This is necessary in order to eventually remove its unacceptable (world) order and – in the most hopeful terms – undo the damage wrought by colonialism and its underlying ideology. Through his particular psychoanalytical lens, Fanon here was referring to the damage done not only to pre-colonial systems and cultures but moreover to the individual, coming to the conclusion that colonialism inflicted severe harm on the psyche of both the colonised and the coloniser.

In my understanding, taking coloniality and the struggle against it seriously therefore involves more than making adjustments to the current world(s) and can only ultimately lead to the radical imagining and shaping of different worlds. In this sense, engaging with decolonisation is always "unsettling" (Tuck and Yang 2012, 3).[9] It is this potential to unsettle that needs to be kept in mind when analysing concrete actions taken in the name of decolonisation and will therefore be a point of reference for my later museum case studies. A similar potential to unsettle has been attributed to the memory of the Holocaust, a link which I would like to stress throughout this volume. But before I return to the inquiry at the heart of this book, in the next two chapters I would like to elaborate further on two more important pillars of coloniality: education and the concept of universal time.

The coloniality of education for the "proper human"

In one of the earliest novels on British colonial destruction on the African continent, author Chinua Achebe (1994) tells the story of Okonkwo, his family and clan, whose "things fall apart" due to the increasing power of the British colonial endeavour in what is now Nigeria. In a conversation between Okonkwo and his best friend Obierika, the two men discuss the impact of the means used by the colonisers to establish their rule. Okonkwo asks whether the "white man" understands their "custom about land", to which Obierika replies

> How can he when he does not even speak our tongue? But he says that our customs are bad; and our own brothers who have taken up his religion also say that our customs are bad. [...] The white man is very clever. He came quietly and peacefully with his religion. We were amused at his foolishness and allowed him to stay. Now he has won our brothers [...]. He has put a knife on the things that held us together and we have fallen apart. (Achebe 1994 [1959], 176)

Around the same time that Achebe's *Things Fall Apart* was published in the mid 1950s, Aimé Césaire was writing his famous essay *Discourse on Colonialism.* What Okonkwo and Obierika observe first hand in Achebe's novel is summarised by Césaire in the gritty manner of his entire anti-colonial manifesto:

> I see clearly what colonization has destroyed. [...] I see less clearly the contributions it has made. Security? Culture? The rule of law? In the meantime, I look around and wherever there are colonizers and colonized face to face, I see force, brutality, cruelty, sadism, conflict, and, in a parody of education, the hasty manufacture of a few thousand subordinate functionaries [...] necessary for the smooth operation of business. (Césaire 2000, 42)

9 However, by this I do not want to suggest a fixation on some kind of decolonial "finishing line" but to stress, in particular, the radical potential of the process.

I am not using these quotations to simply highlight once more the devastating effect of the "divide and rule" policies that were a core feature of colonisation. What I want to recall is instead how the various means of social and cultural control were implemented that laid the foundation for both the colonisation of knowledge and the colonisation of imagination (Quijano 2007, 169). Many scholars have pointed to the immense power of the sort of seduction encountered and described by Okonkwo and his friend in Achebe's novel. What the protagonists of the story, which is set in the late 1800s, experienced, predominantly with regard to religion and customs of law, became a sophisticated system of direct and indirect rule, for with the churches came courthouses, hospitals and trading posts and, most importantly for the constellation I am recapping here, schools. Education in missionary schools was not only dedicated to religion but also to the teaching of Western morals and values more generally, as these schools served the purpose of estranging and assimilating local populations as much as providing basic education in areas such as reading and writing. Many of the encounters with these Western "forms of thought" (Fanon 2001, 38) therefore occurred in educational endeavours, a fact that needs to be taken into consideration when attempting to understand the power structures at play in the realm of memory education. What is more, education not only served (and continues to serve) the purpose of disseminating certain bodies of knowledge but also had a particular function within the security apparatus. On this note, Fanon discerned a close relationship between the task of the police and that of educators, as he ascertained that both of them had the power of coercion necessary to control people:

> In capitalist societies, the educational system, [...] the structure of moral reflexes handed down from father to son, the exemplary honesty of workers who are given a medal after fifty years of good and loyal service, [...] all these aesthetic expressions of respect for the established order serve to create around the exploited person an atmosphere of submission and of inhibition which lightens the task of policing considerably. (Fanon 2001, 29)

This observation can clearly be related to Tony Bennett's assertion (to which I will return in the following) about museums being the complement to prisons because, according to Bennett, they similarly serve to both discipline and form citizens (though by different means) in order to "drive a wedge between the respectable and the rowdy" (1995, 102). I will flesh out this perspective on the museum further on in the next subchapter, but I am referring to it here to point to the role of education as a means to exercise and maintain power, both at home (in the so-called metropolis) and in the colonies – a function which cannot be overstated. Subsequently, the imposition of teacher-student relationships (of which Steve Biko (2017) also speaks in his articles written on apartheid and struggles against it in the 1970s) brought into being a system of domination which maintains influence over the colonised, conquered Indigenous peoples and which did not cease after formal colonisation had ended.

The indirect rule often exercised through education that is inherent in the teacher-students relationship is closely linked to the Euro-modern concept of "the human". This is because the human projected by Euro-modern philosophy is male, *white* and capable of certain cognitive exercises identified as *his* capacity for *rationality* (Nancy 2014; Mignolo 2006). This "human" is fundamental to the colonial matrix of power because, in the eyes of the colonizer, as philosopher Mogobe Ramose explains, "[t]he colonized were not and never had been human beings, [...] because they lacked rationality. Reason or rationality was not part of their nature even though in appearance they looked like human beings. The hallmark of racism then is the claim that other human-like animals are not truly and fully human" (2001, para 11). In a letter to her colleagues in the academy, Sylvia Wynter addresses the immense and often deadly consequences of such a hierarchy that deems those who are not perceived as *white* to be something other, something less than human, or as she puts it, the "lack of the human" (1994, 43). In her letter, Wynter builds her argument around the description of mostly young Black males who were being treated by the Los Angeles police as if there were no humans involved, "N.H.I." – an acronym that police officials used when any "young Black males who belong to the jobless category of the inner-city ghettos" were involved in a case (Wynter 1994, 42). The logic that allows for these young Black men to be considered the "conceptual other" to North American identity and thus treated as such is closely linked to the rationale described above by Ramose. And the very same deadly operation of viewing and treating some as the "conceptual other" was at work during the Nazi era in Europe, when Jews and Roma were being categorised as the "lack of the human" (Bauman 1989; Arendt 2008 [1951]).

Interestingly, Wynter does mention both the dehumanisation of young Black males in the US and that of the Jews in Nazi Germany, thus bringing together realities and experiences that are seldom discussed alongside each other, however connected they might be (Rothberg 2009). James Baldwin once noted in this regard that, for many Black Americans, the Shoah did not come as a shock in the way it did to *white* Americans, because as Baldwin put it, and I would like to quote this passage in full:

> They [*white* people] did not know that they could act that way. But I very much doubt whether black people were astounded – at least, in the same way. For my part, the fate of the Jews, and the world's indifference to it, frightened me very much. I could not but feel, in those sorrowful years, that this human indifference, concerning which I knew so

> much already, would be my portion on the day that the United States decided to murder its Negroes systematically [...]. I was, of course, authoritatively assured that what had happened to the Jews in Germany could not happen to the Negroes in America, but I thought, bleakly, that the German Jews had probably believed similar counsellors. (Baldwin 1962, qtd. in Weinberg 2012)

This observation is remarkable for several reasons: first of all, it was written at a time when not many testimonies by Holocaust survivors had yet been published, nor had many other accounts of what had happened during the Holocaust. Secondly, Baldwin explicitly identifies a connection between those suffering from systemic racism and those who were turned into victims by the Nazis and their collaborators. He is not equating or comparing the events of the Holocaust with the experiences of Black Americans, but rather expressing an empathy that is nurtured by a different understanding of humanness. To Baldwin, the Shoah had once more accentuated what he had long known, that is, how "morally bankrupt" European liberal tradition, or as he put it, "the Christian world" was (Baldwin 1962, qtd. in Weinberg 2012).

This assessment is closely connected to the subject of my investigation because there would be no "humanity" or "human rights" without a common conception of the human being. And the concept of the human being is one that is premised on differentiation. The paradox underlying liberal human rights may thus be phrased as "equal rights to all *civilised* humans" (Gordon 2008, 29; emphasis added). By this logic, colonised people were to be treated like children who needed to be ruled over and given directions, but never engaged with in equal relations, for example, by granting them rights (Césaire 2000). It was from this hierarchal conception of the human and the not-yet-human that the more contemporary dualism of the citizen and the subject arose (Cruikshank 1999; Mignolo 2006). Furthermore, the differentiation between the citizen and the subject (who is yet to become a citizen) is closely connected to a concept important to my analysis, namely that of civil society, which – as I mentioned earlier – is now one of the most important pillars of the liberal democratic order (Mamdani 1996; Villadsen 2016). Before I turn to the micro level of my theoretical considerations and take a closer look at the different conceptions and workings of memory within this duality, I would like to shed some light on one more aspect of the coloniality of knowledge which is intrinsically linked to all ideas of memory – namely, time.

Universal time and democracy as "progress"

The processes of estranging colonised people from their precolonial customs and cosmologies and subsequently subjugating them to Euro-modern modes of being and knowing led to the universalisation of Western temporality as the only existing timeframe. By putting Euro-modernity in the singular and thus by authorising only one "modernity", "history" became the history of the coloniser. As a result, as Frantz Fanon remarked: "The settler makes history and is conscious of making it" (2001, 40). It is therefore impossible to separate the concept of memory from the notion of history and its corresponding temporality. Memory research and acts of memorialisation, as I will argue, rely on the idea of a natural "flow" of time, which presupposes a linearity structured along the parameters of past, present and future, thereby contributing to the "historical operation" (de Certeau 1988). This alone makes memory, its practices and its study, a political project that must be understood as such and examined not only in light of its founding ideas but also its ends.

In his famous novel *Midnight's Children*, Salman Rushdie (2006) writes about people whose word for yesterday and tomorrow is the same and who therefore do not have a grip on time, at least not in the hegemonic sense as an unswerving flow from a past towards a future. As a matter of fact, in many non-European languages, the term for the past and the future is the same (Dhawan 2018), and in some African cosmologies, time is thought of as circular instead of linear (Madlingozi 2015). Thinking about time differently, in more relational terms and finding a perspective on memory that does not need a fixed "past" to turn to will be central to the last chapter of this book in particular. However, it will also be one of the backdrops against which I assess the memory politics I will be focussing on in the following when I ask what conception of time and progress they might imply. This is an important corrective to keep in mind because, even though the idea of objective scholarship, at least in the humanities, has been contested and partly invalidated, Euro-modern epistemology nevertheless understands knowledge as "a detached gaze toward what is other to the self" and furthermore posits "rupture as a condition of knowing" (Allen-Paisant 2020, 9). According to Allen-Paisant, these basic assumptions on which the Euro-modern tradition of thought is based, rely on the "inexorable forward-moving logic of time" (2020, 10). During the Enlightenment, knowledge became strongly inclined towards abstraction and hence disengaged from "nature" (Dhawan 2014). By this logic, "man" (as in both human and male) is destined to dominate nature and must therefore comprehend that it is "other" to him (Horkheimer and Adorno 2002, 7). This does not only yield the classification of humans as either "rational" (able to abstract from and thus rule the natural world) or "primitive" (unable to perform such feats of abstraction and hence subject to domination); rather, this discursive system also posits that there is knowledge to be gained from looking at "the other" – whether as a person, place or period of time. Otherness and the constant identification of what is *other* in contrast to the self is therefore inherent in Euro-modern epistemology, not only with regard to being human but also in relation to time: the "past" is demarcated from the present and future as its "other" (White 2016; Allen-Paisant 2020).

Such an understanding of time and thus of the way our world moves (or, according to Euro-modern logic, progresses) can lead to what Vanessa Andreotti calls the "denial of entanglement" as, according to her, it distorts a sense of "the metabolism we are all part of" (2019, personal communication). Instead, as she explains, imagining our world(s) as constantly moving forwards, and thus not returning to where we came from, creates an illusion of "separability" that leads to the already problematised construction of conceptual *others*. In the context of decolonial approaches to memory, this aspect is particularly interesting because it helps us to understand a core paradox of dominant memory politics, which is the idea that the past, even if we occasionally recall it through mnemonic practices, is a closed entity *other* than our present or future. If we follow Césaire, Western epistemology cannot be separated from what he calls "the principle of rupture and death" (Césaire 1948, trans. and qtd. in Allen-Paisant 2020). This principle requires certain binary concepts such as life/death, past/present and closed/ongoing. In this vein, Nikita Dhawan demands that "retrospective politics […] be replaced by politics of anticipation" (2018) because, as she elaborates in regard to the legacy of slavery, this legacy also lies before us, not just behind us – which, I would add, can be said about the Holocaust as well. In the following subchapter, I will explore how such demands might be included in the realm of memory and museum studies, meaning two strands of social and cultural scholarship which explicitly deal with the forms and functions of representing the past.

Memory and museum studies

> dear head I lose you again I lose my memory I don't recover it don't give a damn since right where I'm mutilated other limbs grow back. (Césaire 1948, trans. and qtd. in Allen-Paisant 2020)

Unlike Aimé Césaire, who claims that he does not "give a damn" about losing his memory, most of the scholarship in social and cultural memory studies deals with the manifold modes of preserving and materialising memories, thereby almost automatically prioritising remembering over not caring for memory. I am intentionally refusing to call the latter "forgetting" because forgetting is already framed as the antithesis to remembering and is thus something different to the ongoing transformation that might occur despite the memory loss described by Césaire. It is a common presumption that we need memory in order to continue living, though too much memory, especially the harmful sort, might petrify us in the same way that Lot's wife turned to stone when she looked back in the biblical story of Sodom and Gomorra (Heyd 2004). Interestingly enough though, if we take a look at non-academic knowledge – literature, for example – or, as argued above, non-Western knowledge systems, we soon find contestations of this concept or idea of memory as the prerequisite for a (better) future. While I do not intend to discuss any of this more explicitly here, before I delve into my review of the canon of (cultural) memory, I nevertheless want to point out that there has been a lack of conceptual work concerned with alternative knowledges of memory.

This means that, in the academic sphere, there has not been much debate about whether or not we should remember – it is merely a question of how, not if we do it: to what extent, motivated by what interests and politics, in which media and over how many generations. In this regard, scholars such as Benedict Anderson and Frantz Fanon, with his emphasis on the colonial space, have theorised the interdependency of history and identity. Focussing on Europe, Anderson has showed how nation states centre their biographies around a founding myth. He conceives of nations as *imagined communities* whose trajectories, which emerge from a distant past and project into a limitless future, encompass a territorially defined population as an essential unity. Elements of this kind of imagined unity, especially in regard to the prominence of a founding myth, are now also said to be constitutive of the so-called international community (Levy and Sznaider 2006; Assmann 2006). Presuming that there is an interdependence between history and identity places value on events and historical figures that resonate with the perception of a supposedly unique culture (e.g., of a group, a nation state, "the West" etc.) and its distinguishing features, such as language and customs. Memory thereby becomes an important trope, and its regulation, promotion, absence or abolition spark many controversies (Traverso 2014). It is thus unsurprising that the subject of memory as a topic of investigation holds a prominent position within cultural studies as well as sociology and history (Radonić and Uhl 2016).

From collective to cultural to public memory

The field of memory studies emerged as a "major focus of scholarly inquiry" in the 1980s (Phillips Casteel 2019, 243). In the beginning, many memory scholars followed the works of French sociologist Maurice Halbwachs (1991 [1967]), 1992 [1966]), whose writings laid the theoretical foundations for memory research as far back as in the 1920s, and remain influential as they are now being translated into English once more. His distinction between individual and collective memory clarified the social and thus societal dimension of memories for the first time. Since then, Halbwachs' theses have been further developed and made fruitful for multiple analyses of contemporary social memory practices by scholars such as Jan and Aleida Assmann (2002; 2006), Astrid Erll and Ansgar Nünning (2008), Mathias Berek (2009), and Ulrike Jureit and Christian Schneider (2011). In the Anglo-American field of memory studies, mention should also be made of the research conducted by scholars like James E. Young (1993; 2000), Jeffrey K. Olick (2007, 2008, 2015). Ann Rigney (2015) and Michel Rothberg (2009, 2011).

Despite the wide-ranging trajectories of contemporary memory studies, it is safe to say that Halbwachs' elaborations on a society's "collective framework" paved the way for a theory of memory that did not focus on memory as something entirely individual but came to understand it instead as something social and thus collective. "Collective memory" therefore refers to the complex social processes through which a society or social group constructs and reproduces its relationship to the past. The concept mainly refers to the cultural practices and social knowledge of the past that influence the emergence, transformation and extinction of social identities (Olick 1999). Halbwachs thus refutes the notion of an independently remembering subject outside of space and time, and thus already provides important indications about the discursive constructedness of memories that, "starting from the present, reach back into the past" (Assmann 2002, 9; my trans.). Concepts such as "cultural memory", coined by Aleida and Jan Assmann (1992; 2002; 2006), and Pierre Nora's "lieux de mémoire" (2001 [1992]) have built on the idea of collective memory as an "umbrella term" for various types of memory that exist within societies, including social, political and cultural memory. Jeffrey Olick also argues for an understanding of collective memory as a "sensitizing concept" (Olick 2007, 1) that synthesises different approaches to memory (especially individualistic and collectivist conceptions). It distinguishes between "bottom-up" or social memory, referring to the ways in which events are remembered by individuals, and "top-down" political memory, referring to the creation of collective identities for political action (Budrytė 2020). And in a model articulated by the philosopher Avishai Margalit (2002), modes of individual and "shared" memories constantly impact each other as they are mediated through communication, institutions and, as I would add, discourse more generally (Margalit 2002; Rothberg 2009, 14–15). For Jan Assmann, "objectivized culture" (1992, 130) has the structure of memory inasmuch as it contributes to collective identities; according to him, it is *cultural memory* that shapes a group's sense of belonging and awareness of its unity and peculiarity. In a way, cultural memory defines "us" against "others", but it also has the potential to reconstruct past identities according to contemporary agendas (Assmann and Czaplicka 1995, 130). In this sense, memory is always guided by the motive of reconstruction; how it is perceived or retrieved, and how it changes is more dependent on present interests than the historical content itself. What is more, there is no memory without certain preconditions since it is always dependent on a network of "contextual knowledge" and can only be conveyed through language. In order to better grasp the various forms in which memory manifests itself and understand their functions within societies, Astrid Erll (2005; 2011) has advanced the study of cultural memory and its media, for example, literature, film or museums. Today, memory studies as a field of scholarly interest deals with the manifold traces and residues of the historical past in the present and has produced many sophisticated volumes on the multiple dimensions of memory that also look at memory's "other", that is, forgetting (Ricoeur 2004; Rieff 2016).

Memory and history were at first seen as irreconcilable because memory was assumed to be subjective, whereas the discipline of history called for objectivity. However, this tension is no longer an issue in memory studies, as most memory scholars believe that there is "a dialectical rather than a mutually exclusive relationship between history and memory" (Eser 2018, para 5). This dispute is especially interesting in connection to earlier work on memory, which was often concerned with the Holocaust. This may well be because, as Andreas Huyssen writes, "[m]emory discourse of a new kind first emerged in the West after the 1960s in the wake of decolonisation [and] accelerated in Europe and the United States in the early 1980s, energized by the broadening debate about the Holocaust [...]" (2000, 22). This means the memory of the Holocaust was not only globalised (Levy and Sznaider 2006) but was also key to the "travels" (Erll 2011) and transmission of memory more generally. Such travels led to the first major shift in focus in memory studies and can be dated to a time when the importance that had been placed on the nation state as a "container" of collective memory had diminished – at least in the field of memory studies (Pethes 2013).

Subsequently, the focus of discussion has shifted to the "transnational transmission of cultural memory" (Phillips Casteel 2019, 243), as many publications on this more recent dimension demonstrate (De Cesari and Rigney 2014; Bond and Rapson 2014). Also responding to this paradigm shift and the issues that it has revealed, Michael Rothberg published *Multidirectional Memory*, in which he explores the question of how the relationship between different victim narratives can be recast and thus how social memory can be shaped less by competition between victims and more by the multidimensionality of memories. Shortly before him, Dan Diner (2007b) published a study on a similar topic, coming to the conclusion that different memories of violence should not be aligned but will instead become more tangible precisely if attention is paid to their differences.

These seminal volumes by Diner, Levy and Sznaider, and Rothberg are of particular importance for my work and have strongly informed it. However, I have come to occupy a position somewhere between the unidirectional and the multidirectional trajectory, as the relevant question for me is not so much concerned with memory's relationality but instead with the conditions under which certain memories appear to be less prominent. That is to say: I want to find out which politics are linked to this phenomenon and how. Therefore, the term that I prefer with respect to the aspects of memory I seek to study is *public memory*, because this formulation points to the importance of the discursive position that memory occupies within society as much as to the politics around it. Public memory, as a result of memory politics, is always institutionalised to some extent and thus implies discursively authorised recollections of histories rather than, for example, literary ones.[10]

Museums as institutions of memory

Memory studies is a field with a diverse range of approaches and topics, with studies on subjects ranging from ecological memory to the memory of happiness, as well as the trauma related to memories of atrocities. Studies that are particularly interested in Holocaust memory are not as dominant in the field as they were originally, although new trends are, of course, still being researched, as this book shows. The historical museum or, more precisely, the memorial museum is regarded as an institution of memory, though not much theoretical work has been dedicated to conceptualising the museum format within a specific memory studies framework to date. Whereas cultural theory is increasingly being applied in museum studies, and while the museum has become popular amongst cultur-

---

10 How this understanding relates to the overall perspective of discourse theory and governmentality will be explained in a subchapter as well as in the later synthesis of my theoretical approach at the end of this chapter.

al theorists like myself, the field of museum studies has developed more or less separately from memory studies and only occasionally in collaboration with it (Bal 1996; Mason 2011). Still, some notable work at the "interface" between memory and museum studies has been conducted by Silke Arnold-de Simine (2013), Liliana Radonić (2016), Joyce Apsel (2019) and Amy Sodaro (2018). All of these works, as well as Stephan Jaeger's publication *The Second World War in the Twenty-First-Century Museum* (2020), have informed this study, as they not only bring to the fore the special features of the memorial museum as a genre but also provide nuanced accounts of specific content and constellations in and around these museums.

A decade before what is often referred to as the "memory boom", during which academic as well as popular engagement with the topic of memory spiralled (Echterhoff and Saar 2002), museum scholars identified a "museum boom" that, from the 1970s onwards, saw constant increases in visitor numbers at museums across the world (Baur 2010, 7). While people generally seem to know what a museum is, scholarly work on the topic stresses diversity: the variety of focusses (e. g., anthropological, historical, technical, art or natural history museums), the various generations of museums, whether a museum has a collection or not and what size it is, if it is privately owned or state-run (Baur 2010, 16–19). This means that, on the one hand, most people have some idea of what museums are, but not everyone has the same idea when they picture a museum. Thus, to state the obvious, there is no such thing as *the* museum – in the singular. Instead, there are many, multiple and astonishingly diverse museums – in the plural. Given the complexity of museums as institutions and thus of museum studies in relation to memory studies, the following section primarily serves as a brief introduction to key publications and concepts that will allow me to distinguish between the types of museums (or memory institutions) that my analysis is concerned with while nevertheless providing some examples of the most important characteristics ascribed to museums generally.[11]

---

11 A lengthy discussion of etymological changes or, more generally, the history of the museum as a term and concept can, for example, be found in Paula Findlen's (2004) work as well as in the early introductory work by Edward P. and Mary Alexander (1979). Sharon Macdonald's and Helen L. Leahy's (2015) edited four volume *International Handbook of Museum Studies* provides an excellent overview of numerous issues concerning the expanding field. Melanie Blank and Julia Debelts (2002) analyse German lexical entries for the term museum, while similar research has been conducted for the English-speaking world, especially Great Britain and North America, for example, by museum theorist Marjorie Schwarzer (2012). A good overview of the overall development of museum studies can also be found (in German) in Joachim Baur (2010): *Museumsanalyse. Methoden und Konjunkturen eines neuen Forschungsfelds.*

Until the late 1990s, museums were primarily of public and scholarly interest due to the objects and collections they put on display, a focus that was soon criticised for its limitations (Vergo 1989; Macdonald 2010). Subsequently, the academic discipline of museology transformed into the interdisciplinary field of museum studies that increasingly researched museums themselves as a society's "artefacts" instead of primarily exploring the artefacts shown within a museum (Baur 2010, 7). We could say that museum studies, like memory studies, developed into a critical endeavour aware of its own political implications – both tangible and intangible – as questions about "what was researched, how and why, and, just as significantly, what was ignored or taken for granted [...] came to be seen as matters to be interrogated [...] with reference [...] to wider social and political concerns" (Macdonald 2010, 3). In this vein, there have been many studies that look at the museum as a cultural institution, covering various aspects such as museums' "urge to collect" (Pearce 1994), their potential to function as "contact zones" (Clifford 1997), their "exhibitionary complex" (Bennett 2015) and educational purposes (Falk and Dierking 2000), or more generally, the role(s) they play in today's societies (Karp and Kratz 2006; Bose et al. 2011). Many of these studies have identified a principle that is attributed to museums as institutions, which elevates them to the realm of an "objective knowledge" that has been selected, ordered and chosen for representation in order to meet greater societal needs. Here, again, we can draw a parallel to memory, which is also often perceived as a high moral good that attests to a society's "maturity" (Barkan 2000; Barkan and Karn 2006). Similarly, museums were long believed to be beneficial to all members of society because they served "truth", whether about nature, our planet, about "other cultures" or historical events.[12] This idea of the museum might not be as strong today as it once was, especially during the Renaissance, but, as I will contend elsewhere in this study, knowledge put on display in a museum still grants authority to the narratives exhibited as well as their subjects and objects.

One core theme in many studies of museums that is also pertinent to studies of public memory is therefore the *story* that the museum tells and the rhetoric that it uses to narrate whatever its subject is (Bal 1992). Another aspect closely linked to the stories on display is the museum's mandate or overall agenda, which Mieke Bal describes as "telling, showing, showing off" (1992) in her semi-

---

12 Upon closer inspection, however, it becomes plain to see that most museums – especially the traditional ones generally located in the metropolitan areas – were not designed to be easily accessed by all members of society. Instead, a number of them demarcated (and still demarcate) the many boundaries that structure our unequal societies. An assessment of this aspect of museums can, for example, be found in Clifford 1997 as well as Bennett 2004.

nal article on the American Museum of Natural History. More precisely, she illuminates the act of "collecting as a form of domination" which relegates museums to "an era of scientific and colonial ambition" (Bal 1992, 560). The aforementioned founding myth at the heart of imagined communities can be understood as serving a similar aim of attributing greatness to one's own group, but, in declared contrast to the issue described by Bal, many contemporary museums and other memory institutions derive their agenda of narrative construction from their newly assumed role as actors of social change.[13] However, it is questionable whether this new mandate resolves former colonial entanglements or, more generally, practices of domination, a matter that requires further scrutiny (Bennett 2004; Perla 2021). Bal has spoken in this context about the "double status" of the museum, which comes to function as a "museum to the museum" (1992, 560). As she explains, it ends up serving as

> a preserve not for endangered species but for an endangered self, a "meta museum": the museal preservation of a project ruthlessly dated and belonging to an age long gone [...]. Willy-nilly, such a museum [...] speaks to its own complicity with practices of domination while it continues to pursue an educational project that, having emerged out of those practices, has been adjusted to new conceptions and pedagogical needs. (Bal 1992, 560)

What Bal observes about older, more traditional museums – namely that, even after they attempt to renew themselves, they still carry the burden of their old selves – also holds true for many recently established institutions. As a result, there is a growing number of sites that no longer make explicit reference to their institutional designation in their names in order to emphasise that they are *not* museums. This, for example, applies to the Johannesburg Holocaust & Genocide Centre, one of the three sites I will look at later on. The museum scholar Joachim Baur (2010) explains that such explicit acts of moving away from the title "museum" are a consequence of the various associations mentioned above. Newer museums in particular want to avoid the designation in their name due to their desire to distance themselves from the more classic notions of the museum, for example, the idea that a museum is an almost sacred space where the visitor quietly observes but does not interact, or the notion of the museum as an institution that presents wisdom that we ought to consume instead of engaging with it in order to foster dialogue on socially relevant matters.

Here, it once more becomes clear where memory scholarship and activism overlap because, on the societal level, memory, especially that of genocide

13 I will come back to the idea of a museum being an active part or player within society in chapter 4.

and the Holocaust, is most often evoked in order to stimulate social dialogue about responsibility (Sternfeld 2013). In chapters 4–8, I will take a closer look at this new trend in museums that, by looking at the Holocaust, attempt to engage in societal matters such as struggles for social justice and human rights issues. However, my focus will not be on the "public expectations of museums" (Pabst 2016, 135) but on a memory and museum discourse that shapes their missions and view of themselves as actors who accept social responsibility. But before that, a discussion of the discursive operation of public memory is required to illustrate both the questions and the assumptions guiding this research.

Memory as a discursive historical operation

I have shown above how approaches to the study of memory differ, even within the field. I will now provide a brief account of my understanding of memory, which makes use of Michel Foucault's discourse theory and analysis, and can be related to his discussions of governmentality. That is to say that I consider public memory in all its forms and functions to be a discourse of knowledge, meaning a discourse that shapes, regulates, limits and produces a certain knowledge. It is a discourse that allows statements to be made about the past but also about the present and the future (Foucault 1970). Not every historical event, eyewitness account or archival record is granted the authority required for it to find its way into a museum, for example, or for its commemoration to find its way into the public calendar (Zerubavel 2003). This indicates something very important about the Foucauldian concept of discourse: it is essentially constituted by the factors "power, knowledge and truth" (Mills 1997, 17).

Foucault saw discourse as "practices that systematically form the objects of which they speak" (1972, 49). In this sense, all the techniques and practices of governmentality are inevitably entangled with the discourses that produce, shape and regulate them. Hence, one of the core questions underlying my analysis is: how does the discourse that regulates public memory affect and condition specific truths about the past but also about the present and future? And furthermore, how is it narrativised within each museum space? Michel de Certeau once stated that "[f]iction is the repressed other of history" (1986, 22); we therefore need to take into consideration the "emplotment" of historical events, as Hayden White (2016, 55) has referred to it. This is key for any analysis interrogating how past events are transformed into consumable stories (Allen-Paisant 2020), but that is not at all to say that history itself is mere fiction, or either true or false. Rather, it means that a discourse produces the narratives that circulate about the past and eventually manifest themselves as public memory, because it brings about the things with which it is concerned. Any discourse can thus be best understood in its relation to those things, which is why I am providing examples of the relationship between discourse theory and public memory and not simply paraphrasing it in an isolated chapter. As Sara Mills explains, "A discursive structure can be detected because of the systematicity of the ideas, opinions, concepts, ways of thinking and behaving which are formed within a particular context, and because of the effects of those ways of thinking and behaving" (1997, 17). Therefore, approaching memory as discourse means examining how the discursive framework demarcates the boundaries within which we negotiate the acceptable ways to think and speak about certain past events, how to commemorate them, and how to give them specific meaning in contemporary society (Landwehr 2009, 2012). Foucault wrote the following about this:

> Truth is of the world; it is produced by virtue of multiple constraints [...]. Each society has its regime of truth, its general politics of truth: that is the type of discourse it harbours and causes to function as true: [...] the techniques and procedures which are valorised for obtaining truth: the status of those who are charged with saying what counts as true. (1979, 46)

Accordingly, some knowledge is generally considered more authoritative than other bodies of knowledge; what we believe to be true about our world(s) depends on the discourses that structure, assemble and regulate a "regime of truth". Different bodies of knowledge nevertheless exist within societies and might potentially come into conflict with each other. This can be illustrated by an example that is closely related to the subject matter of this book: in Germany, public knowledge of the history of the Holocaust is largely based on thorough research conducted over the past seventy years by numerous scholars. But it is also very much informed by family memories and identities that might contradict some of the scholarly findings. Nevertheless, private memories and identities have not only been passed from generation to generation but, from the early postwar period onwards, have been woven into the fabric of Germany's public memory, its institutions and its programmes (Diner 1996; 2007b). This means that "[w]hat can be said or not about something is neither absolutely fixed (because it varies historically) nor is it open to the whims of the moment" (McHoul and Grace 1993, 23). This is particularly interesting when it comes to interrogating the political dimensions of memory. Because, as I claimed in my introductory chapter, in the context of public memory, history is often invoked in a specific function: as the "final arbiter of right and wrong" (Scott 2020, 1). Politicians and state representatives from across the political spectrum employ memory, especially that of the Holocaust, to show that they are on the right side of history and are legitimised by the course that it has taken. This moral dimension of history, and thus memory, is based on the idea that our history is a universal phenomenon that unfolds independently of our intentions and follows a linear, progressive evolution. This ontology has already been scrutinised in the context of coloniality, and Foucault (1977) also pointed to the problematic references made to history that seem to lead us in a certain direction and to pursue specific ends. Instead of insisting on its linearity and presupposing a teleological evolution, he suggested contemplating the ruptures and contradictions of history:

> History becomes "effective" to the degree that it introduces discontinuity into our very being – as it divides our emotions, dramatizes our instincts, multiplies our body and sets it against itself. "Effective" history deprives the self of the reassuring stability of life and nature, and it will not permit itself to be transported by a voiceless obstinacy toward a millennial ending. (Foucault 1977, 153)

What Foucault calls "effective history", and what we might understand as a more relational conception of histories, is something entirely other than a clear-cut case to which one can refer as an "arbiter of right and wrong". This is because it denies reassurance instead of offering it, and thus falls foul of the project of transmitting its meaning for eternity. By juxtaposing Foucault's critical reading of history with the diagnosis of hegemonic usages of history proposed by historian Joan W. Scott (2020) in her recent book on "lessons from history", we gain further insight into the ways in which historical discourse functions: by thinking about the past as an instructive case instead of emphasising its "discontinuity", events in the past seem to unfold as a unidirectional chain that allows us to use history to guide our actions in the present.[14] It is from what actually happened in the past that lessons can be learned, as the logic identified by Scott goes. In this way, the past is meticulously distinguished from the present in order to create different futures that will still conform to history's progressive and necessary direction (Scott 2020, 3). This understanding and utilisation of history is what Michel de Certeau (1988) called the "historical operation", which can be related to other critical works on history and the process of constructing it, especially those by Hayden White (1987, 1978; also see Paul 2011). According to this perspective, historians (and I would add memory activists and entrepreneurs) often create the past through their representations of history because they decide what to consider noteworthy and how to eventually turn it into a consumable story.

The questions raised by a discourse-theoretical approach to history and public memory therefore do not cast doubt on the historical events themselves but

---

14 This aspect of the historical operation is especially pertinent to the analysis and outlook offered in chapters 8 and 9.

instead seek answers to how we think about the past, how we interpret it, which narratives and instances of the past are favoured over others and where the limits and possibilities of all statements about the past lie (Foucault 1979, 46). More generally, Sara Mills argues that any analysis of discourse

> should be concerned with the mechanics whereby one becomes produced as the dominant discourse, which is supported by institutional funding, by the provision of buildings and staff by the state, and by the respect of the population as a whole, whereas the other is treated with suspicion and is housed both metaphorically and literally at the margins of society. (1997, 19)

The aim of discourse analysis is consequently not to research a specific institution, ideology or theory but rather to focus on the practices, mechanisms and conditions that make their existence possible in the first place, grant them authority or render them irrelevant. Investigating memory as discourse analysis facilitates the assessment of how closely truth and knowledge about the past are connected to power. Each constitutes and depends on the other, and this led Foucault to draw the conclusion that power itself is not primarily restrictive but can also be highly productive because it formulates possibilities of behaviour and offers forms of subjectivity: "The individual is not to be conceived of as a sort of elementary nucleus [...] on which power comes to fasten [...]. In fact, it is already one of the prime effects of power that certain bodies, certain gestures, certain discourses, certain desires come to be identified and constituted as individuals" (Foucault 1980, 98).

This productiveness of power that constitutes certain subject positions is highly relevant to my analysis and decisively informed my close reading of programmes for global citizenship in chapter 4 as well as my case studies.

What is more, in the discursively conditioned historical operation, the present is historicised and simultaneously determined by what it lacks, thereby imagining a future that overcomes this deficiency. Thus, the history that materialises at sites of public memory must not be understood as history unfolding on its own but rather as the effect of its materialisation that constructs notions of past, present and future, and establishes relationships between them. These relationships are the foundation of how we can refer to the past and subsequently of what can be learned from the past. These "lessons of history" – in the case of Holocaust memory, often called "lessons for humanity" – are part of a moral history that comprises a representation of differences. Scott summarises this effect as follows:

> There is an unresolvable tension in the very word history between moral imperatives and political practicalities: the *lessons of history*, after all, not only expose errors that demand

> correction, evils that require repudiation, but also remind us of human imperfection, of the necessary compromises of politics, and the impossibility of securing peace on earth. (2020, 4)

Every time history is invoked as the legitimation for political decisions or projects, a "historical operation" is at work. It is the repudiation of "a certain (constructed) past in order to clear an opening to the future [...] as a way of providing moral legitimation for the operation itself" (Scott 2020, 4–5). Thus, the overarching question for the analysis undertaken from the theoretical angle mapped out here is how the historical operation works as a politics of memory.

A decolonial study of memory from the perspective of global governmentality

This volume aims to illuminate how memory is utilised as a tool of government. To this end, the analytical perspective informing the overarching questions of my study is that of global governmentality. However, as I have explained, there is no theory or methodology that explicitly maps out what global governmentality is concerned with or how to approach a possible topic of investigation from this analytical viewpoint. By supplementing the theoretical angle of governmentality with decolonial theory, the focus becomes more precise, adding weight to assessments of universalised Euro-modern modes of government. The interaction between these theoretical perspectives gives us a deeper insight into politics of citizenship and the impact of coloniality as it, for example, shows that certain aspects of current governmental techniques, especially the management of "difference", were first tried out in the colonies (Mamdani 1996). Moreover, a dialogue with decolonial perspectives enriches and makes studies of global governmentality more complex in the sense that, even though both discourses challenge the many binaries on which conventional analyses of global politics are premised, the decolonial lens invites us to envisage the world differently, as an interconnected space discursively constituted by actors who exist contemporaneously to each other. What is more, if we seek to understand the implications of the governmental means that target future horizons of hope, it is key to look at the coloniality of dominant imaginaries that strengthen "the single story" rather than create openings for pluriversality.

Subsequently, the additional inclusion of theoretical considerations about memory and museums as specific sites of memory but also of government helps us to better understand how these mechanisms work on the micro level. In order to make these theoretical deliberations more tangible and to apply them to the sites of my investigation, namely human rights museums, I want to evoke two claims mentioned earlier about the "nature" of the museum: that of the museum as a site of government and that of the museum as a Western institution. In his renowned book, *The Birth of the Museum*, museum scholar Tony Bennett (1995) argues that museums are sites of government that, as I mentioned above in relation to the dual role of education, complement prisons in their function of disciplining citizen-subjects. Bennett explains this claim as follows:

> The museum, viewed as a technology of behaviour management, served to organize new types of social cohesion precisely through the new forms of both differentiating and aligning populations it brought into being. [...] If [...] the prison served the purpose of depoliticizing crime by detaching a manageable criminal sub-class from the rest of the population, the museum provided its complement in instilling new codes of public behaviour which drove a wedge between the respectable and the rowdy. (Bennett 1995, 101–102)

Bennett proposes a view of the museum that focuses on its capacity to disseminate knowledge and, along with it, governmental rationale. His observations about the construction of hierarchies amongst citizen-subjects are especially salient today, as my work will show. Unlike many other museum scholars, Bennett continuously examines "the public museum alongside a parallel series of exhibition apparatuses [...]. These jointly comprised a complex distinguished by a particular set of knowledge/power relations which provided a counterpoint to those informing the operations of Foucault's disciplinary archipelago" (Bennett 2018, 19). Accordingly, the museum is deeply conditioned by the power-knowledge nexus and is moreover an important player in the politics of truth. The public museum, according to Bennett, used to (and still does, as I will contend) not only help to order things and bodies of knowledge according to Enlightenment ideals and evolutionist thinking in gendered and racial hierarchies, but moreover primarily served the purpose of stimulating the voluntary "self-reform" of visitors (2018, 19–20). In this sense, as Bennett concludes, museums became important agents for "civic education" and are even "civic engines" themselves. The issue of "civic education" is now familiar and reminds us both of the techniques of the self and of the role of education as part and parcel of colonial "civilising" missions. Does this mean that the museum stems from the very logic of "civilising" those who allegedly lack the ability to become "proper" humans or citizens?

In her article on "deprovincialising the museum", museum scholar and curator Nora Sternfeld (2016) recalls a conversation between herself, her students and Bonaventure Soh Bejeng Ndikung, the founder of the art space *Savvy Contemporary: The Laboratory of Form-Ideas* and the newly appointed artistic director at the *Haus der Kulturen der Welt,* both located in Berlin, Germany. One of Sternfeld's students had asked Ndikung whether or not the museum was a Western institution (implying in her question that it was). Ndikung responded by asking the student: "Is the museum a Western idea, or is the idea that the museum is a Western idea a Western idea?" (Sternfeld 2016, 200). The view proposed by Ndikung challenges the premises on which a common reading and historiography of the institution of the museum is based because it opens up new potential ways of thinking about what the museum has been and could yet become. This alternative viewpoint will be pivotal to an experiment I call *the Museum of Doubt*, to which the ninth chapter of this book is dedicated. More generally, the brief overview of museum historiography and theory provided in the third subsection of chapter 2 points to the first aspect problematised by Ndikung and Sternfeld, namely that most accounts of the evolution of the museum begin in nineteenth-century Europe (Bennett 1995). There is thus no easy answer to Ndikung's challenge, and the student's assumption is very relatable as what are presumed to be the first museums did clearly serve the purpose of "accumulating time" (Foucault 1986, 24) by means of collecting everything that was regarded as constitutive of Western culture. Furthermore, museums soon became spaces of demarcation, where the West's "others" were depicted in sharp contrast to the "civilised" and "cultivated" societies of Europe (Breckenridge and Appadurai 2015). The aforementioned division of museums into different genres (art museums, history museums, ethnographic museums etc.) is also, according to Mieke Bal (1996), a result of the Western tradition of thought, which divided the world and its inhabitants into the "civilised" (who make history and produce art) and the "savages" (whose history is not recognised and whose art is not considered to be art).

Though clearly important, these issues are not the most central to my argument about the museum as a Western institution.[15] What I want to emphasise instead is related to Bal's notion of "exposure" as well as Bennett's suggestion that we understand museums as "civic engines". This is because, however compelling the emphasis on the museum is – even though it might not be a Western idea after all – the hegemonic notion of the museum's entanglement with Eurocentrism is as strong as ever. Bragato and Gordon have argued that, through different modes of coloniality, Eurocentrism has established itself as a global phenomenon with profound consequences, because it

---

15 Many museums across Europe as well as some in settler-colonial societies have established working groups to learn more about their colonial entanglements. Published works that specifically cover the problem of museums and the colonial past and present of their collections are, for example, Fairweather 2018; Kravagna 2015; Aldrich 2009; Henare 2005; Coombes 1994, 2017.

> expresses the specific rationality of the new global standard of power established in Euro-modernity through colonial relations. Eurocentrism is a binary, dualistic perspective of intersubjective and cultural relations between Europe and the rest of the world codified in a set of categories (East/West, primitive/civilized, [...] irrational/rational, traditional/modern). (Bragato and Gordon 2018, 4)

The institution of the (Western) museum was designed to contribute to this very codification of categories and boundaries because, as we have already seen, the museum, at its very core, is an operation of knowledge. A museum is assigned authority over knowledge: it accumulates and assembles, includes and excludes, and (re)orders knowledge, which it then displays and thus disseminates. In this sense, museums expose knowledge by presenting and revealing "truth", and their "acts of exposure" can be understood not only as "showing" but also as a form of "telling" (Bal 1992). To ensure that this exposure is effective, museums organise the gaze to govern the eye (Bennett 2018, 170) and set both the direction and pace of time, which is, at least in the case of historical museums, most often trapped in progressivist thinking (Kazeem 2009). Moreover, museums have the ability to shape imaginaries, an important aspect of coloniality that is very relevant to this analysis. Of course, the museum can also be a space of disobedience (Ndikung 2016, qtd. in Sternfeld 2016), has "radical democratic potential" (Prottas 2020, 210) and agency (Kazeem et al. 2009).[16] But even a self-reflective, critical museum is in danger of propping up modes of coloniality simply because of the nature of exposure – namely, *telling* – and the many long-standing assumptions and practices of representation.

In conclusion, attempting to perform a decolonial analysis of public memory from the perspective of global governmentality opens up multiple fruitful aspects that enrich the investigation, make it more complex and thus – hopefully – help to make it less likely to fall into the many traps of a "single story". Nevertheless, the difficulty of this undertaking is reflected in this very account of my theoretical and methodological framework, in which I use a division that is common, but not unproblematic, in scholarly work on memory, the Holocaust and (anti-)colonialism, namely that between memory studies (specifically in connection to Holocaust studies) on the one hand and decolonial and postcolonial studies on the other (Gilbert and Alba 2019). As one of the first scholars to have critiqued this separation in Anglophone academia, Michael Rothberg (2009) explicitly criticises the lack of engagement with postcolonial topics in Holocaust (memory) studies. He furthermore attests a predominantly metropolitan focus to memory studies and claims that "cultural memory studies may have inadvertent-

16 I will discuss some of my own thoughts about this potential further in chapter 9.

ly done as much to reproduce imperial mentalities as to challenge them" (Rothberg 2013, 364). The scarcity of dialogue between the two areas of scholarly interest is surprising when looked at from the field of decolonial thought, where, as mentioned in the previous chapter, anti-colonial thinkers have made references and drawn parallels to the Holocaust since the 1950s. Since the publication of *Multidirectional Memory,* Rothberg's criticism has prompted more work that explicitly tries to bring together decolonial theory and studies of (Holocaust) memory, although they remain on the margins. As Sarah Phillips Casteel explains, and I agree with her,

> [a]ttempts to effect a rapprochement between postcolonial and Holocaust studies must inevitably confront thorny issues surrounding the Holocaust's status as a yardstick for other historical atrocities as well as fears that the global distribution of Holocaust memory will result in the erasure of authentic historical knowledge of the Shoah. (2019, 247)

This quotation sums up many of the considerations I have mapped out in this chapter, but it is rich in presuppositions which need to be unpacked before I rely on them in my analysis. For this reason, before I move on to the analytical part of this volume and explore the particular mechanisms of power at play at the juncture between Holocaust memory and the global human rights project, I would like to use the next short chapter to disentangle the nexus of these two discourses.

3 The Emergence of the Holocaust-Human Rights Nexus

As stated in the introduction, underlying my research is the presupposition that there is an interdependence between Holocaust memory and the human rights project. This nexus has, in turn, been nurtured by various mnemonic practices and memory policies (McQuaid and Gensburger 2019). However, since the interconnectedness of these two fields is not widely recognised, this claim needs further elaboration. In this chapter, I will begin by briefly historicising the emergence of the Holocaust-human rights nexus in order to point out how necessary it is to investigate its political implications. To this end, I will cursorily look at the two fields separately, the memory of the Holocaust on the one hand and human rights on the other, before then mentioning some of the most important developments that have cemented their amalgamation.[1] By first addressing both discourses separately I also want to substantiate the claim that they have not always been closely connected and have only been linked to each other rather recently in relation to broader political changes and concerns (Moyn 2014). In this way, I will illustrate the rise of the human rights paradigm in relation to the ways in which "the Holocaust trope" and its images began to "travel" into other political contexts (Huyssen 2018) in order to eventually provide an understanding of the role played by the nexus in today's political culture. These clarifications will then bring me to the aspect of the nexus most relevant to my overall topic: the memorialisation of the Holocaust in human rights museums.

Public memory of the Holocaust and its universalisation

Part of what Stuart Hall (2011b) called the "national culture" of Euro-modern nation states is, as I explained in my theoretical considerations, a conception of time that is divided into past, present and future. One discursively constructed product of this conception of time is the idea of history as the biography of an *imagined community.* Similar to the biography of an individual, a shared history serves first and foremost to provide meaning within a national culture. Much of what is considered "culture" is explained by making reference to the past as it is represented in traditional rituals, in a certain lifestyle or in particular laws that

1 I do not, however, claim completeness but have only picked the milestones that are directly linked to the overall topic of this book.

https://doi.org/10.1515/9783110788044-005

derive their legitimacy from the past. However, this past is not a product that accumulates uniformly or "naturally" in the course of time. Rather, a society's past is a product of discourses, its representation often the result of controversial power and knowledge structures (Reichel 1995). Here, "memory strategies" (Reichel 1995, 26) come into play which are supposed to create a balanced chronology, a harmony between past, present and future. The connection between the "national culture" of a nation state and its materialisation in practices of remembering is not always immediately clear. By symbolically memorialising the past in icons, monuments and museums, or even in public statements, historical realities are constantly being repressed, erased and restored at the same time. Therefore, the position that National Socialism and the Holocaust have occupied in Europe and in the wider world since 1945 has changed again and again. Depending on the individual nation states and their respective practices of public memorialisation, the Shoah has been assigned varying positions in the landscape of remembrance.

Primo Levi, who was persecuted as a Jew and deported to Auschwitz, tells the story of a recurring dream that he and other prisoners in the camp constantly had of being back home with their families and wanting to report on the unimaginable things that were happening to them in Auschwitz: "[...] I cannot help noticing that my listeners do not follow me. In fact, they are completely indifferent; they speak confusedly of other things amongst themselves, as if I was not there. My sister looks at me, gets up and goes away without a word" (Levi 1996, 60). This nightmare became a reality for many survivors, both within their families and in wider society, because, for over forty years, hardly any space was created in which survivors of the Shoah could have reported, could have "borne witness", although many saw precisely this as their duty to all those who had been murdered (Levi 1991, 167–169; Agamben 2002, 13). The deliberate, planned attempt to completely eradicate European Jewry seemed both morally and intellectually incomprehensible, and thus no conventional ways of coming to terms with the past appeared to be suitable (Adorno 1997; Postone 2005). What made the matter of Holocaust memory even more difficult was both a lack of awareness and the refusal to sincerely acknowledge the victims and their immense suffering – an acknowledgement that would have also included a recognition of responsibility or even guilt for the mass atrocities committed. On the societal level, there was the question of how to speak about such horrendous crimes and what it might mean to publicly commemorate and mourn in a democratic secular society. Such fundamental considerations about how to memorialise the Holocaust seem almost unimaginable today, as we see all around us well-established, though not uncontested, landscapes of memory dedicated to commemorating the Holocaust and other genocides across Europe, North America and of course Israel, as well as in the Balkans, Cambodia, Taiwan, South Africa and Rwanda (Schoor and Schüler-Springorum 2016), a phenomenon that is today often referred to as transnational memory (De Cesari and Rigney 2014).

But in the immediate postwar years and during the Cold War, there was not yet any mention of a shared, transnational memory; collective memory moved in purely national contexts – if memory of the Holocaust was indeed assigned any relevance at all (Levy and Sznaider 2006, 27–29). It is only since the end of the bloc confrontation in 1989/1990 that there has been a visible change that has increasingly lifted the memory of the Holocaust out of its "national containers" (Levy and Sznaider 2006, 24). This interpretation has been contested by Michael Rothberg (2009, 2019), who, as mentioned above, has emphasised the many earlier references to the Shoah across the globe, most prominently in relation to anti-colonial and abolitionist critique. However, it is certainly only since the beginning of the new millennium that questions of how to appropriately commemorate and "correctly" interpret the Shoah have been discussed in a more global context – increasingly within a broader human rights context, in which the Holocaust has come to function as a negative point of reference. A telling example of this trend is the official narrative about the consolidation of postwar Europe, according to which the European Union rose out of the ashes of a desolate war-torn continent which had been brought to its senses by the shock of the Holocaust. This metaphor of Europe as a phoenix was employed by the former President of the European Council, Herman Van Rompuy (2012), in a speech he delivered after the European Union was awarded the Nobel Peace Prize in 2012. More generally, as Michael Rothberg and Yasemin Yildiz note, "the continent's post war unification [...] has taken place via the explicit rejection of the Nazi past [...]. Collective memory of the Holocaust has functioned as a point of reference for a post-fascist Europe and the basis of a human rights regime [...]" (Rothberg and Yildiz 2011, 34).

The Kosovo War of 1998/1999 is another case in point and is often mentioned as a key moment on the way to the globalisation of memory. Indeed, the war in Kosovo was the first military intervention to be carried out in the name of the "lessons of the Holocaust" and the protection of human rights (Levy and Sznaider 2006, 194). Through implicit and explicit comparisons to the Shoah, the conflict came to be understood as a moral confrontation, and, in Germany, politicians and the media dared for the first time to draw parallels to the Shoah in order to justify their involvement. In this context, the imperative of "never again Auschwitz" was suddenly no longer confined to references to the historical atrocities committed by the Germans but served as a cipher to prevent future genocides (Levy and Sznaider 2006). This trend was further strengthened by another discursive event in the wake of the new millennium: the international

Stockholm Holocaust Conference (26–28 January 2000), which testified to the important role that Holocaust education still had to play (Kroh 2008). Its declaration states that "[t]he Holocaust (Shoah) fundamentally challenged the foundations of civilization" and that "the unprecedented character of the Holocaust will always hold universal meaning" (The Stockholm International Forum on the Holocaust 2000). Furthermore, the signatories undertook to encourage "the study of the Holocaust in all its dimensions", to promote "education about the Holocaust in our schools [...] and in our communities" and to commemorate "the victims of the Holocaust and to honour those who stood against it".[2]

Not long after the generalisation of Holocaust memory, which was an important discursive strategy to help make German participation in the Kosovo War acceptable, and, shortly thereafter, the reaffirmation of the importance of Holocaust education, the globalisation of Holocaust memory culminated in the establishment of International Holocaust Remembrance Day: in 2005, the General Assembly of the United Nations confirmed the global importance of Holocaust memory by officially adopting an international memorial day, which has since been observed on 27 January, the date that Auschwitz was liberated. A great deal of scholarly work has already been produced on UN Resolution 60/7, which made the memorial day official, but I would nevertheless like to recall its primary content in order to illustrate my argument. Half of the ten preambles to this resolution explicitly refer to the Universal Declaration of Human Rights and two more to the Convention on the Prevention of Genocide. Thus, the intertwinement of Holocaust memory on the one hand with the advancement of human rights on the other was officially and universally institutionalised by the decision to introduce International Holocaust Remembrance Day. In the resolution text, the choice to officially commemorate the Holocaust was formulated as mutually reaffirming respect for human rights and thus the fact "that the Holocaust, which resulted in the murder of one-third of the Jewish people, along with countless members of other minorities, will forever be a warning to all people of the dangers of hatred, bigotry, racism and prejudice" (United Nations 2005). Support for the resolution also encountered demands to extend its scope. The representative from Venezuela, Imeria Núnez de Odremán, and Maged Abdelfattah Abdelaziz, the Egyptian representative, advocated that not only the victims of the Holocaust but also victims of anti-Christian and anti-Muslim persecution, such as in Kosovo or Srebrenica, be commemorated (Schoder 2012, 5). The Malaysian representative, Hayati Ismail, agreed that "[t]he resolu-

2 I will look more closely at the Stockholm conference as well as the developments that resulted from it in chapter 4's subsection on global Holocaust memory education.

tion should be broadened to incorporate not only the lessons of the Holocaust but also other acts of genocide, ethnic cleansing and war crimes" (Ismail, qtd. in Schoder 2012, 5). Indonesian representative Muhammad Anshor added, "It would be preferable if the intention to institute Holocaust remembrance within the United Nations system also gave simultaneous attention to other tragedies" (Anshor, qtd. in Schoder 2012, 5). Eventually, Resolution 60/7 was passed without any of the broadenings of scope put forward by some representatives, and so, the Holocaust was institutionalised as a clear shared point of reference worldwide. Along with the addition of this new commemorative event to the global calendar, an outreach programme was established which conceptualises the annual observance day together with corresponding educational projects. Without passing judgement on whether this was a positive development or not, it must be noted that the process of globalising Holocaust memory produced a set of norms or a standard for how to approach the history of the Holocaust, the means by which it should be remembered and what conclusions should be drawn from its memory (David 2017).

My intention with this brief genealogy is by no means to convey the impression of a coherent development towards the historical reassessment and transformation of the Shoah and its memory, as it was more a shift in discourses that led to the universalisation of Holocaust memory. In turn, the more recent history of human rights is increasingly being linked to that of international law, with the Nuremberg War Crimes Tribunal (1945–1949) being repeatedly declared as its point of departure (Teitel 2016). In this genealogy, it appears as if a new morality emerged with the end of the Second World War and the Allied victory over Nazism, which has been continuously advanced and consolidated ever since. While historian Samuel Moyn (2012, 2014) notes that the human rights agenda that was increasingly being discussed in the 1940s was *not* in fact an explicit response to the Shoah and thus did not aim to prevent genocide in the future, the Nuremberg trials were nonetheless retrospectively inscribed into the history of human rights. The tribunal has come to function as a positive founding myth in much the same way that the Holocaust was inscribed into European and even global historiography as a negative reference.[3] In an essay on forgiveness, Jacques Derrida directly links the emergence of the global paradigm of a morally charged human-rights project to the universalisation of memory described above, which, according to him,

> authorised, with the Nuremberg Tribunal, the international institution of a juridical concept such as the "crimes against humanity". [...] Even if words like "crimes against humanity"

3 The latter in particular will be discussed in the interpretation following this chapter.

> now circulate in everyday language, that event itself was *produced* and authorised by an international community on a date and according to a figure determined by its history. This overlaps [...] with the history of a reaffirmation of human rights, or a new Declaration of Human Rights. (Derrida 2001, 29)

Derrida maintains that the international stage, as it had been reshaped after the events of the Second World War, was constituted largely by a new "urgency of memory", which was itself conditioned by the rise of the human rights paradigm. He concludes – and I would like to use this assertion as a stepping stone to my explications on human rights – that "the concept of 'crimes against humanity' remains on the horizon of [...] geopolitics" (Derrida 2001, 30).

The human rights paradigm as a global morality

At the beginning of the 1980s, Black queer feminist Audre Lorde famously said, "The master's tools will never dismantle the master's house" (1984, 110). In our current age, one of these tools – at least this is what its critics often posit – is the human rights paradigm (Mutua 2016; Whyte 2019). Considerations of this claim will serve as a common theme in the following chapters, but I do not intend to discuss it in isolation but rather to keep it in mind as a backdrop to my examination of the Holocaust-human rights nexus. I would simultaneously like to emphasise the ambivalence of the human rights project, of which I am critical mostly due to its underlying logic and political implications, but which I certainly do not intend to reject entirely. However, the discussions carried out by scholars like Wendy Brown (2004; 2006), Costas Douzinas (2000; 2007; 2013), Didier Fassin (2012), Jessica Whyte (2012; 2017; 2019), Makau Mutua (2009; 2016) and Joseph R. Slaughter (2007) have shown me that human rights are much more than the actual rights formulated in the 1948 Universal Declaration of Human Rights and all its corresponding documents and additionally drafted declarations (such as the Convention on the Rights of the Child or the Declaration on the Rights of Indigenous Peoples). The human rights project can instead be perceived as a much broader phenomenon and, in its close relationship with Euro-modernity and, more recently, neoliberalism, as one of the most powerful paradigms of our time (Brown 2004, 2015; Moyn 2018; Whyte 2019). Whilst I cannot fully delve into the immense body of work on the ambivalent history or many paradoxes of human rights, I will briefly summarise here how I understand human rights myself and from which critical scholarship on human rights I have derived this perspective. I will mainly do so, perhaps in a somewhat unorthodox manner, by looking at some of the contradictions and ambiguities of the human rights project to give the reader a sense of the ways in which human rights function as a discourse of power and normativity that is deeply rooted in liberal democratic policies and philosophy.

In many introductions to human rights (Ishay 2008; Sommer and Stellmacher 2009; Joas 2011; 2015), their "evolution" (Lauren 2011) is divided into roughly three generations or dimensions: the first generation is considered to have had its starting point closely following the French Revolution in the mid-eighteenth century, the second arose about a hundred years later in the nineteenth century, and the most current, the third generation of human rights, is said to have emerged around the middle of the twentieth century (Fremuth 2015, 67–69). I am most interested in the third generation, which is currently the most influential – in international law and also more broadly as a public discourse (Hunt 2007; Moyn 2012).

It is commonly accepted that the origins of human rights can be found in Enlightenment ideals and subsequent developments such as the French Revolution (Tedeschini 2019). That human rights are universal is another widely accepted attribute, though one that was not formulated until the drafting of the Universal Declaration of Human Rights (hereafter UDHR) (Sommer and Stellmacher 2009, 13). In this sense, human rights law can be understood as an internationalisation of what Makau Mutua has called "the obligations of the liberal state" (2016, 12). By this he means the duty of each nation state to "police" itself. Only in the case of the alleged failure of such self-regulation is the international structure called upon, and the accused nation state becomes the target of human rights mechanisms, from scrutiny to intervention to international tribunals and courts (Mutua 2016). However, Samuel Moyn challenges this narrative of the constant progress of human rights and, even though he agrees that the institutionalisation of human rights took place in the late 1940s (Eckel 2014), he dates their actual rise to relevance much later. He argues that, in the late 1970s, when both the socialist project and anti-colonial struggles had lost their drawing power, it was human rights that remained as a domain in which to seek a better future (Moyn 2012). However, this perspective is rather Eurocentric as it only starts at the point in time when the radical claims for human rights coming from the global South and its newly liberated post-colonial states had fallen silent (Whyte 2019; Tedeschini 2019).

Despite a notion of "shared power" at the newly founded United Nations that made it possible for claims emanating from the global South to be heard, Mutua and other critical scholars of human rights and international law, such as Luis Eslava and Sundhya Pahuja (2020), as well as Nicola Perugini and Neve Gordon (2015), remind us that "in fact, international law started as a racist project" (Mutua 2016, 13). Nation states, mostly in Western Europe, considered themselves civilised and thus superior, and viewed themselves "as God's gift to the rest of humanity" (Mutua 2016, 13), a position with which these states legitimised not only the exploitation but also the "policing" of the rest of the world by means of colonisation, the primary method for enforcing Euro-modern norms and installing them as global standards. While some of the human rights formulated in the UDHR – foremost maybe the right to life – of course cannot be written off that simply as Euro-modern principles and indeed hold the promise of serving the most vulnerable, other fundamental human rights, like the right to property, do invite such decolonial critique less ambiguously. The reason for this is not so much the ideological underpinnings of this particular right or the general human rights outlined above but the many instances in which current Indigenous land claims have been dismissed with recourse to Article 17 of the UDHR, which includes the human right to (individual) property, thereby hampering decolonisation processes (Sayın et al. 2017).

Interestingly enough, various delegates from the Soviet bloc as well as from Latin American nation states were already criticising the inherent inequality and hierarchy of the UDHR at its birth. These delegates specifically pointed to the theory and practice widespread among colonial powers that have allowed them to categorise the people on this planet into superior races who are meant to rule and inferior races that must be subordinated or even eradicated (Whyte 2017). The absurdity of using phrases such as "civilised nations", they argued, stood in sharp contrast to the emphasis on equal rights and non-discrimination that many Western delegates put forward as core principles, which are the values for which the UDHR is still being praised today. Jessica Whyte reminds us that "[w]hen the UK tried to retain this language by pointing to the long, established lineage of civilisational hierarchies, it was forced to reckon with the delegate of India, who knew well the historical consequences that had followed from European assumptions of superiority" (2017, para 21). This is an important insight because it illuminates a contradiction at the heart of the concept of "all members of the human family", as it was called during the UDHR's drafting process. The Western states that were simultaneously the colonisers did not think of colonial subjects as members of this family; when they spoke about "everyone" they did not mean those whom they had categorised as inferior. This has far-reaching consequences even today because, in the words of Costas Douzinas, "Despite the claims of liberal philosophers, [...] bare humanity offers no protections. Human rights, we could conclude, do not belong to humans; they help construct who and how one becomes human" (Douzinas 2009, para 7). Douzinas' evaluation is similar to the aforementioned decolonial criticism of the categories "human" and "humanity", and reveals once more the contradiction at the heart of Hannah Arendt's famous phrase about "the right to have rights".

This right, Arendt suggested, would be the necessary precondition for gaining the protection of any other universally binding human rights,[4] because, as Ferit Güven puts it, "for those who were at the margin of the society, it has always been a possibility that their existence will lose all the 'privileges' and 'rights' lent to them" (2015, 7).

In order to not only receive but also retain the rights they had been granted, the recipients of those right were required to meet the standards that had been set and acclimatise to them. Ayça Çubukçu sums up the conundrum underlying the human rights paradigm and relates it the conception of "the human" as follows:

> on the one hand, liberal articulations of human rights are "founded" on the assumption that one is born a human being, and therefore entitled to human rights by birth, on the other hand, such conceptions of human rights attach particular qualities to the concept and person of the human. [...] Strikingly, in these humanist formulations, what all humans around the world share is a capacity for humanity: what is common to humans is, primarily, a potential humanity that requires cultivation, development and fostering. (Çubukçu 2017, 255–256)

The paradox here is that not all humans have the right to be human but instead need to earn their entitlement. The implication is that where rights can be granted, they can also be taken away, a supposition which divides the people sharing this planet into those dispensing norms and rights on the one hand and those trying to live up to the requirements in order to achieve or retain the privileges of being human on the other. At the juncture with Holocaust memory, the idea of such a "capacity for humanity" towards which subjects need to be guided and thus empowered to partake in its benefits is surprisingly salient, as I will show in the course of this analysis.

Despite the fundamental contradiction at the heart of universal human rights,[5] the UDHR was accepted by forty-eight of the fifty-six delegates present

---

4 A very thoughtful examination of Arendt's thinking about "the right to have rights" can be found in a publication of the same name by DeGooyer et al. (2017).

5 There were more controversies than the one detailed here. Another dispute between the Soviet bloc and the United States, for example, arose in relation to the opposing emphases on either social and cultural rights (which the USSR delegates wanted to strengthen) or civil and political rights (for which the US advocated). These opposing interests even resulted in the drafting of two different resolutions, which were only negotiated and enshrined in international law in 1966. For more on this issue, see Eric D Weitz' (2019) book on the roles that individual nation states' interests played during the period in which the UDHR was being drafted and implemented.

in Paris on 10 December 1948 and is celebrated and invoked even today throughout the world and by various political orientations. The adoption of the declaration paved the way for present-day human rights policies and is considered to be one of the most important moments of postwar history, rather like the Nuremberg trials (1945–1947) and the signing of the Convention on the Prevention of Genocide, which was adopted just one day before the UDHR.[6] Considering the close proximity of the defeat of Nazism in Europe to the introduction of these new international principles, it stands to reason that these very principles were articulated as a direct, immediate reaction to the events of the Second World War, especially the Holocaust.

As has been noted before, even though it was met with some contestation, this familiar, much-cited storyline nonetheless adds retrospective moral weight to human rights because it clearly positions the UDHR on the "good" side of history (Eckel 2014; Moyn 2014). As a beacon of hope in a still unjust world, human rights have served and continue to serve the marginalised and ill-treated around the world in their struggles for justice. And yet the appeal to human rights, however strong the case, does not ensure social or even political change. One reason for this is that, on a global level, human rights are currently not usually categorised as legally binding laws but instead as "principles" or "ideals", which is accompanied by numerous enforcement problems (Femuth 2015, 69). In this sense, the ideal that the human rights discourse supports is very much dependent on the "good will" of those dispensing the rights, even more so when their own political interests are at stake.[7] In relation to this specific character, Douzinas defines human rights as follows: "Human Rights are a hybrid category, which introduces a number of paradoxes at the heart of society by bringing together law and morality" (2009, para 3). There is an interesting parallel to which I would like to point here: in discussing the paradoxical nature of "learning from history", the constant tension resulting from the fusion of politics and morality is reminiscent

---

6 A lengthy discussion on the further development of international law in the context of decolonisation can be found in the edited volume on the "Battle for International Law" by von Bernstorff and Dann (2019).

7 In this regard I would once more like to point to the situation of refugees dying during their attempts to cross the Mediterranean Sea as well as to the human rights activists risking their lives in the struggle to save them. Not only are these refugees being reduced to "bare life" that is not considered worthy of rescuing or granting refuge to, but sea rescue missions are also being criminalised instead of supported, which is resulting in activists being sent to jail and their boats demolished. This is not simply a case of human rights being neglected but one that shows how human rights discourse operates within a certain political rationality which depoliticises issues such as the right to asylum and even the right to life itself, just as Hannah Arendt predicted (Sciurba and Furry 2017).

of the tension involved in a similar coupling at play in human rights discourse. The ways in which both subjects – human rights and the lessons to be learned from history – are related to the moral arena will thus be of great interest for the following analysis. Unsurprisingly, the fusion of (international) law and morality at the heart of human rights has interested researchers from the fields of law and the humanities since their rise to influence, which was roughly twenty years ago, at the beginning of the new millennium (Moyn 2012). It is precisely this amalgamation of law and morality that has since become a powerful means for setting standards (Mutua 2016), which is most interesting to me precisely because it is in the guise of a global universal standard or morality that the Holocaust-human rights nexus takes full effect (David 2020).

The many public commemorations and condemnations of the evils of Nazism which I outlined above go hand in hand with exhortations to become better human beings with qualities that are very similar to the qualities attributed to the ideal human enshrined in the logic of human rights and humanity. This is especially interesting in regard to the ways in which human rights discourse has been fused with Holocaust memory, as I will show in my next chapter on global education and human rights museology. However, before we embark upon the analytical part of this book, I would like to conclude this very brief genealogy of the Holocaust-human rights nexus with a few general remarks.

Implications and effects of the Holocaust-human rights nexus

Memory scholar Andreas Huyssen has remarked that "most national memory projects are organisationally linked to transnational debates in museology, memorial design competitions, human rights activism, and mnemonics" (2018, para 2). The two previous subchapters support this claim and add another important aspect: projects and practices for Holocaust memory across the globe are discursively linked in the sense that they rely on a body of knowledge that has been disseminated within the human rights project and beyond, as well as through various Holocaust-related mnemonic practices and memory politics. Scholars and memory activists have raised concerns that the universalisation of Holocaust memory is not primarily invested in commemorating the victims but is rather about constructing a new shared or collective memory, one that is "above conflict" and transcends past and present in order to allow for future-looking politics (Sznaider 2008, 69). It does indeed stand to reason that the globalised memory described in the paragraphs above is more about learning lessons from the past than it is about earnestly engaging with the causes and effects of the actual historic events. This "[...] transfer of the historically specific Holocaust to a future-oriented globalised politics, on the basis of which human rights in general can be claimed [...]" (Sznaider 2008, 156–157) has standardised the discursive practices of memory and prepared the ground for the process of universalising memory in the name of democracy and peace. Lea David introduced the term "moral remembrance" (2020, 1) to describe these systematised ways in which various nation states across the world are addressing their pasts, namely the human rights abuses that are part of their history. According to her, these standards rely on a "global system that creates values and norms" which is "deeply rooted in human rights memorialisation practices" (David 2020, 12–13). In a comment similar to Derrida's observation about "cosmopolitan forgiveness" (2001), David notes that there is an expectation generated by these global standards which strongly impacts the mnemonic practices of today's nation states. The logic is as follows: if a state truly wants to come to terms with its past, it needs to follow certain steps, of which the implementation of moral remembrance is an important one. If adopted properly, as David describes the rationale, the model of moral remembrance serves as an "insurance policy against the repetition of massive human rights abuses" (2020, 2). These morally charged mnemonic standards entail dealing with or "amending" the past (Karn 2015) (e.g., through the work of history commissions and forensic archivists or the establishment of truth commissions), followed by a *duty to remember* (e.g., erecting monuments or introducing days of remembrance), which will subsequently lead to *justice for the victims* (often granted on the rather abstract level of recognition, though less often manifesting itself in financial reparations or restitution). As a result, "global injustice memories are [...] intimately connected to an implicit or explicit global 'we', with moral responsibilities that extend beyond national boundaries and identities" (David 2020, 7). In this way, the discourse of global harmony and the responsibility to secure peace often seems like it is looking back at history due to the way that it evokes the lessons learned from the past, although it is simultaneously quite ahistorical in the sense that it only very selectively refers to certain pasts, excludes others from the narrative or is ignorant about established facts that do not serve its storyline (Sznaider 2008; Madlingozi 2015).

This has been emphatically demonstrated by Wendy Brown (2006) in her study of the Simon Wiesenthal Center Museum of Tolerance, which has been a major inspiration for my work here. She points out that tolerance, the value around which the museum in Los Angeles was conceived, is a contemporary discourse of "depoliticization" (Brown 2006, 109). Moreover, the Museum of Tolerance generalises conflicts and negates their specificities through this very mechanism of depoliticisation. She explains her conclusion as follows:

> The Museum of Tolerance not only promulgates a politics that it dissimulates through the rubric of tolerance, it also promulgates a discourse of depoliticization that is itself a means by which the politics of tolerance – the operations of tolerance as a discourse of normativity and power – are dissimulated. [...] The process [...] produces a more generic depoliticization of conflicts and of scenes of inequality and domination (Brown 2006, 142).

The term depoliticisation here refers primarily to the effect produced when a political conflict is portrayed as being the result of intolerance rather than dominance so that the context is shifted, power mechanisms are obscured, and the political problem is reinterpreted as one between intolerant and tolerant individuals. Even military interventions, as Brown argues, are justified not least on the grounds that the political systems being fought are intolerant regimes. The context in which a conflict arose no longer plays any role analytically; the discursive conditions that produce an (in)tolerant attitude in the first place are not considered. What is more, demands for human rights and tolerance (or human rights by means of tolerance?) are based on an understanding that regards social differences between people as "natural" and assumes that everyone reacts to "difference" either with prejudice or with acceptance. Moreover, this discourse makes it possible to attribute the same decontextualised trigger – namely, prejudice – to every form of oppression and dominance up to and including genocide, and then to extract the same "lessons" from it: more democracy, more tolerance, more human rights. In this way, it becomes possible to explain a collection of extremely diverse phenomena by one and the same pattern, which excludes important historical and political analyses and legitimises various forms of intervention in the name of human rights (Brown 2006, 143). The question of whether this holds true for practices of Holocaust memorialisation within human rights frameworks generally as well as in the particular museums I studied will guide us throughout the following chapters.

4 The Interplay of Holocaust Memory and Human Rights Museology

The main focus of this chapter will be on what I will call *memory education*. This term indicates that public memory is not only informed by but also mediated through education. The construction and negotiation of knowledge about past events and also about the lessons to be learned from them take place to a large extent in history-based teaching. The "generation of post-memory" fills in its lack of lived experience and personal memories by means of didactics, whether in schools or museums.[1] As part of the many manifestations of the "universal urgency of memory" (Derrida 2001, 28), there has been, on the one hand, a noticeable "global proliferation" of memorial museums (Sodaro 2020, 13) dedicated to the victims of violent histories that thus have a "strong commemorative dimension" (Carter 2017, 5). At the same time, global Holocaust education is also becoming more widespread, with an increase in the number of programmes and guidelines being offered to educators and policymakers around the world (Kaiser and Storeide 2018). In this context, it is almost impossible to distinguish between historical education about Nazism or the Holocaust on the one hand and its mnemonic practices on the other. By this I mean that such education simultaneously nurtures and promotes public memory, which is why I understand institutions which focus on global Holocaust education and those primarily dedicated to its memorialisation as being reliant on each other and therefore analyse them side by side.

Today's history museums no longer solely display the heroic stories of imagined communities. Instead, they often add stories of past failures to their exhibitions, thoroughly woven into a narrative of liability and the need for atonement. A similar trend can be observed in many educational settings, where learning about past wrongdoings and case studies of atrocities serve to strengthen learners' understanding of and respect for democratic principles. This is because many "parts of the world have now begun to recognize the history of the Holocaust as an effective means to teach about mass violence and to promote human rights and civic duty, testifying to the emergence of this pivotal historical event as a universal frame of reference" (Fracapane and Haß 2014, 10). As a result,

1 I borrow this term from Marianne Hirsch, even though I am aware that she uses it to describe "the relationship that the 'generation after' bears to the personal, collective, and cultural trauma of those who came before" (2012, 5). She does not, as I do here, include all that came after as she was not referring to the historical period of the descendants of the perpetrators and bystanders but only to that of the victims.

https://doi.org/10.1515/9783110788044-006

Holocaust memory and its materialisation in educational programmes and museum exhibitions has become ubiquitous, with the consequence that one might easily think that such manifestations have been in place for a very long time. However, institutionalised Holocaust education is a rather recent phenomenon: in Europe it has only been about twenty-five years since the Holocaust was introduced to national school curricula – England being the first country to make it a mandatory subject of study, and only after a period of "long and hard (work) on the ground" (Pearce and Chapman 2017, 224). This holds true for Germany as well, where the struggle for institutionalised sites of memory and education on the subject lasted at least until the end of the 1990s (Wüstenberg 2017). Other countries such a Poland have recently even limited the public memory of the Holocaust by law and reduced its content in favour of a Polish narrative of victimhood, which makes it a criminal offence to emphasise Polish collaboration during the Holocaust (Belavusau 2018). Holocaust teaching initiatives and initiatives to establish museums and monuments in its memory outside of Europe (with the US being an exception) are even more recent, as the examples of Canada and South Africa will show. All of this is testament to the complicated and inconsistent evolution of Holocaust education and the museification of the Holocaust that, despite its global institutionalisation, still remains contested and is still being disputed in many local, national and supranational contexts (Kaiser and Storeide 2018; Rothberg 2021).

What is interesting, however, is that the foundations for the proliferation of Holocaust memory education had already been laid in the immediate postwar period, when both the United Nations Educational, Scientific and Cultural Organisation (UNESCO) and the International Council of Museums (ICOM) were founded in response to the destruction wreaked by the Second World War. On 16 November 1945, the UNESCO constitution came into force. The document opens by declaring

> [...] that since wars begin in the minds of men, it is in the minds of men that the defences of peace must be constructed; that ignorance of each other's ways and lives has been a common cause, [...] through which their differences have all too often broken into wars; that the great and terrible war which has now ended was a war made possible by the denial of the democratic principles of the dignity, equality and mutual respect of men [...]. (United Nations Treaty Series 1947, 276)

The war that is being referred to as "terrible" is the Second World War, which lasted from September 1939 to September 1945.[2] During the war, the Allied Forces had already declared that they were fighting against Nazi Germany and its collaborators in the name of democracy, against intolerance and the denial of freedom (Puckett 2019, 52). Since the moment of its constitution, the organisation has continued its work in the name of "democratic principles" – with programmes such as *Education for International Understanding* (1974), with which UNESCO first aimed for global standards in history textbooks – in order to advance a moral episteme that had not yet come into being in 1945: universal human rights. Ever since, its central aim has been to contribute to what is now conceptualised as education for peacekeeping (Kaiser and Storeide 2018, 805). In a similar vein, the emphasis on historical consciousness has prevailed in UNESCO's work. Although it has shifted its focus from the Second World War in general to the Holocaust in particular, UNESCO continues to turn to this infamous period in history, which means that, in a sense, Holocaust memory education has always been entangled with broader educational schemes from early on and has always been charged with the attempt to secure a better, more peaceful world, though the vision for the future has not always been as standardised as today.

Like UNESCO, the International Council of Museums (ICOM) was established in the period immediately following the Second World War, between 1946 and 1947. It was primarily founded to discuss and advance the "educational role of museums, exhibitions, the international circulation of cultural goods and the conservation and restoration of cultural goods" (History of ICOM). According to a definition adopted by ICOM in 2007, the museum is "a non-profit institution" that "acquires, conserves, researches, communicates, and exhibits the tangible and intangible heritage of humanity and its environment for the purposes of education, study, and enjoyment" (Museum Definition 2007). In this vein, ICOM soon began offering training to museum staff across the globe, thereby bringing the idea of the museum itself as well as techniques of conservation and aestheticisation to societies outside of Europe and North America. In this way, there was a universalisation of the museum and its purpose which is still productive of today's "mindful" museums that revolve around global issues such as climate

2 On the European continent, the war officially ended on 8 May 1945 with Germany's unconditional surrender, though it was still being fought in other parts of the world, namely in the Pacific region. The acts of war outside of Europe culminated in the detonation of the first atomic bomb over the Japanese city of Hiroshima on 6 August 1945, followed by a second one over the city of Nagasaki a few days later. Japan surrendered on 2 September 1945, which marked the end of the Second World War (Overy 2005; Beevor 2012).

change, social justice and "cultural diversity" (Janes 2010, 325). Over the years, ICOM and many of its members have supported UNESCO's initiatives, drawn on its recommendations for exhibitions and adapted some of its educational materials to the museum setting. In this sense, museums have long played an important role not only in local civic education but also in the context of global educational endeavours. In a recent meeting initiated by UNESCO with twelve museum directors from around the world, UNESCO's Assistant Director-General for Culture Ernesto Ottone said, "We need museums more than ever, the pandemic has highlighted their vital contribution to social cohesion, the economy and creativity. [...] We must do everything possible to ensure that museums retain their important function as meeting places of inspiration, sharing, and cultural mediation" (Ottone 2021, qtd. in UNESCO press release 2021). On the one hand, this statement is the result of the constant threat that museums are facing, namely that of losing their impact. However, in relation to the theoretical considerations about museums, it is Ottone's reference to "social cohesion" in particular as well as to the museum's role in enabling "cultural mediation" that is noteworthy in the context of this book and that will stay with us throughout the following chapters. Overall, global education as it is envisaged by the UN and many NGOs in the education sector as well as ICOM is an "education that opens people's eyes and minds to the realities of the world, and awakens them to bring about a world of greater justice, equity and human rights for all" (Europe-wide Global Education Congress 2002).

As I will show, Holocaust programmes have become intrinsically linked to the goal of cautioning people across the globe about "the realities of the world" – whatever that may entail – and raising awareness for human rights. These programmes are therefore connected with international relations and the global political economy but often primarily operate as a technocratic pedagogical endeavour carried out in schools, churches or museums, and undertaken by teachers and community educators. But while the aims of global Holocaust education are closely related to the local institutions of civil society, which often initiate such programmes, Holocaust memory has been authorised on the political level by supranational bodies such as the UN, the Council of Europe and the International Holocaust Remembrance Alliance (IHRA). In one of the few scholarly publications on the function of these institutions and their interplay, Kaiser and Storeide note that "promoting international norms for Holocaust remembrance and education has taken place in a governance system that at least loosely connects norm entrepreneurs across multiple levels from the national to the European and global" (2018, 806). We are thus witnessing an increase in standardised programmes and recommendations devised by specialists in Holocaust history and pedagogy that are being offered to educators and policymakers around the world. These programmes, as my analysis shows, not only provide historical content but also present the desired responses to their teachings, which supposedly strengthen democratic consciousness.

On a similar note, museums and their pedagogical efforts do not exist in a vacuum but rely on, and in turn influence, other players active in the field. I have therefore come to the conclusion that, in order to understand human rights museology as far as Holocaust memory is concerned, it is important to look at these memory authorities, which produce knowledge about the Holocaust-human rights nexus and engage in its educational endeavours. I would like to keep in mind the notion of "norm entrepreneurs" throughout the discussion and shed some light on the rationale underpinning key publications and programmes launched by UNESCO and the IHRA.

Global education against ignorance

Let us begin this section by looking at two particularly noteworthy aspects of the introduction to UNESCO's constitution: firstly, the interpretation of the Second World War as a war against gross inequality and for the "mutual respect of men"; and, secondly, the underlying assumption that the reason that this war (and others before it) broke out in the first place was not socioeconomic, nor was it driven by the will to expand territory, exploit labour or eventually exterminate supposed "other races", but was instead simply the result of "ignorance". Simlarly, Benjamin Ferencz, who had been the chief prosecutor at the 1947 *Einsatzgruppen Trial* (one of the subsequent trials carried out by the International Military Tribunal in Nuremberg)[3] and was later actively involved in the establishment of the International Criminal Court in the Hague, called the atrocities committed against Jews, a "tragic fulfilment of a program of intolerance and arrogance" (Ferencz 2018).

This perspective on war and, in particular, the Holocaust is very common and can be found throughout pedagogical projects that teach democracy, human rights and citizenship education by drawing on historical case studies. At the same time, it has been widely criticised by critical human rights scholars as well as scholars from the fields of Holocaust and genocide studies. Historian Berber Bevernage criticises the underpinnings of such an understanding of war and conflict as an "antimaterialist ontology, [...] one in which historical conflict is not primarily caused by materialist interest or structural injustices but conflict-

3 More on this trial as well as on Benjamin Ferencz himself can be found in chapter 5.

ing identities and perceptions" (2018, 81). This is a very important observation which points to the neoliberal technique of moralising and individualising political issues such as (armed) conflict as well as the responsibility for preventing such conflicts. As I have already indicated in regard to the Holocaust-human rights nexus, when they are viewed through a lens like tolerance (or intolerance), which is more of an attitude in the individual "minds of men" (United Nations Treaty Series 1947, 276) than a systemic structure or force within a society, matters of inequality and violence tend to be understood as something caused by personal prejudice (Brown 2006). Consequently, many programmes on the Holocaust which have been conceptualised around tolerance, advocating for individual empowerment and raising awareness of ignorance, do not engage enough with the complexities of the political, systemic and "materialist" structures of inequality and violence that have led to past conflicts and genocides as well as those still taking place today. In the following I will therefore not only introduce the core of UNESCO's and the IHRA's programmes but also examine whether these critical aspects can be identified in their publications. I will pay special attention to the means by which this tendency towards individualisation and depoliticisation might influence memorialisations of the Holocaust in human rights museums.

UNESCO's human rights and citizenship education

UNESCO highlights the transformative power of education and sees lifelong learning as a fundamental part of active citizenship and sustainable development. After education for international understanding, another concept began to permeate the discussion: human rights education (HRE). This is closely tied to the ideal of global citizenship, which is presented as the antidote to ignorance. This can be attributed to another shift in focus articulated by the United Nations at the beginning of the 2000s, namely the move from a "culture of reaction" with regard to genocide towards one of active prevention (Annan 2004). Because of its transformative as well as preventive potential, HRE has been presented ever since as a desirable "global educational philosophy" that encourages all endeavours for a more peaceful and just world (Zembylas and Keet 2018). It reflects the efforts of the Council of Europe and the UN to "promote human rights, democracy and the rule of law", and its overarching vision is formulated as follows:

> Learning in education for democratic citizenship and human rights education is a lifelong process [that includes] training, awareness-raising, information, practices and activities which aim, by equipping learners with knowledge, skills and understanding and develop-

> ing their attitudes and behaviour, to empower them to exercise and defend their democratic rights and responsibilities in society, to value diversity and to play an active part in democratic life, with a view to the promotion and protection of democracy and the rule of law. (Kerr 2013, 8–9)

This quotation clearly shows the connection being established between desirable citizenship and HRE, and that it is not possible to make a clear-cut distinction between citizenship education on the one hand and human rights and democracy education on the other. Michalinos Zembylas and André Keet thus identify an interdependence between human rights, democracy and citizenship in education, as all three themes are grouped under the rubric "education for democratic citizens" (2018, 1). The UNESCO 2030 Agenda also highlights the importance of global citizenship education and gives the following brief definition of its basic aims:

> While the world may be increasingly interconnected, human rights violations, inequality and poverty still threaten peace and sustainability. Global Citizenship Education (GCED) is UNESCO's response to these challenges. It works by empowering learners of all ages to understand that these are global, not local issues and to become active promoters of more peaceful, tolerant, inclusive, secure and sustainable societies. [...] It aims to instil in learners the values, attitudes and behaviours that support responsible global citizenship [...]. (UNESCO/Global citizenship education 2016)

The link between preventing violence and advancing active global citizenship is apparent in both quotations, and they are both particularly rich in their emphasis on participation, on playing an "active part" in society. This furthermore suggests a desire for an active civil society which contributes to peacekeeping by combating all forms of discrimination.

According to these definitions, citizens living in a democracy clearly have rights, which they are encouraged to claim when threatened, but they also have obligations. Democratic global citizens are expected to participate actively in society, to behave in accordance with its values and to respect its laws. In an effort to advance these universal goals, various bodies within the United Nations as well as national and international NGOs have developed programmes on key topics such as sustainability and peace in the past twenty years (Andreotti 2014), thereby adding to the salience of human rights and citizenship education (Coysh 2018). Examined from the analytical perspective of governmentality and keeping the techniques of the self in mind, the vocabulary employed by UNESCO in the above quotations is immediately reminiscent of "the will to empower" that Barbara Cruikshank (1999) has identified as inherent in contemporary democratic discourse. Wording such as "instil in learners" or "developing their [the learner's] attitude and behaviour" in particular exposes the governmental technique of influencing the subject's conduct.[4]

What is more, these educational endeavours have been connected to Holocaust memory from the outset and aim to "mobilize civil society for Holocaust remembrance and education, in order to help prevent future acts of genocide" (UN General Assembly 2005). For this reason, in addition to its HRE programmes, UNESCO passed another resolution on the promotion of Holocaust memory, and the aim of educating global citizens has also been prominent in its recent publications on Holocaust education. The two pedagogical concepts, global citizenship education and Holocaust education, are presented as being "naturally" affiliated with each other, as this passage from a policy guide on Holocaust education and preventing genocide shows: "Learning objectives [of Holocaust education] align with approaches to Global Citizenship [...]. Many educators, scholars and advocates believe that studying the Holocaust can help students develop valuable knowledge, skills, values and attitudes. Intended outcomes can range from knowledge acquisition to behavioural change" (UNESCO 2017, 38). That is because, according to Irina Bokova, the Director-General of UNESCO, teaching and learning about the Holocaust will help to "raise awareness about a shared history, to promote human rights everywhere and eliminate all forms of discrimination and violence" (2014, 5). Bokova does not elaborate on issues such as the sense in which history is "shared", which history she is referring to or how such an awareness will prevent atrocities from taking place. Instead, UNESCO writes the following about its Holocaust programme:

> Building on UNESCO's strong convening power, its role in shaping the international education agenda and its large networks, the main objectives of the programme are as follows: Raise and maintain awareness about the legacy of the Holocaust among education stakeholders, through remembrance and advocacy activities [and] develop policies and systems that are supportive of education about the Holocaust and other genocides. (2017)

This assessment of its own role gives some indication of how influential the norms developed by UNESCO are in the realm of global education. The title of the programme, "Education for Holocaust Remembrance", is furthermore suggestive of a link I would like to emphasise here once more: the binding of memory to education and vice versa. This amalgamation is powerful, especially on an emotional level, as I will demonstrate throughout my case studies. According to UNESCO, the realms in which Holocaust education as global citizenship education is supposed to achieve the most are "cognitive, socio-emotional and behav-

4 I will elaborate further on this aspect in chapter 8.

ioural" (Stevick 2018, 8). The socio-emotional domain which then impacts on the behavioural one, as the reasoning goes, stimulates "a sense of belonging to a common humanity, sharing values and responsibilities, empathy, solidarity and respect for differences and diversity" (UNESCO 2017, 15). It becomes apparent that UNESCO's programmes evoke a "sense of belonging" coupled with a feeling of responsibility for a "common humanity" by engaging with the history of the Holocaust and its *lessons for humanity.* Similar lessons are conveyed by the IHRA, to whose work I will turn next.

The International Holocaust Remembrance Alliance in promotion of global citizenship

The Stockholm International Forum on the Holocaust, which took place in 2000, and its Declaration and the ensuing establishment of the Task Force for International Cooperation on Holocaust Education, Remembrance and Research remains relevant for contemporary international organisations concerned with Holocaust memory (Allwork 2015). The task force, which changed its name to the International Holocaust Remembrance Alliance (IHRA) in 2012, currently comprises thirty-five member countries and eight observer countries (IHRA/Our Structure). All of these member states set up delegations and take turns holding the precedency of the organisation, and meet annually and report back to the IHRA about the development of Holocaust remembrance and education in their respective countries.[5] Due to its international structure, the IHRA claims to be "uniquely placed to take the lead on issues related to Holocaust education, research and remembrance in the international political arena" and, moreover, calls, though in rather vague terms, for "appropriate forms" (IHRA/Our Structure) of Holocaust remembrance and education across the globe.

In the same manner as UNESCO, the IHRA also combines Holocaust education with present-day issues relating to genocide prevention, as it states on its website,

> The IHRA's network of trusted experts share their knowledge on early warning signs of present-day genocide and education on the Holocaust. This knowledge supports policymakers and educational multipliers in their efforts to develop effective curricula, and it informs government officials and NGOs active in global initiatives for genocide prevention. (IHRA/Our Structure)

5 For an account of IHRA's structure and all its activities, please see its website: https://www.holocaustremembrance.com (accessed 2 June 2022).

The IHRA calls this work "historically-informed policymaking" and, in order to realise its goals, develops and promotes numerous resources for educators amongst its member countries and beyond to "serve as practical educational tools" (IHRA/Working Definitions). These materials are backed by charters and recommendations that primarily address policymakers. The programmes are presented under recurring topics such as "sensitising", "awareness raising" and "reflection", while their "key arguments for teaching and learning about the Holocaust" rely on the conviction that

> this study [of Holocaust history] can prompt learners to develop an understanding of the mechanisms and processes that lead to genocide, in turn leading to reflection on the importance of the rule of law and democratic institutions. This can enable learners to [...] reflect on their own role and responsibility in safeguarding these principles in order to prevent human rights violations that are liable to explode into mass atrocities. (IHRA/Why Teach About the Holocaust)

It is apparent that, like UNESCO, the IHRA intends to motivate people across the globe to become "active citizens" who reflect upon the prejudices and stereotypes they might hold, ideally unlearn them and also motivate others to do the same. In this sense, the IHRA also advocates for "behavioural changes" (UNESCO 2017) in order to strengthen democratic principles. A recent statement published as a reflection on the implementation of the IHRA's "Recommendations for Teaching and Learning about the Holocaust" reads: "After all, it is an important part of 'counter[ing] the influence of historical distortion, hate speech and incitement to violence and hatred.' That is, Holocaust education remains fundamental to the preservation of democratic values and pluralistic societies" (2020). Notably, the IHRA also states that "[t]eaching and learning about the Holocaust can help learners to identify distortion and inaccuracy when the Holocaust is used as a rhetorical device in the service of social, political and moral agendas" (2020). By identifying this advantage of Holocaust education, the IHRA is implying that its engagement is neutral and hence not something carried out "in the service of social, political and moral agendas". This assertion of non-alignment with any political agendas will stay with us throughout the analysis to follow, as it is also a common assertion in the field of human rights education, in which both educational formats present themselves as being free from any power relations or ideological commitments (Coysh 2017). The examples given above show how a particular *operation* of history is performed through the close ties between Holocaust memory on the one hand and advocacy for the moral principles of liberal democracy on the other. Such a normative idea about the "proper" reasons for learning about Holocaust history as well as the best ways of teaching it can be found in all publications by UNESCO, the

IHRA and many other partner organisations, and is meant to be globally endorsed. They share the aim of safeguarding democratic principles and follow the approach of trying to touch the "hearts and minds" of lifelong learners (UNESCO 2017, 105).

What is noteworthy in this context is that, despite the concepts of *the citizen* or *citizenship* being overt in all of these programmes and publications, no explanation is given of the implications or underpinnings of the ideal they present. This absence is revealing and can be seen as adding emphasis to Barbara Cruikshank's (1999) findings on the making of the citizen-subject, most importantly to her insight that, in democratic discourse, the citizen is not something one simply becomes by holding legal citizenship but something that is actively produced by various means. This notion of the citizen is a product of power relations that aim to guide and shape, rather than merely to control, the actions of others. My research is therefore driven by the question of whether these efforts to activate and guide subjects to become "voluntarily compliant citizens" (Cruikshank 1999, 19) can also be found in other institutions that engage with memory, such as museums. Or to put it differently: with the help of my case studies, I hoped to learn about the different ways in which memory education conducted "on the ground' contributes to the broader exercise of citizenship education.

Human rights and memorial museums

Since 2019, about fifty years after first articulating a universal definition of the museum, the ICOM has been in the process of identifying museums' social responsibilities and potential to act as agents of change and reevaluating its definition of the museum (Brown and Mairesse 2018). The scholars and museum professionals seeking its renewal argue that the current definition no longer speaks the language of the twenty-first century (Small 2019) as present-day museums should be improving participation in processes of democratisation and thereby focussing more on museums' roles as social players and social justice advocates instead of – as was traditionally the case – solely on their collections (Janes 2010; Brown and Mairesse 2018). The new definition that was drafted by the ICOM in the spirit of UNESCO's Sustainable Development Goals (McGhie 2019) and that was put to a vote in 2019 at the annual ICOM meeting reads as follows:

> Museums are democratising, inclusive and polyphonic spaces for critical dialogue about the pasts and the futures. Acknowledging and addressing the conflicts and challenges of the present, they hold artefacts and specimens in trust for society, safeguard diverse mem-

> ories for future generations and guarantee equal rights and equal access to heritage for all people. Museums are not for profit. They are participatory and transparent, and work in active partnership with and for diverse communities to collect, preserve, research, interpret, exhibit, and enhance understandings of the world, aiming to contribute to human dignity and social justice, global equality and planetary wellbeing. (ICOM/news 2019)

Even though the delegates at the 2019 meeting in Kyoto could not agree to adopt this definition, it is nevertheless instructive of what museums nowadays are meant to be and also provides insight into what museums aspire to become. The category of museums being discussed in this book unmistakably aligns with the new definition, as all three of my case studies seek to protect democratic values and, in particular, to champion human rights.

The evolution of these *mindful* or *conscious* museums dates back to before the ICOM proposed its museum definition, to the same period as other instances of human rights advocacy became institutionalised, i.e., the late 1990s and early 2000s (Janes 2010; Petrunina 2019). Museums dedicated to documenting human rights abuses – like acts of genocide – or to the significant advances that have been made in the field – such as the granting of civil rights – have proliferated since the veritable museum boom of the 1980s, a development which is now reflected in the ICOM's proposal for a new museum definition (Carter 2019).[6] Since the early 2000s, more and more institutions have been choosing to self-identify as *human rights museums.*[7] Jennifer Carter and Jennifer Orange have termed this shift in museums towards a human rights framework "human rights museology" and have described it as an

> evolving body of theory and professional practices underlying the global phenomenon of museums dedicated to the subject of social injustices, one that is fundamentally changing the form and nature of museum work. Human rights museology acknowledges the potential for museums to engage in campaigns against human rights violations, at the local, national, and international levels. (Carter and Orange 2012, 112)

Moreover, they identify different applications of the concept of human rights (as a predominantly juridical framing or one that primarily understands human

6 By making explicit reference to rights, social justice, global equality and planetary wellbeing, the proposed definition marked an approach very different to previous definitions structured around the principal functions of museum work that have served the museum community since the ICOM's inception in 1946 (Carter 2019). For more on this, see also the following sub-section.

7 Japan is an interesting exception to this emerging phenomenon as it is the only nation state that was already opening human rights museums in the 1980s and 1990s (Carter 2017).

rights as a cultural asset in the service of humanitarianism) as well as both the continuities and discontinuities in references to human rights made in older generations of conscious museums. The new type of museum is generally marked by its dedication "to the subject and field of human rights as the foundation of these institutions' missions and mandates" (Carter 2017, 1). Consequently, some of these institutions have been established within the context of specific historical acts of violence committed on national soil and address this history from a combined historical memory and human rights perspective. In such cases, museums are often born of transitional justice mechanisms and subsequent peace initiatives, and one of the important parts of this new museum agenda is "moral remembrance – the standardized set of norms, promoted through human rights infrastructures at the world polity level" (David 2020, 4).

What is more, in all instances, as in the global educational endeavours for human rights, an activist approach is at the core of this new museology, with the purpose of engaging in issues of social justice and motivating others to do so as well. This activist approach appears to be the answer to the threat of "irrelevance" that museums of the twenty-first century face. Furthermore, as Robert R. Janes writes:

> It is increasingly vital that museums generate the requisite purpose and will to participate more consciously in the world around them, as the warning signs of our collective vulnerability continue to accumulate. [...] Along with the willpower required to reduce consumption is the greater need to transform the museum's public service persona defined by education and entertainment to one of a locally-embedded [sic!] problem-solver, in tune with the challenges and aspirations of the community. (Janes 2010, 173)

He concludes his idealistic call for more mindful museums with a plea to museum professionals around the world to live up to this potential and create museums that serve their communities as "stewards" instead of remaining "spectators" (Janes 2010, 184). While Janes addresses museum boards and executives with his call to transform the museum itself into an activist in the service of society, human rights museology is also very much concerned with engaging visitors in issues of social justice and sustainability.

Conscious museums generally claim that they are trying to be self-reflexive and to employ their power carefully because they are aware of how "museums construct and present ways of seeing and understanding that not only *reflect* but also *shape* collective values" (Sandell 2016, 135). Nevertheless, as Tony Bennett (1999) has persuasively argued, it has always been an important task of museums to *programme* – in other words: to shape – the behaviour of their visitors in a certain way and in line with dominant political rationale (Bennett 2019, 101). There is, however, a noteworthy distinction between the ways in which traditional art or science museums *operate* on the souls of their visitors and the ways in which so-called conscious museums do. Whereas the former often creates a sense of "civilisation" and its supposed assets more generally, the latter strongly relies on cultivating a sense of shared values by mobilising affect and employing strategies of empathy (Carter 2017). In the following, I will explain why it is precisely the museums that "curate difficult knowledge" (Lehrer and Milton 2011) and engage with "difficult heritage" (Macdonald 2016) that are prone to adopting the ideal of the conscious museum and its affect-driven activist approach. In the following I will consider at greater length the phenomenon that a strikingly large number of human rights museums include exhibitions on the Holocaust in order to understand the implications of the "conscious museum" and its specific modes of "moral remembrance".

* * *

Both history and memorial museums present a "past made present" (Rothberg 2009) in line with contemporary "politics out of history" (Brown 2001). The narratives to be found in a museum's exhibits are based on discursively regulated historical facts that depend on a particular politics of knowledge and a particular "regime of truth". Therefore, history museums can be seen as reflections of an official narrative of the past. They are in this sense active players that archive, constitute, authorise and make available what is acknowledged as history at a certain time and in a certain place (Carter 2017). What is more, "the act of display is always simultaneously one of definition and attribution of value. […] Museums materialize values and throw processes of meaning-making into sharp relief […]" (Mason 2011, 18). In this vein, memorial museums add value to specific narratives about the historical events and victims being commemorated and thus have the ability to strongly influence formations of collective memory while at the same time revealing the memory politics at play in the respective contexts of a society or community (Williams 2007). In a museum, it is therefore possible to observe what has been selected for display and what has been left out – or only superficially presented – as well as to get a sense of how the official narrative about the past has changed over time. For this reason, museum spaces are not neutral but instead always suggest favoured storylines that enshrine moral obligations and thus provide instruction on citizenship. Silke Arnold-de Simine speaks in this regard of the double function of "mediating memory" and writes the following about the interplay constitutive of memorial museums:

> The investment of museums in memory, which can be witnessed in museum theory and practice alike, is motivated by the conviction that mere knowledge about the past does not suffice to prevent the perpetuation of violent and traumatic histories. The ethical imper-

> ative to remember is taken to its literal extreme: visitors are asked to identify with other people's pain, adopt their memories, empathize with their suffering, re-enact and work through their traumas. Museums take on the role of facilitators in that process by providing experientially oriented encounters with the help of multimedia technologies. (Arnold-de Simine 2013, 1)

This is a very important observation which illuminates a specific function of memorial museums that aims to strengthen visitors' capacity for empathy through memory. In order to evoke such feelings, museums need to find ways to engage their visitors in certain ways and convey meaning in a way that goes beyond simply documenting historical events. In this sense, the emplotment of a historical narrative gains importance as it serves to stimulate such "meaningful encounters". This has to do with a tendency which does not value the act of memorialisation as an end in itself but calls for a relational approach which links the suffering of those being commemorated to the realities of the present. In this sense, practices of memorialisation gain a preventive character that attaches more importance to learning lessons from history than to merely honouring victims. The "ethical imperative to remember" is therefore derived from a dedication to the present and the future, and only partially to the past. Connected to this is a change in focus observed by Alison Atkinson-Phillips, who claims that "public memorials are not just about the dead anymore" but instead also commemorate "lived experiences" and thereby gesture towards the future (2020, 1).

In their assumed ability to "build bridges of compassion and solidarity", museums are being expected to take on more responsibility for "social justice" (Christensen 2015, 13–14) and to contribute more to developing the social conscience. On this note, it is interesting, though not at all surprising, that the transformation taking place within museology towards a human rights agenda first took shape in memorial museums (Arnold-de Simine 2013).[8] There is no single, unalterable definition of what makes a memorial museum, nor a human rights museum. However, the IHRA, which released a specific charter on memorial museums in 2012, states, "Memorial museums are responsible to protect the dignity

8 Scholars working in human rights museology have identified the prominent United States Holocaust Memorial Museum (USHMM), which opened in 1993, as the first memorial museum to make this shift from chronologically displaying Holocaust history to highlighting aspects of this history while gesturing towards a more "conscious" future: "The addition in 2009 of the 'From Memory to Action' gallery to the otherwise [...] historical trajectory of the Museum's tripartite Holocaust narrative [...] signals a fundamental innovation in both the Museum's discursive, and its museographic strategies" (Carter 2017, 3). In doing so, the USHMM decided on a "campaignist perspective" that can be viewed as an "important precursor to the broader typology of human rights museums" (Carter 2017, 3).

of the victims from all forms of exploitation and to ensure, beyond conventional history lessons, that the interpretation of political events inspires critical, independent thinking about the past" (IHRA/International Memorial Museum Charter 2016). This claim indicates that there is a productive connection between teaching the past and the way that museums might contribute to the aim of educating critically thinking citizens by means of history. Moreover, the IHRA identifies the importance of binding principles for memorial museums, which it attributes to the danger of the politicisation and nationalisation of memory, also providing a similar reason for the importance of their universal Holocaust education programmes. Its 2012 charter on memorial museums links the Universal Declaration of Human Rights with the ICOM's code of ethics and posits that "co-existence of different commemorative imperatives" can only be achieved if the institutions and surrounding communities agree on "a shared set of positive values". The importance of lessons from the past is subsumed within the statement that "modern memorial museums are contemporary history museums with a special obligation to humanitarian and civic education" (IHRA/International Memorial Museum Charter 2016). However implicit, the assumed utility of history education for fostering shared values and a sense of belonging to a common humanity is ubiquitous in the IHRA's charter as well as on the ICOM's memorial museum committee, which has also pledged allegiance to "the UN Charter's universal ethical and political principles" as well as "to universal human and civil rights and the careful preservation of cultural assets" (International Memorial Museum Charter 2016). This illuminates how, by defining themselves as responsible for issues of justice and tolerance, memorial museums pioneered, albeit less explicitly, the agenda of new human rights museology. Amy Sodaro draws the following conclusion about the complex expectations directed at these museums:

> Memorial museums are intended to be about both memory and thinking in the form of historical understanding; they are also aimed at inspiring emotional, affective responses and empathy. [...] Their most lofty goal is to prevent future genocide, human rights abuses, and violence, and in their robust efforts to do so, they radically depart from many other forms of commemoration. (Sodaro 2018, 162–163)

The gist of "historical understanding" with its aspiration of "critical thinking" which will help prevent violence in the future is what interests me most in this book. This is because, in a similar vein, many newly established human rights museums combine aspects of the memorial museum with socio-cultural or other interdisciplinary approaches to human rights. In this sense, the hybrid form of memorial / human rights museum is intended to "morally educate" visitors to internalise an ethics of "never again" (Sodaro 2018, 163) and to simultaneously engage visitors to actively participate in making "never again" a reality. While these two perspectives, memorialisation and activism, were first thought to be in tension or conflict with each other (Huyssen 2011), the practice of combining the two discourses has become rather salient, as my case studies will show.

Learning from the Holocaust in human rights museums

The importance of museums in the construction of collective memory has already been noted, as has the museum's ability to help shape visitors' understanding of values and democracy more broadly. In an article on the "Future of Holocaust Education", Australian scholar Avril Alba assigns museums a special role as institutions that not only convey historical content but that have also "deeply influenced the overall development of Holocaust education". She explains her claim that "the global reach of these programs is only set to increase" as follows:

> While much Holocaust education takes place in the classroom, it is without doubt Holocaust museums, and those museums that extrapolate from the Holocaust to broader topics such as genocide and human rights, that have emerged as leaders in this field. Not content to run education programs solely for site-based visits, these institutions also often offer a range of programs directly connected to school syllabi [...]. (Alba 2020, 600 – 601)

Despite this impact on Holocaust education, Alba asserts that there is a paucity of scholarly work that focuses on or, more precisely, evaluates "museum-based Holocaust education programs" (2020, 606). However, there have not been many assessments of the role museums play in the realm of Holocaust programmes in civic education. In her attempt to offer an evaluation of such programmes, Alba describes a "tension" which

> arises between these institutions' traditional role as social history museums and their educational remits. The latter often involves a process of universalization to connect the history of the Holocaust to the needs of the target groups [...] that these institutions seek to reach. Extrapolating "lessons", universal, ethical directives from this history, thus emerges as a common theme. (Alba 2020, 606)

This tendency to universalise both Holocaust history and its lessons is apparent throughout the educational frameworks that I have presented as well as in the broader context of memorial museums.

Within the human rights framework, Holocaust memory and education are invoked as a "benchmark" for "the dangers of prejudice" and are also found to be useful to "promote peaceful coexistence" between various members of society (Gilbert and Alba 2019, 1). If we look across the globe, we thus find numerous initiatives to commemorate the Holocaust, to learn lessons from its history, to compare it to other somewhat loosely related or even entirely different histories and to accommodate it in local museums. Most of these independent, state-sponsored and even international museum initiatives rely on the Holocaust to harness the power of tolerance and shape active citizens who are sensitive to the need to respect human rights and democracy. It is thus safe to say that the Holocaust trope has become an integral part of the contemporary democratic imagination. This does not mean that it is necessarily being actively remembered across the globe, but it might, in some instances, serve as a metaphor for an abstract memory of the worst atrocities of which humans are capable. Due to this status, Holocaust exhibitions can be found in many human rights museums all over the world, and many Holocaust museums now also have "human rights" or "tolerance" in their names, indicating that their exhibitions go beyond merely commemorating history and are thus relevant to the present and the future (Alba 2015; Alba et al. 2018). What is notable in this context is the progressivist thinking that is often involved, which makes use of events in the past in order to suggest that it is from this history that "a world learns how to move forward". This title of an exhibition at the Dallas Holocaust and Human Rights Museum in the United States is just one example of many that put forwards and thereby constantly underscore the idea of history as a forward-moving set of instructive cases from which we can draw lessons for a better future (Karlsson 2018). In this context, exhibitions about human rights and their evolution often serve to show "just how the world progressed in the years following the Holocaust" (Dallas Holocaust and Human Rights Museum).

Carter identifies a common thread amongst both older and newer museological human rights trends, which she describes as a "transversal teleological discourse of optimism that their architectures (in a metaphorical sense) ultimately seek to convey" (2017, 15). In this spirit, museums as communication systems, as curators of "meaningful encounters" and earnest reflections on our societies not only contribute to narratives about the past and the present but also envision and substantiate the kind of future that is being shaped (Honoré Gatera 2020). Museologist Jennifer Carter has stated that, in a museum, "human rights are communicated through the choice of subject matter, and the scale on which this subject is addressed throughout the museum" (2017, 15). On this note, it is also important to take into account what subject matters are less preferred or viewed as less likely to stimulate fruitful discussions on human rights. In this sense, human rights museums which focus on this specific constellation of (Holocaust) memory and teachings on human rights seem to bring to the fore a specific body of knowledge not only about the past but also about the direction in which history will evolve if we manage to extrapolate the "right" lessons from it. In this way, Holocaust memory is globally elevated to the status of "best practice" and most valuable lesson for humanity; this is a development that might be taking place at the expense of more regional historical references that still have an impact on racial power dynamics today, such as genocides or other forms of racial violence that took place on local soil. I will examine the extent to which this also holds true for the museums that I have chosen as my case studies in the next three chapters. However, before I finally turn to the museums themselves, I would like to map out my research design for my case studies and link it to the findings set out in this chapter.

The *emplotment* of the Holocaust – research design

It soon becomes evident that the realm of museum studies, with its various interdisciplinary academic inquiries and methods, is as divergent in terms of its focusses as museums themselves. I have already shown how important additional educational programmes and their role as general "civic engineers" are to museums. This applies even more in the case of museums that seek to convey specific lessons. Their involvement in global educational programmes make evident their will to engage citizen-subjects in the name of democracy. Engaging others and oneself in such ways and to such ends might be neither a bad nor good thing, but what the analysis of governmentality teaches us is that engagement is, in any event, a political act. This political nature will become even more tangible when we examine specific institutions of memory and how they are utilised in support of democratic rationality. As I have explained, my focus on museums stems from the premise that educational institutions in general and museums in particular disseminate political rationalities. Tony Bennett (1995) identifies museums as places that nurture tactics of self-governance and that exhort the visitor to live in a more moral way. And since human rights have risen to the status of global morality, it is not surprising to see this reflected in the branch of human rights museums that, since the early 2000s, have invested in the work of human rights and contributed to its advocacy.

As a consequence, I have taken a perspective which understands museums as sites of government, as places that advance tactics of the self in order to motivate their visitors to live their lives in a more moral way. Against this backdrop, I am pursuing a critical investigation of museums that is methodologically informed by cultural studies and, more precisely, cultural analysis (Mason 2011). This means that I understand culture as a signifying practice (Hall 2011b) which, in the context of museums, leads me to look at these institutions, their exhibitions and accompanying materials as *texts*, and thus as places primarily concerned with the production and dissemination of specific knowledge. Walter Benjamin (2002) once illuminatingly wrote that history decays into images, not stories, and it is in museums in particular that these images, as selected accounts of history, are the result of a complex of power-knowledge relations that cement the narration of such images of history by reintegrating them into an overarching storyline. In this regard, Hayden White commends Saul Friedländer's famous volume on *Nazi Germany and the Jews* for managing to abstain from the temptation of a complete story, meaning that Friedländer "does not emplot a single course of events, and resists the imposition of stereotypical structures of meaning that would allow any 'domestication' of the facts" (White 2016, 56).

White's observation suggests that it is rare but nonetheless possible in historical writing to "narrate without narrativizing" (2016, 56), whereas museums, so it seems, cannot dispense with the construction of a storyline. In this sense and following White, "emplotting" difficult histories amounts to domesticating them or, in other words, serves to tame the past in order to make it accessible and consumable. In this way, presenting content "in a rather unambiguous manner takes preference over the contingency of meaning in many museums" (Bose et al. 2011, 114; my trans.). I would like to use these critical points as a foil against which to examine the three human rights museums around which my research is centred. To what extent do they pursue the noble goal of celebrating peace and human rights to which many memorial and human rights museums have ascribed? Moreover, how does this agenda impact the narrative about Holocaust history and its lessons displayed in museums, and has this history been *tamed* in any way? Finally, with my assessment of global educational programmes in mind, what effect does memorialising the Holocaust in each of the three human rights museums have on formulations of citizenship? Do the museums touch on this issue at all, implicitly or explicitly, through their exhibits or their educational programmes?

To answer these questions, I have primarily examined the overall *emplotment* of the Holocaust within the framework of human rights museology and have tried to understand how it might effect or enable a particular influence on the visitor's behaviour. I will therefore focus on the narratives that weave together Holocaust memory with human rights, instead of, for example, the different objects that are on display or how the visitors perceive the exhibits. As proposed by cultural analyst Mieke Bal (1992), I will address the narrative that each museum constructs and applies, as well as its rhetoric and plot. Bal conceptualises museum displays as a "sign system" that works "in the realm between the visual and the verbal, and between information and persuasion, as it produces the viewer's knowledge" (1992, 561). This means that I will look for narrative structures and devices, strands, storylines and plots, and my main focus will be on the interplay between the actual texts, the collocation of displays and the specific topic of the Holocaust within the larger museum context as well as the visual (media) features used to support the storyline. I will also concentrate on selected educational materials and programmes that serve to make museum visits more meaningful and deepen understanding of the information disseminated throughout the museums. In all three cases, I will begin by introducing each museum in its societal context before looking at, firstly, the narrative of the exhibitions and, secondly, the educational materials provided by each museum. In this way, I intend to grasp the overarching link between Holocaust history and human rights as it is forged by the institutions in question. This research design is reflected in the recurring structure of the chapters on the Memorium Nuremberg Trials, the Canadian Museum for Human Rights and the Johannesburg Holocaust & Genocide Centre. Overall, the case studies will serve to draw out larger underlying themes related to the Holocaust-human rights nexus and its normative concept of citizenship.

5 The Memorium Nuremberg Trials: Promoting the Rule of Law

The Memorium Nuremberg Trials is a relatively small museum in the south of Germany. It is not as well known as other memory institutions concerned with Nazi rule and the Holocaust, and has to compete with much larger sites in Bavaria such as the memorial at the former Dachau concentration camp or, in Nuremberg itself, the former Nazi Party Rally Grounds. Nevertheless, I found it compelling to conduct a study of the Memorium as it addresses a period of history at the crossroads between wartime and postwar history, between the national and the transnational, and between the singular and the universal. But before I delve into this first case study, I would like to make one important disclaimer, namely that I was only able to visit the Memorium once, in the summer of 2018, before deciding to postpone further research trips to Nuremberg until the extensive ongoing renovations and planned enlargement of the museum had been completed. Then the global Covid-19 pandemic hit Europe, rendering all further museum visits impossible. I therefore had to rely in part on the *virtual* tours being offered by the Memorium.

While all three case studies are meant to contribute to a better understanding of the correlation between global mnemonic practices and educational endeavours, and to make tangible the way in which the Holocaust-human rights nexus manifests itself within museums, the Memorium also provides valuable insights into the particular German version of the Holocaust-human rights nexus. As I have already explained, all forms of memorialisation are conditioned by society and its various institutions, which are themselves shaped and regulated by the discourses of knowledge that constitute any regime of truth. Thus, not all aspects of history find their way into public memory, as decisions about what to include and what to exclude depend on the broader context of retrospective politics – both national and transnational. Accordingly, in order to grasp the specific setting in which the Memorium is situated, I will begin by providing a biography of the museum – by which I mean not only an account of the history of the site itself but also of the history that it puts on display. The reason for this is that it is not only the origins of the Memorium that we need to understand within the broader context of German memory politics but also, since memory is a "present tense exercise" (Meral 2012, 30), all the devices and practices used to detail Nazi crimes within the museum space, as we might otherwise not understand the gaps or particularities of their emplotment.

https://doi.org/10.1515/9783110788044-007

From remorse to activism?

Even though the formation and transformation of (West)[1] German public Holocaust memory has been influenced by global developments such as the bloc confrontation and the consolidation of a new European order (Diner 2003), it is nonetheless a very specific case that is intrinsically structured by the fact that Nazism emerged in Germany and that the Holocaust was planned and perpetrated by Germans (with the help of their collaborators). In this sense, the enormity of personal involvement in the crimes to be remembered, the ensuing questions of guilt and innocence, and the hope that it would somehow be possible to repair the past by mnemonic means feature strongly in German narratives about the past, though less and less often than they used to (Brumlik et al. 2000; Jureit and Schneider 2010).

With regard to the Holocaust-human rights nexus, I have explained the trend towards transforming the Holocaust into a negative point of reference. A telling example of this is the official narrative about the *Grundgesetz, the* German constitution. The German Federal Republic, as one of the two successor states to the so-called "Third Reich", adopted the *Grundgesetz* as an antidote to National Socialism and its ideology. Even though a large number of Nazi continuities – from laws that were passed and utilised by the Nazis to clerks and politicians who had served under National Socialism – could still be found in Germany despite the Basic Law, the official account portrays it as evidence of the strong opposition in which the Federal Republic stood to the Nazi state and its unjust laws (Haardt 2019). Making explicit reference to Germany's past in order to provide legitimacy to its contemporary constitution has become the norm, a reference which is frequently evoked in official politics and that can also be found at the Memorium. Yet the ways in which Germany has dealt with its Nazi past and the many present-day forms and functions of Holocaust memory are by no means coherent but instead marked by frictions and numerous disputes. Some of the many examples of this contested subject are early debates about *Stunde Null* (zero hour) in the 1950s, which proclaimed a completely new beginning after the German defeat of May 1945 (in the sense of getting a second chance as an innocent nation rather than acknowledging responsibility for the past and present of Nazism), the *Historiker Streit (historians' dispute)* of 1986 about the singularity of the Holocaust (Fischer and Lorenz 2007) and the ongoing "*catechism debate*" trying

1 I will not go into any detail about memory culture and politics in the former German Democratic Republic, even though they were, of course, in many regards different to those in West Germany.

to bring together discussions about Nazism and colonialism.[2] Nevertheless, German public Holocaust memory has embraced the international human rights framework, though perhaps not as unambiguously as the US memory landscape. Various mnemonic practices carried out by memorial sites, memory activists and politicians alike attest to this shift towards the more universalised approach to the topic of the Holocaust outlined in chapter 3. But unlike, for example, in the US context, the human rights framework is being questioned yet again among practitioners in the German field of Holocaust memory. That it has nonetheless found its way into official politics will be illustrated in the following subchapter by looking at the example of the politician Heiko Maas (Social Democratic Party) and some of his many references to Holocaust memory. I have chosen to proceed by discussing a specific example due to the complicated nature of German memory politics past and present, which can only be very selectively addressed here.

Maas, who served as Germany's Foreign Minister from 2017 until 2021, and who had been the Justice Minister in the previous cabinet between 2013 and 2017, has – like no other German politician before him – relentlessly emphasised Germany's duty to remember the Holocaust and its lessons. In his inaugural speech in March 2018, Maas stated that his main reason for going into politics was Auschwitz (Federal Foreign Office 2018). This is a curious and rather unusual statement for a German politician, but it provoked only a few reactions and even fewer inquiries seeking to clarify what Maas had actually meant. Shortly after Maas delivered his inaugural speech, he visited Israel, where he met with survivors of the Holocaust and explained to them why he had declared Auschwitz to be his motivation for becoming a politician: while researching his family history, he was unable to find anybody who had fought against, or even mildly resisted, Nazi rule and therefore decided to go into politics in order to play an active part in preventing atrocities like the Holocaust from ever happening again (Frehse 2018). Shortly after meeting with the survivors, Maas expressed a similar view in the guestbook of Israel's national Holocaust memorial, Yad Vashem. He emphasised not only his personal responsibility but that of the entire nation state of Germany, writing, "Remembrance must never stop. Germany bears responsibility for the most ferocious atrocities in the history of humanity. The Shoah remains a warning and gives us a mandate to stand up for human rights and tolerance" (tagesschau 2018; my trans.). By making such statements, Maas actively distances himself and, along with him, Germany more generally

2 An excellent overview of the events connected to how Germany dealt with its past between 1945 and 2002 can be found in a lexicon on this topic assembled by Fischer and Lorenz (2007).

from the Nazi past. In doing so he implies that, instead of feeling any possible repercussions of that past in the present, Germany has learned its lessons and is committed to the international community and its principle of the rule of law. This was also explicitly expressed by Maas in his inaugural speech, which he continued by mentioning Germany's candidacy for a non-permanent position in the United Nations Security Council, which would lead to the "challenging responsibility for maintaining world peace as well as international security. Whoever sits there [in the Security Council] needs to be prepared for having to make tough decisions: It was like that in the case of Iraq in 2003 as it was concerning the intervention in Libya 2011" (Federal Foreign Office 2018). In the space of four sentences, the German foreign minister moved from Auschwitz to present-day humanitarian campaigns and military interventions, suggesting, as in his entry in Yad Vashem's guest book, that the latter was somehow connected to the former. An emphasis on Germany's special responsibility for human rights resulting from its perpetration of the Holocaust is not new, nor is it unique to Heiko Maas. Moreover, German politicians often express similar sentiments about the state of Israel, to which Germany believes that it bears a special responsibility.[3] Still, the many references to the lessons to be learned from the Holocaust uttered by Maas are remarkable and, I would claim, symptomatic of a rather new trend within German memory politics that explicitly links Holocaust memory to democracy education and human rights activism.

In 2017, when he was still the Minister of Justice, Maas had demanded that refugees should be educated and tested on Holocaust history before being granted legal status in Germany. His call was mainly directed at refugees from allegedly "un-democratic", mostly Islamic countries and was intended to ensure that they unlearn the prejudices that Maas (and with him many other Germans) assumed that they harbour (Maas 2017).[4] His remarks need to be understood in relation to the concerns often expressed in Germany about hatred for various minorities being "imported" by refugees, who, it is claimed, lack respect for the val-

3 Statements in this regard abound and are made whenever German politicians meet with Israelis. Former Chancellor Angela Merkel, as well as the former President of Germany, Joachim Gauck, have declared Germany's unconditional solidarity with and responsibility for Israel in light of the past. In 2019, this commitment resulted in a disputed law against the Boycott, Divestment and Sanctions (BDS) campaign and provoked a heated debate about current German Holocaust memory (Moses 2021; Brumlik 2021).

4 From 2015 onwards, a time that saw large numbers of refugees from Syria, Afghanistan and Northern African states seek refuge in Germany (and Europe more generally), there were many accusations against newcomers, claiming in particular that the men had close relations with terrorist organisations, were antisemitic and were threatening (German) women's rights and safety (Hess et al. 2017).

ues of a free and democratic Germany (Castro Varela 2015a). Such expressions of concern only work against the background of a European Union that considers itself to be a "peace project" at heart, a place where Germany has become an important player (Castro Varela 2015b). What is more, Maas' statements and expressions of accountability regarding the Holocaust indicate that he assumes that Germany has fully internalised the desire to promote human rights in a way that many of the people who are seeking refuge there have not. Accordingly, what Maas says is conditioned by a certain discourse that has become widespread since the so-called "long summer of migration" (Hess et al. 2017) in 2015 and by the general discourse on security, and the norms and values of contemporary Germany. In this context, Germany is often referred to as a particularly good example of responsibly addressing a difficult past – in terms of the legal measures it has enacted and even more in its practices of memorialisation (Barkan and Karn 2006). What is more, Germany's own assessment of its history has advanced so far that it has led Maas to demand that Germany's "others" also learn from the Holocaust. His attitude implies that Germans have now learned enough to qualify them as teachers of tolerance (Castro Varela and Ülker 2020). This argumentation is once again linked to the global tale of the success of international law and human rights, due to which it is now commonly accepted that the Second World War against Nazi Germany and its collaborators was a "campaign for social justice" (Moyn 2014, 77), a campaign that is still ongoing (though of course by different means) and that Germany, now transformed into a democratic nation state, has at last joined. This aspect is especially interesting in regard to the Memorium, which I will now introduce. In a way, the museum perpetuates at least some aspects of this view and precisely dedicates its exhibition to the transition from a world ravaged by war to one in which the rule of law has succeeded – or will succeed eventually if we all take part in the process.

From guilt to atonement? Documenting the Nuremberg Trials at a historical site

Although it is not officially a museum, the Memorium, which opened in 2010, has all the features of one and will therefore be regarded here as a museum space. It is located in Nuremberg, Germany, a city that is well known for being the location of the Nazi Party Rally Grounds (*Reichsparteitagsgelände*) and the place where the Nuremberg Race Laws of 1935 were enacted. Nuremberg is closely associated with the NSDAP, the Nazi Party, and its rally grounds, parts of which were turned into a documentation centre in 2001. Four years later, in

2005, the board of trustees of the Nazi Party Rally Grounds Documentation Centre then launched the Memorium Nuremberg Trials project, which took another five years to be realised. The history that is represented at the Memorium is marked by a very specific entanglement between German perspectives on the Nazi era and those of the Allied victors. It is thus unsurprising that a large amount of scholarly attention has been paid to the Nuremberg trials, from legal scholarship to works by historians and memory scholars, who explain the importance of these international trials and the role they have played in the writing of history (Teitel 2000).[5]

Due to Nuremberg's importance during the twelve years of Nazi rule, the Allies chose to hold the International Military Tribunal that tried twenty-two Nazi war criminals in that very city, adding another event to Nuremberg's Nazi heritage. The International Military Tribunal (IMT) trials held in Nuremberg between 1945 and 1947 involved the prosecution of four criminal offences. The offence which is most important today was the offence of crimes against humanity.[6] Though the legal category of crimes against humanity was first introduced by the IMT in Nuremberg, the trials were not concerned with the Holocaust. Instead, the tribunal was established to bring those Nazis to justice whom the Allies considered to be the "masterminds" behind the murderous regime. Though the main leaders of the Nazi regime had to answer for their crimes before the IMT, the Holocaust itself did not feature in the indictment (Schabas 2008). The follow-up trials in 1946 and 1947 were, to a certain extent, dedicated to atrocities connected to the Holocaust but cannot be compared to the Auschwitz trials of the 1960s either, which dealt solely with the genocide of European Jewry (Diner 1996). Nonetheless, the storyline present in German public memory (although somewhat less so at the Memorium itself) draws a direct connection between the new criminal category and the Holocaust. It perpetuates the aforementioned "founding myth" of Europe as the phoenix which rose from the ashes of the Second World War to take up its designated role as a peace project and accepts that the criminal charge of "crimes against humanity" was the right response to the Holocaust. However contested this storyline might be (Moyn 2014), it is still plain to see how impactful the immediate postwar period was on the formation of global

5 Some noteworthy publications in this regard are Schabas 2008; Bloxham 2001; and Tusa and Tusa 1984.

6 The other criminal offences prosecuted at the IMT were war crimes, crimes against peace and conspiracy to commit those crimes. The latter two charges were introduced to the field of international criminal law in Nuremberg in order to encompass the mass crimes committed by the Nazis (Zentrgraf 2013).

public memory discourses. In this regard, I will once again quote Derrida, who observed the following (as already quoted in chapter 3):

> Even if words like "Crimes against Humanity" now circulate in everyday language. That event [the Nuremberg trials] itself was *produced* and authorized by an international community on a date and according to a figure determined by history. This overlaps but is not confounded with the history of a reaffirmation of human rights, or a new Declaration of Human Rights. (Derrida 2001, 29)

This important assessment not only points to the role played by international tribunals in constructing narratives (Aksenova 2017) but also to the need for Derrida's "figure determined by history", a figure that could function as a point of reference and, over the years, became more and more productive of the universalised version of Holocaust memory and its entanglement with the human rights project. What is more, the military tribunal played an important role in this particular form of "judicial history writing" (Aksenova 2017, 52–54) because the trials heard a large number of witnesses and were preceded by the collection of thousands of documents. In this sense, they already served as an instrument of (selective) history writing. Therefore, like Derrida, Natan Sznaider (2008) and Dan Diner (1996) also see the Nuremberg trials as a key event that contributed on multiple levels to the development of a global, as well as a specifically German, historical narrative.

As I have shown, the tribunal is remembered above all for the impulses it provided in the development of international law: for the first time in the history of international politics, the highest state officials of a country had been brought before an international court. Ultimately, it is these steps in the development of international law to which the tribunal of Nuremberg owes its historical importance, namely the extension of punitive power and the punishment of official authorities by international law, including the definition of a new crime (Zentgraf 2013). The category of crimes against humanity differs significantly from the traditional categories of international law, which were war crimes and crimes against peace. As Robert Fine explains, "While the latter generally treats states as subjects of right and upholds the principle of national sovereignty, the former treats individuals as subjects of right and encroaches on national sovereignty" (2000, 293). In legal terms, using newly introduced categories of law in the attempt to deal with the crimes committed during National Socialism presented a problem. A prohibition against retrospective legislation would have prevented successful trials, and it was only the extent of the atrocities to be tried that justified its application. In this regard, as Henrike Zentgraf (2013), historian and former head of the Memorium points out, the separation of the categories of law and justice, i.e., legal and moral criteria, was suspended in Nuremberg, as a criminal prosecution on the basis of new criminal offences would not have been possible otherwise. That the indictment was nevertheless permitted could only be understood from an "ethical historical point of view" (Zentgraf 2013, 9). By this she means the widely held conviction that criminal prosecutions had been absolutely necessary in order to respond legally to the mass crimes, as they were an indispensable reaction to the "immeasurable suffering" the Nazis had caused (Zentgraf 2013, 9–10). Even though the call for legal responses to the Nazis' crimes was rejected by several intellectuals, among them Hannah Arendt and Vladimir Jankélévitch, Zentgraf's is a very interesting observation which I would like to emphasise as it brings to the fore how moral categories have been part and parcel of the Holocaust-human rights nexus from the outset. The issue of retrospective justice and its legitimacy is also very illuminating in regard to the changes that have taken place in German narratives about the past, as it was only after the transformations of the 1980s and 1990s that culminated in the reunification of the two German states that the German Federal Republic officially accepted the verdicts handed down in Nuremberg (Schabas 2008). Before that, the trials – which now serve as an example of the dawn of a new democratic conscious – were denounced as unlawful victors' justice (Werle 2006). Bearing in mind how recent this change in narrative was, the function of the trials in both contemporary German and global storylines about the tribunal is even more noteworthy. On a global scale, the trials are primarily remembered in the form of an

> Anglo-American tale of liberal triumph in which the high-minded U.S. chief prosecutor, Robert H. Jackson, along with representatives of the other Western powers, put the desire for vengeance aside and gave the Nazis a fair trial before the law – marking one of "the law's first great efforts to submit mass atrocity to principled judgment" and ushering in a new era of international human rights. (Hirsch 2008, 701; quoting Douglas 2001, 1)

Germany adapted a similar narrative at the beginning of the 2000s, thereby placing the memory of Nuremberg in the broader context of human rights. Although Nuremberg was regarded as a Nazi stronghold in the 1930s and 1940s, contemporary Nuremberg has given itself the label "The City of Human Rights". Several memorials and documentation centres, and the Street of Human Rights designed by Israeli artist Dani Karavan, proclaim the city's rejection of Nazism and its Nazi heritage in favour of a new identity. Thus, by facing up to its past, Nuremberg has tried to transform its overall story in line with the aforementioned tale of triumph, deploying similar narrative devices as those used by Heiko Maas. When the Memorium was formally opened, the storyline behind Nuremberg's (and more generally, Germany's) claim to a new identity was expressed very clearly in the news reports of the day: "Von Schuld und Sühne" ("Of Guilt and Atonement"), for example, was one of the headlines (Przybilla 2010). One might wonder if the journalist who chose that headline was aware of Jean Améry's (1966) famous collection of essays, *Beyond Guilt and Atonement*, in which the philosopher and Auschwitz survivor rejects all attempts at reconciliation. What is more, Améry claimed the right to nurture resentment towards the perpetrators of genocide instead of forgiving them in pursuit of a harmonious future.[7] This leads to the question of whether this oversimplified transition from Nazism to a culture of human rights, from guilt to atonement, is also present at the Memorium, in both its exhibition and its educational materials, or whether the museum displays a different plot. The following subchapters are dedicated to the museum's content, in particular the ways in which it addresses the Holocaust in relation to human rights.

The Memorium is dedicated to a period of German and indeed global history which really only began in 1945, after the Allied victory over Nazi Germany. It focuses on the Nuremberg trials as a historic event and solemnly presents the perpetrators and their crimes while also looking at the tribunal's legacy. As the museum itself states, the aim of the exhibit is to *document* rather than to represent the trials, which is why the curators have refrained from presenting any objects and instead primarily rely on texts and photographs illustrating the textual information. This, so they reason, will enable visitors to draw their own conclusions about the tribunal, its verdicts and the overall prosecution. This does not mean, however, that reading is the primary means of gathering information, as there is also original video and audio material from the trials included in the exhibit. And yet, what could be regarded as a museum object is the courtroom in which the trials themselves were held. Since March 2020, room 600 is no longer in use by the court, and visitors can now actually enter it. The courtroom can also be visited digitally now, with various options to zoom in and learn more about its original appearance during the IMT in comparison to today. During my first visit in 2018, the courtroom was still being used for court procedures, so it was only possible to peek into it through four small windows located in the exhibition space. This was an interesting set-up, the exhibition being located in the attic above the courtroom and the visitor thus looking down into it and being given the impression of also looking down on the people on trial there. Even though this was probably an unintended result of the exhibition's location rather than an intentional effect, I immediately got a feeling of righteously looking down upon the perpetrators who had been prosecuted there over seventy

7 I will discuss Améry's thoughts on resentment and its potential for memory politics further in chapter 9.

years before – as if I, as a member of a democratic society that had faced up to its past, and even more so as an individual who had decided to come to such a museum to engage further with this past, was entitled not only to observe the trials but also to sit in on them in judgement. It might well be that this was just my impression, but the window seemed like an interesting device in any case. It invited visitors to imagine that the actual military tribunal was taking place before their eyes, thereby perpetuating the very particular perspective of an observatory.

Before the courtroom became part of the Memorium, the Nuremberg Municipal Museum had begun offering public tours of it on the weekends. An undated press release from the Municipal Museum states that "these tours enjoyed increasing popularity every year. It became particularly clear during the numerous events for the 60th anniversary of the start of the trial, how deeply Court Room 600 is rooted in the international cultural memory, as a venue of jurisdiction on immeasurable injustice" (Museen der Stadt Nürnberg 2010, 5). This is a very interesting observation, on which I will follow up towards the end of this chapter. Whilst the quotation above suggests some sort of enthusiasm for the knowledge rooted in "international cultural memory", the Memorium itself tries to avoid taking any kind of emotive approach or engaging the visitors in ways that go beyond the subject of the exhibition. In this sense, it is, as intended, a documentation centre rather than a museum – a site dedicated to imparting historical information as objectively as possible. Is this at all possible, particularly in a museum space? And can the Memorium stay true to this principle?

Justice versus revenge

As the main exhibition space at the Memorium is located in the attic of Nuremberg's *Justizpalast*, the main courthouse, it has no natural light, which makes its overall appearance seem very dark. Only the large display panels, all of them parallelograms, are brightly illuminated, with white and light-blue backgrounds. The displays are slanted at different degrees and different angles, mirroring the angular ceiling and making the visitor feel like they are floating about. This technique of making visitors feel slightly disoriented is supposed to reflect the immensity of the paperwork that was produced for the trials – such a large amount that one might get lost in the attempt to work through it. Most of the display panels in the museum's permanent exhibition discuss the International Military Tribunal (IMT), the London Statute[8] on which it was based, the different trials and their key protagonists – the prosecutors, judges, defendants and their lawyers. Here, the panels not only detail the events of the trial but also give insight into the various prosecutors' strategies and intended outcomes, which differed depending on the Allied country they represented. In this way, visitors also learn about the political differences between the parties involved in the prosecution, especially the latent tension between the US and the Soviet Union. Interesting in this regard is the framing of the formation of the tribunal around the question of "Retribution or Accountability?", which mainly concerned the Allied powers' decision to hold trials instead of indulging in a campaign of vengeance. Thus, what is stressed here is the shared aim of all four Allied powers to let justice prevail over revenge, a goal stronger than all political differences.

The exhibition furthermore allocates some space to the witnesses who appeared in court and details the impact of the trials on German society and the various international responses to them. The different units of the exhibit include panels on the history immediately leading up to the trials, focusing primarily on "The Path into War", meaning the history of the Second World War, which Nazi Germany started on 1 September 1939 with its attack on Poland. However, the timeline providing additional information on this history starts before 1939, the first entry being on a secret speech about "Lebensraumgewinnung im Osten" (the land grabbing or occupation of foreign territories in the east) delivered by Adolf Hitler as early as February 1933 – even before the NSDAP was voted into power in March of that year. It also includes another secret speech from 1937 in which Hitler informed the heads of the Wehrmacht, the German army, about his plans for foreign policy and the 1938 annexation of Austria. By providing detail about such events, the Memorium emphasises one important aspect that has been frequently contested in Germany, namely the fact that many Germans could have known – and in fact did know – about plans for war as well as those for persecution and subsequent executions long before they were actually realised. On the same note, this part of the exhibition points out not only that the Wehrmacht was involved in devising and implementing these plans from early on (which again, many Germans denied well into the 1990s) but also that the logic which drove those plans was, from the beginning, openly antisem-

8 The *London Statute* or *Charter of the International Military Tribunal* is the formal agreement between the United Kingdom, the United States of America, France and the Union of Soviet Socialist Republics on the prosecution and punishment of the "major war criminals of the European Axis". The declaration was signed by the four Allied powers in London on 8 August 1945 and ratified by nineteen more governments. The document was the first of its kind aiming to establish common ground for an international criminal tribunal (UN 1951).

itic and racist (Welzer et al. 2002; Frevert 2003). This unambiguous perspective on the crimes committed by the Nazis and their collaborators, of which only very few were eventually tried in Nuremberg, is a core feature of the exhibit at the Memorium. For this reason, the museum can be seen almost as an antidote to many German family narratives about the Nazi era. However, the prime focus on the perpetrators on trial simultaneously risks perpetuating the tale of the small evil clique that took over Germany and ruled ruthlessly without any support from society at large (Bajohr and Wildt 2009).

Along with the accounts of the history leading up to the trials, the Memorium displays some of the news coverage of the trials and provides detailed information about the penalties handed down. Visitors learn about the importance of media coverage in conveying information not only about the trials but also about the atrocities committed. In this way, as the panels suggest, the world was informed about what had happened in Europe and established it as an indisputable fact. In this part of the exhibition, visitors also find more information about how the Germans dealt with their Nazi past in the years during and after the trials, with one panel discussing the question of "victors' justice" – the main argument employed by many Germans against acknowledging the tribunal's legitimacy – and therefore also its verdicts. Another related panel, which addresses the impact of legal proceedings on the process of coming to terms with the past more generally, is of particular interest. Important trials that are claimed to have impacted how Germany deals with its past are the 1961 Eichmann Trial held in Jerusalem and the Auschwitz Trial held in Frankfurt between 1963 and 1965. The latter was one of the first trials carried out at a German court and led by a German prosecution. The Auschwitz Trial was moreover the first trial in Germany to deal explicitly with the Holocaust and German responsibility for it. This shows that, even though the mnemonic narrative about the Nuremberg trials suggests otherwise, the IMT did not address the Holocaust, even though it was there that the legal category of crimes against humanity was first used.

Down the corridor and next to the restrooms in a rather dark corner is another, much smaller part of the exhibition that looks at the Tokyo Trials (also known as the International Military Tribunal for the Far East) of 1946. On another grey wall we find printed in white the seven "Nuremberg Principles". These guidelines were officially formulated and adopted by the International Law Commission of the United Nations in 1950, which codified them into principles of international law. That these core principles of international law are still referred to as the "Charter of Nuremberg" adds weight to the narrative which identifies Nuremberg as the birthplace not only of these principles but also of an international awareness of the importance of the rule of law more generally.

In this same area of the exhibition, there are a few more panels that provide an overview of the twelve subsequent trials held between 1946 and 1949 at the US military court only. These trials prosecuted functionaries like Nazi concentration camp doctors and members of the so-called death squads (*Einsatzgrupp*en).[9] It was only with regard to the follow-up trial against the *Einsatzgruppen* that the organised mass murder of Jews and Roma found explicit mention at Nuremberg. Back then, those murders were still viewed as part of the larger course taken by the war and not as genocides that had been carried out alongside and, at times, even despite the war.[10] The Memorium does not bring up the issue of whether or not the IMT and its follow-up trials were or should have been concerned with the Holocaust. As a matter of fact, the Holocaust is hardly mentioned at all anywhere in the exhibition but is nevertheless present as a backdrop to the museum's overarching narrative.

"Make law, not war": From Nuremberg to the Hague

The last gallery at the Memorium is titled "From Nuremberg to The Hague" and dedicated to the further development of international criminal law. A detailed timeline informs visitors of significant events in the history of international law, the first one being the signing of the London Statute in 1945. This founding moment was followed by the adoption of the Convention on the Prevention of Genocide and, just a day later, the Universal Declaration of Human Rights in December 1948. Marked by a gap of several decades, the timeline then shows how it was only after the end of the bloc confrontation that international law was effectively put into action again, namely with the 1993 establishment of the International Criminal Tribunal for the former Yugoslavia and the 1994 Tribunal for Rwanda. Unlike the IMT in Nuremberg, both of these ad hoc tribunals explicitly

---

9 The *Einsatzgruppen* were special units acting as part of the Security Police within the National Socialist system. They were deployed from the beginning of the war in 1939 in Poland, and, from 1941, in the Soviet Union in particular to carry out the mass murders of Jews which were committed in very large numbers outside the extermination camps (Friedländer 2009).

10 For a long time, this remained the primary perspective on the Holocaust: understanding it as something that was inherent to the war instead of being driven by a separate logic. However, scholars like Hannah Arendt have long argued that, though the war made the massive scope of the executions possible, the Holocaust needs to be understood for its specific rationale and as an endeavour that was at times even *more* important to the Nazis than winning the war. This she explains, firstly, with the costs of the systematic killings, especially the deportations and the extermination centres, which not only exceeded the Nazis' budget but were kept going when the war had already clearly been lost (Arendt 1989; Diner 2003; 2007a).

addressed the crime of genocide and could therefore be described as standing in contrast to the IMT instead of being tribunals that followed in its footsteps. Interestingly enough though, the museum displays primarily focus on the genocides committed in Srebrenica and Rwanda but do not make any reference to the fact that the Holocaust was *not* an issue in its own right at the Nuremberg Tribunal. As a result, instead of explaining this important difference between the tribunals, which testifies to the rather recent importance of earnestly condemning the crime of genocide, the Memorium traces the penalties issued at the later ad hoc tribunals back to the IMT. It does so by evoking the case of Nazi publicist Julius Streicher, who was convicted in Nuremberg of inciting antisemitic hatred, a crime later codified as the "direct and public incitement to genocide" and tried as such at the Tribunal for Rwanda. In this way, the timeline presented at the Memorium conforms to the linear narrative of progress with regard to the rule of law, which eventually culminated in the opening of the International Criminal Court (ICC) at the Hague in 2003.

This impression is further propagated by the display opposite the timeline that traces the biography of Benjamin Ferencz. Once the prosecutor at the Einsatzgruppen trial (1947), he was the only one of his colleagues present at the Nuremberg trials who had witnessed the founding and opening of the ICC and even worked there for a few years. Ferencz, at the age of a 102, seems to embody this very storyline, which has been relentlessly emphasised in his many public appearances as an advocate for social justice – and especially in the notable number of recent documentaries about his life and achievements.[11] What is more, by drawing a direct line from Nuremberg to the Hague, from the IMT to the ICC, the gallery, however small it might be, plays a significant role in emplotting Holocaust memory within the Memorium. It represents a bridge from the past to the present and closes with a final section that is titled "Justice Matters", which was curated in cooperation with the ICC. It is mainly these last two galleries which conform to the overall plot of the Memorium, assembled to emphasise the importance of the rule of law. But of course, this overall storyline only works against the backdrop of a detailed account of the IMT, which, in the way it is presented at the Memorium, leaves no doubt that legal prosecution was the necessary and also most virtuous response to Nazi crimes. A panel discussing the more ethical and philosophical contestations of this response, such as those of Hannah Arendt, could have complicated this assessment. However, the Mem-

11 The Google results for Ferencz immediately display a number of films about him, both fiction and non-fiction: most of them have similar titles which already suggest the enormous importance of what he did and achieved, like "Prosecuting Evil", "Watchers of the Sky" or "A Man Can Make a Difference".

orium has chosen to convey the simpler and more predictable storyline which confirms the importance of the rule of law, with Nuremberg as its birthplace. The additional materials and programmes offered by the Memorium only underscore my reading of the museum, especially because they draw links to the human rights project and the Holocaust that are much less explicit in the exhibit.

On 20 November 2020, the Memorium, in partnership with the city of Nuremberg, celebrated the seventy-fifth anniversary of the opening of the IMT trials in historic courtroom 600. Since this event had to take place at the height of the Covid-19 pandemic, only a few distinguished guests, most of them Bavarian politicians,[12] were able to attend the event in the courtroom, which meant that most of the speakers sent in their words in commemoration of the tribunal via video. The first address to open the celebration was sent by Benjamin Ferencz. It was Ferencz as well who, in 2010, gave the speech to mark the opening of the Memorium Nuremberg Trials. Ten years later, he began his speech by recalling the Einsatzgruppen trial in which he had been chief prosecutor at the age of twenty-seven and in which, as he stated, the defendants, who showed "no remorse whatsoever" during the trial, were convicted for "cold blooded murder" (Ferencz 2020). He then turned abruptly to the present and continued his address by reminding his audience of the wars that are still going on today, in which "young people" kill "other young people, whom they don't even know". Ferencz described this continuity as "madness", a madness which he has spent his entire life fighting and which, as he concluded, everyone needs to first of all acknowledge and then "do whatever you can" to stop. The plea to do "whatever you can" for a world that "needs a lot of changes" is not, however, as open ended as it might appear but instead clearly defined: Ferencz closed his talk with his life motto, the slogan "make law, not war", a fight we must "never give up" for which he wishes his audience "the best of luck" (Ferencz 2020). A common memory move is applied here in Ferencz' welcome address, namely that which was identified by Joan W. Scott (2020) as the "the historical operation" at the foundation of most lessons from history. Turning to the IMT, to which Ferencz had not only been a witness but where he had also played an important role (more precisely, at one of its subsequent trials), adds extra weight to his assessment of the present and the conclusion he draws from it, which is precisely to "make law, not war".

12 It should be noted in this context that the German province of Bavaria, the *Freistaat* Bayern, is (and has been since 1957) politically dominated by the CSU, the smaller and often even more conservative partner of the Christian Democratic Union, whose members and leaders frequently make racist and sexist statements and introduce discriminatory policies (Hamm 2018).

The next important speaker to follow Ferencz at the celebratory event was German President Frank-Walter Steinmeier, who not only thanked Benjamin Ferencz for his words and his enthusiasm for making the world a better place but also emphasised at the very beginning of his speech how much positive influence Ferencz, with his "wisdom", had had on Germany, Europe and the world. Steinmeier evoked the image of ruins, of Germany and "the old order" in ruins, and also the rule of law having been in ruins at the point in time at which the IMT convened for the first time. He then spoke of the sites where the horrendous crimes were carried out, the names of which had not been well known before the trials. However, instead of mentioning the sites of major war crimes, Steinmeier named Auschwitz, Buchenwald, Theresienstadt, Sachsenhausen and Dachau as well as some other lesser-known sites of the Holocaust. All of these sites, as he cautioned, testified to a "will to extermination" that was inherent to the Nazi system. With these words, Steinmeier made explicit a key feature of the narrative underlying the work of the Memorium and the public memory of the Nuremberg trials discussed here, namely the belief that the IMT, and with it the international legal order that was founded anew in Nuremberg, was established in response to the Holocaust. Moreover, as Steinmeier claims in his concluding remarks, the prosecution of the crime of genocide would not have been possible without Nuremberg. In this sense, the same tale of success which structures the narrative at the Memorium was conjured up in the speeches delivered on the occasion of the seventy-fifth anniversary of the IMT hosted at the museum, making the connection to Holocaust memory even more apparent.

Another positive effect of the trials, according to Steinmeier, was that Germans were no longer able to make excuses for the atrocities committed during the Nazi era but instead had to begin a process of reform and catharsis. This is historically far from accurate as, for one, the period of denial and sugar-coating went on for much longer than just the few years immediately following the end of the war and, secondly, the hope for atonement cannot be so clearly distinguished from the refusal to accept guilt and responsibility (Jureit and Schneider 2010).[13] It is interesting to note how the German president also employed the Christian motif of purification or atonement that had already been identified as constitutive of Nuremberg's rather recently presented self-image as the "City of Human Rights". But how are human rights integrated into the narrative of the

13 In their extensive study on the "illusion" of how Germany has successfully dealt with its past, Ulrike Jureit and Christian Schneider build their argument around the wish for redemption, which they identify as the engine for much of German public Holocaust memory.

Memorium and how does a reference to human rights function in the construction of the overarching storyline?

Paving the way for human rights at Nuremberg

As part of its educational material, there are videos on the Memorium's website (all of them in German) that provide answers to some of the questions most frequently asked by visitors. One video responds directly to the question "What do the Nuremberg trials have to do with human rights?" and immediately answers in very plain terms: the tribunal at Nuremberg was when the world first learned about the horrendous crimes committed by the Nazis, and since the institutionalisation of human rights was a direct response to those crimes, the Nuremberg trials and human rights are directly connected to each other. This point is reiterated later in the video when the speaker states that human rights – and she holds a printed version of the Universal Declaration of Human Rights towards the camera – had been invented so that such terrible atrocities like those of the Nazis and their collaborators would never happen again. In order to let the suggested historic importance of the UDHR unfurl its power, there is a moment of silence, and instead of the speaker in her office, we now see a black-and-white picture of the pillars designed by Dani Karavan for Nuremberg's Street of Human Rights. Each of the pillars has one of the articles of the UDHR inscribed into it (though not all thirty articles are present in his artwork) and, for the sake of comprehensibility, so that all viewers will know why they are now seeing this image, a large heading "Allgemeine Erklärung der Menschenrechte" ("Universal Declaration of Human Rights") appears. We are then provided with an account of Article 1 and its relevance, which, in light of the sentence about all humans being "endowed with reason and conscience" (UDHR), leads the speaker to point out the moral compass that each and every human supposedly has. We are then told that it was this very same moral compass, this consciousness, which led the members of the United Nations to craft the UDHR. Human rights are not only explained in their connection to the Nuremberg trials but also presented as a great gift to all of humanity, aiming to bring about a more peaceful world. The video thus both serves as an educational tool and conveys enthusiasm for human rights causes. At the end of the video, appealing to the viewer's very personal conscience, the speaker asks with a bright smile which human right is our favourite and why. In this vein, the Memorium utilises various techniques to motivate visitors not just to passively consume the information it provides but rather to take an active stance regarding the lessons they should learn from history.

Another teaching module addresses a similar question within the exhibition space. Here, the main question is whether human rights were the international legal response to the crimes of National Socialism. The visitors are guided through the exhibition with a special focus on the human rights violations committed during the Second World War. This is an interesting way to retrospectively interpret Nazi crimes, for during the period when the crimes were committed, there had already been international legal frameworks in place but no such thing as institutionalised human rights. It is, however, a recurring phenomenon in Holocaust-related pedagogy and the bodies of public memory with which it is fused that the atrocities of the Nazis, and especially the Holocaust, are framed as human rights abuses. While from today's perspective, the crimes certainly did violate numerous human rights, it is at the same time a narrative strategy that needs to be understood in its capacity to add value to the coupling of Holocaust memory with the human rights project. This is because it underscores the need for a strong human rights agenda and consciousness in order to prevent such appalling crimes from being committed in the future – the core lesson promulgated by the Holocaust-human rights nexus.

After the guided tour through the Memorium, the aforementioned module, which was developed in partnership with the city of Nuremberg's Human Rights Bureau and the Centre for Human Rights, then has participants reconvene and discuss the extent to which the hope for a brighter future secured by international law and respect for human rights has been fulfilled. Additionally, it asks what impact human rights have on contemporary politics and how human rights affect the everyday lives of the participants. If the groups have enough time, they are asked to go to the Street of Human Rights in the city centre and look at the UDHR articles inscribed there. This shows how the pedagogical programmes offered by the Memorium make use of other features of Nuremberg's human rights infrastructure, thereby contributing to the city's transformative narrative. Generally speaking, I found that most of the educational programmes made the leap to the present, as almost all of them ended with a discussion of the contemporary relevance of the Nuremberg Tribunal. Another of the Memorium's educational programmes even goes beyond present-day issues that could be related to the Nuremberg trials and strikes a more visionary note, asking participants to come up with their own ideas for an international justice system, challenging them to develop something like an international court. However, whatever ideas of their own the visitors might have, the exhibition's design ensures that their responses remain within the framework of liberal democracy and in respect of its most important virtue, the rule of law.

Throughout, the Nuremberg trials are unambiguously presented as a positive point of reference – we could even go so far as to say that they are the founding myth – for today's international community and its objectives, namely the rule of law and international respect for human rights. The pedagogical material at the Memorium is also interesting because it points to an aspect mentioned at the beginning of this chapter, that is, the role that such tribunals play in the process of assembling and thus writing history as well as their power to disseminate knowledge about the past. In this way, the Memorium, in its specific function as a museum, keeps on dispersing the knowledge shaped during the trials and fuses it with contemporary discursive truths about the tribunal and its influence on the development of human rights and international law. Even though it is seldom mentioned in the exhibition, the Holocaust trope is omnipresent – and not only for someone searching for it like me. During a 2018 conversation I had with Henrike Claussen (formerly Zentgraf), the former head of the Memorium, she told me that many of the visitors, especially the international ones, come to the Memorium expecting to find a historical site directly related to the Holocaust. This expectation is, I suspect, fed by the existing body of knowledge about the trials that I have already discussed as well as their relationship to the Holocaust and the impact they have had on the development of human rights that circulates within global public and cultural memory. Therefore, the Memorium – even though it presents a more nuanced historical account than that which finds its way into public memory – not only promotes the narrative of the successful rise of the respect for human rights but also aims to encourage the development of new human rights advocates who will advance the rule of law in the future just as Benjamin Ferencz calls upon us to do. What is more, the tacit emplotment of Holocaust memory within the history of the IMT as well as the explanations offered about the relevance that this history still holds today – as that of an evil past which was put on trial in Nuremberg – is distinguished from the hopeful future made possible by the proceedings that took place there. These unprecedented proceedings and the ways in which they have come to be memorialised provide a persistent view of the morally superior Allied victors who resisted any temptation of revenge and instead chose to enforce justice through law against all odds, thus ensuring "the progressive direction of history" (Scott 2020, 27) and building the foundation for today's culture of human rights. The Holocaust-human rights nexus thus relies on this tale of success while simultaneously reiterating it, giving moral legitimacy to its current politics.

In the following three chapters, I will ask to what extent human rights museums elsewhere in the world contribute to upholding this founding myth of the universal human rights project, how the Holocaust is related to it and what larger function any references to Nuremberg might have in the other two museums I studied.

6 The Canadian Museum for Human Rights: Prescribing Benevolence

The Canadian Museum for Human Rights (CMHR), where I spent four weeks in the autumn of 2018, is located in the city of Winnipeg, in the central Canadian province of Manitoba. Even before it opened in 2014, the CMHR, to date the world's largest human rights museum and the only national Canadian museum outside the capital city of Ottawa, had attracted the attention of many scholars interested in human rights museology. There is thus already a notable body of scholarship available on this institution, produced, for example, by Winnipeg-based museum theorist Angela Failler (2015; 2019) and the initiative *Thinking through the Museum*, as well as Failler's co-author Amber Dean (2015; 2019). One edited volume on *The Idea of a Human Rights Museum* has been assembled by Busby et al. (2015) and includes a number of essays that seek to assess the potential and limits of the new museum. Other publications on the CMHR that touch upon the role played by Holocaust content compared with representations of other genocides at the museum include an article by Dirk Moses (2012), an article by the two curators of the CMHR's Holocaust exhibit Clint Curle and Jeremy Maron (2018), and a discussion by Olena Hankivsky and Rita Dhamoon (2013). Other noteworthy critical assessments of the ways in which settler colonialism and Indigenous genocide are included in the museum have been published by former CMHR curator Tricia Logan (2014) and by a renowned expert on difficult knowledge and the possibilities of curating it, Erica Lehrer (2015). The origins of the museum and the process of its establishment have also been controversially discussed in numerous Canadian newspaper articles (cbc news 2011), and a more recent scandal that evolved out of discrimination accusations was even reported in the *New York Times* (Porter and Austen 2020). Looking at these publications, the CMHR's relevance for my research is clear, especially since it has not yet been analysed from a governmentality point of view nor in terms of the specific forms and functions of its Holocaust exhibition. Moreover, the CMHR provides insights into the practices of Canadian Holocaust memory (Anderson 2017), the ways in which this memory might be favoured over the more controversial history of Indigenous genocide and the reasons why this may be so.

Towards a "human rights culture"

The CMHR was born out of a private initiative of Canadian politician, media mogul and entrepreneur Israel "Izzy" Asper, who, according to the website of

https://doi.org/10.1515/9783110788044-008

the Asper Foundation (which he also founded), first had the idea for such a museum in the year 2000. However, despite what the official CMHR website writes about its own history, Winnipeg-based Israel Asper did not initially have a museum dedicated to the history and celebration of human rights in mind. Instead, what he was first aiming for was to establish a large Holocaust museum like the United States Holocaust Memorial Museum in Washington DC, to which the Asper Foundation had been organising trips for high school students for many years. Asper wanted his hometown of Winnipeg to have its own museum on the Holocaust and to promote Holocaust memory across Canada more generally. When he first announced his plans to erect a museum in Winnipeg in the late 1990s, Asper received support from the Canadian Jewish Congress but not from any other state institutions. In 2000, in partnership with his daughter Gail Asper, he first considered founding a tolerance museum like the one in Los Angeles (MacNabb 2014) rather than a dedicated Holocaust museum. Eventually, in April 2003, the Friends of the Canadian Museum for Human Rights, in joint partnership with the Government of Canada, the Province of Manitoba, the City of Winnipeg and the Forks North Portage Partnership, announced their intention to establish the Canadian Museum for Human Rights in Winnipeg (Asper Foundation/Canadian Museum for Human Rights). The concept for the museum was inspired and motivated by the extraordinary impact of the Asper Foundation's Human Rights and Holocaust Studies Program. It took yet another five years, until 2008, for the state of Canada to join the project; state funding and national museum status were thus only made available after Asper and his associates agreed to widen the scope of the museum to encompass human rights more generally (Moses 2012). In order to provide support for the CMHR plans, the Canadian government had to pass a bill which changed the Museum Act "to include the first new national museum in more than 40 years, and the first ever to be built outside of the national capital region" (CMHR/Our History). In a report by Arni Thorsteinson, who chaired an assessment of the CMHR commissioned by the Ministry of Canadian Heritage, the CMHR was praised as the first of its kind:

> The Canadian Museum for Human Rights will be the first museum for human rights, not only in Canada, but also for the world. It is a new concept for a museum that can best be described as an "idea" museum. An "idea museum" is more about concepts and less about collections of objects. CMHR's mission crosses the conventional museum boundaries and its mandate is bold and purposeful. It has the potential to serve as our national brain trust, intellectual fountain and knowledge depository for human rights – an institution that engages and empowers Canadians and visitors from all walks of life to combat prejudice, intolerance and discrimination. (Thorsteinson 2008, 1)

Propelled by these arguments as well as by the prospect that such a museum might help advance Canada's image as a progressive and tolerant society, the former conservative government under Stephen Harper approved the founding of the CMHR as an authority on the subject of human rights. On a similar note, the authors of the report strongly supported the effort to make the CMHR a national museum, which was intended to become, if not the first human rights museum in the world, at least the largest of its kind. The framing of the CMHR as an "idea museum" is moreover very interesting, especially in contrast to the memorial museum originally intended. The image of a place of ideas gives the CMHR an almost visionary aura that is emphasised throughout the recommendations in the report, which continues as follows:

> Human rights are for all and the responsibility to nourish and protect these rights rests with everyone. The CMHR will not be the sole authority on this topic, but the museum may ultimately guide individuals to their own call to action for the promotion of human rights in Canada and around the world. [...] The historical context is an essential prerequisite for placing the human rights journey in its proper perspective. History is both an endowment and an empowerment for future generations. (Thorsteinson 2008, 1)

Here, the presentation of the reasons why elements of a historical museum are considered indispensable for promoting an understanding of human rights and the importance of the idea is striking. The tone is similar to that of the memorial museums mentioned earlier, which were among the first of their kind to weave together memory and human rights activism. How this connection plays out at the CMHR was therefore of particular interest to me.

Internationally, the CMHR is affiliated with the Federation of International Human Rights Museums (FIHRM), which, in close cooperation with the United Nations, encourages its members to participate in the shift taking place in museology towards an emphasis on "lived experience" with the intention of evoking empathy by telling stories of formerly oppressed groups (Christensen 2015, 13). The FIHRM's mandate is testament to the new trend within museology outlined in chapter 4, as it aims to support museums to accept greater responsibility for "social justice". In other words, it advances the claim that museums in general and memory institutions in particular should make more of a contribution towards developing the social conscience. And the role envisaged for museums is for them to help their respective societies and communities to take positive action towards promoting inclusion or, as it is formulated by the CMHR, "a human rights culture". In line with this self-imposed mandate, the CMHR advertises itself as follows: "The Canadian Museum for Human Rights is the first museum in the world solely dedicated to the evolution, celebration and future of human rights." (CMHR 2014) It furthermore praises itself in an official video as an "amazing gift" to all Canadians and to international visitors. Nevertheless, after undergoing many changes in its mission and focus, the CMHR faced vehement protests when it opened in 2014 and is still an object of criticism.

At the time of its opening, the resistance it encountered was mostly a result of the museum's location on so-called Treaty One Territory, in this specific case the traditional land of Anishinaabe, Métis, Cree, Dakota and Oji-Cree nations, a traditional meeting place that is now occupied by the large museum (Dean and Failler 2019).[1] In addition, activists from the community around Shoal Lake 40[2] launched the *Museum of Canadian Human Rights Violations*, with which they intended to "encourage" visitors to ask uncomfortable questions about Indigenous/settler relations after being confronted with "how 100 years of Canadian indifference plays on in real life" (Facebook page of the Museum of Canadian Human Rights Violations). Of particular concern was the immense amount of water used inside the CMHR, labelled as "healing" and given special prominence in the CMHR's Garden of Contemplation. Yet, despite the almost religious meaning attributed to the water used in the CMHR, the museum gives no account of the "First Nation end of the pipe" (Museum of Canadian Human Rights Violations). At first, the CMHR entirely rejected the criticism that it was participating in this sort of "Canadian indifference" (Dean and Failler 2019), before gradually changing its strategy – for example, at the beginning of its virtual tours developed due to the Covid-19 pandemic – to publicly acknowledging its location on "ancestral land" and the fact that its water supply comes from Shoal Lake 40 First Nation. However, this recognition makes no mention of the opposition voiced by Indigenous communities to the erection of the museum on traditional land in the first place – which was largely ignored during the process of creating

1 For more on the issue of Indigenous land and the numerous debates surrounding it, see, e.g., Gray and Gardner 2016.

2 Shoal Lake 40 First Nation is an Ojibwa or Ontario Saulteaux First Nation located in the Eastman Region of Manitoba and the Kenora District of Ontario. At the beginning of the twentieth century, parts of this land were annexed by the city of Winnipeg, which built an aqueduct on the traditional land in order to convey clean drinking water to Winnipeg. Over time, the Ojibwa village was displaced and relocated to an artificially made island, which resulted not only in the inexcusable isolation of the First Nation but also in the deprivation of clean drinking water. This was due to a boil-water advisory under which Shoal Lake 40 was placed from 1997 to 2021, suggesting that the community's water was (potentially) contaminated. While the water on its way to Winnipeg was treated at a water department, the people of Shoal Lake 40 had to rely on expensive bottled water instead. Tom Anderson, an elder from the community, summed up the injustice as follows: "We find a disconnect between what the city [of Winnipeg] achieved and what the impacts were for us" (Bernhardt 2019). For more information, see also the Shoal Lake #40 website (https://www.sl40.ca, accessed 3 June 2022).

the museum and might call for the museum to take a more self-reflexive approach to the issue that goes beyond mere recognition. In addition to acknowledging the land and water, the museum could also acknowledge its own flaws and ignorance towards Indigenous perspectives, which have challenged the museum from the outset and which, if they had been taken seriously, might have led to the museum relocating to a less prestigious but also less contested location (Gray and Gardner 2016).

Despite the many disputes and scandals, the CMHR has attracted a large number of visitors from across Canada and beyond, and has received numerous accolades and awards. Overall, the CMHR is monumental not only in its architecture and design but also in terms of its size and content. This monumental quality suggests in and of itself the importance of the museum's official mandate: to celebrate human rights as humanity's highest good, its beacon of hope for the future. The CMHR addresses the subject and field of human rights by going beyond a primarily commemorative framework – at least at first glance. But at the same time and in some kind of relation to the new museum, a number of national memorials in the capital region of Ottawa were either newly constructed or altered during the Harper period.[3] Amongst these new monuments were Canada's first National Holocaust Monument, which was only realised after continuous debates that took place between 2011 and its finalisation in 2017. Thus, reiterating that monuments not only represent certain events and people in history but also reveal much about the time in which they are erected, it is curious how many new sites of memory were commissioned within such a short period of time. Edward Said once made the following remark about harnessing the power of public memory: "The invention of tradition is a method for using collective memory selectively by manipulating certain bits of the national past, suppressing others, elevating still others in an entirely functional way. Thus, memory is not necessarily authentic, but rather useful" (Said 2000, 179). In this regard, as the report on the CMHR suggests, an emphasis on human rights and Canada's contribution to their proliferation appeared as a welcome addition to Canada's memorial and museum landscape. Accordingly, granting the CMHR the status of national museum and building national monuments dedicated to the victims of the Holocaust and the victims of communism are forms of (re)inventing Canadian tradition with an emphasis on it being a tolerant nation. It is thus interesting to contemplate for a moment the fact that a conservative government was advocat-

3 Stephen Harper and his Conservative Party of Canada were in office from 2006 to 2015. Along with the CMHR and the Holocaust Memorial, monuments commemorating both "the War of 1812" and the victims of communism were also commissioned (Weeks 2015).

ing for memory in the name of freedom and equality, and to think about the correlations between these different monuments and the CMHR.

The Canadian tradition on public display is one of championing freedom, peace and human rights, and of always standing in opposition to what is considered extremism – in the case of the monuments: Nazism or Communism (Weeks 2015). As former Prime Minister Stephen Harper put it in a speech delivered at a fundraising event in 2014: "Know that evil comes in many forms and seems to reinvent itself – Nazism, Marxist-Leninism, today, terrorism – they all have one thing in common: The destruction, the end, of human liberty. Ideologies that promise utopias lead to the opposite, hell on earth" (Harper qtd. in Kranjc 2015). Here, Harper, who only a few years before had stated that Canada had "no history of colonialism", not only oversimplifies twentieth-century history and wrongly equates Nazism with (presumably) Soviet communism but also implicitly denies the present-day human rights ideology that, in fact, tends to promise (neo)liberalism as "the last utopia" (Moyn 2010). Instead, Canada's political motives for fighting against historical Nazism and communism as well as for commemorating both as similarly horrifying and murderous ideologies are framed by Harper as something entirely apolitical that benefits all (Canadians and beyond). It was with this larger political context in mind that I visited the CMHR, not only looking to answer the broader questions identified in my research design but also to pinpoint the particularly Canadian issues surrounding (national) identity and memory.

"Idea museum" or memorial museum?

The close connection between narratives about the past, their public framings and the aim of building the human rights culture envisaged by the CMHR is evident in different struggles for representation within the museum. As mentioned above, the CMHR was, from the outset, planned as a Holocaust museum. This aim, however, had to yield to the broader and more future-looking human rights framework. The decision about which human rights abuses to feature in the museum was made with this broader scope in mind and with the help of an independent advisory committee.[4] In due course, the committee recommended that the CMHR position the Holocaust as "a separate zone at the centre of the muse-

4 The Content Advisory Committee's final report can be accessed online and provides a list of all members as well as their deliberations and recommendations: https://publications.gc.ca/collections/collection_2011/mcdp-cmhr/NM104-1-2010-eng.pdf. (21 June 2020)

um, showing the centrality of the Holocaust to the overall human rights story" (Content Advisory Committee 2010, 62). Similarly, a bill which was introduced by the Minister of Canadian Heritage to realise the cooperation between the museum and the Federal government determined that the CMHR would "house the largest gallery in Canada devoted to the subject of the Holocaust" (Mahabir 2008, qtd. in Hankivsky and Dhamoon 2013, 904). Until then, it had been the Montréal Holocaust Museum which had widely been considered the institution that would take on this pedagogical and commemorative role through the strength and reach of its educational programming (Carter 2017).

As soon as the first details about the museum's content reached the public, various interest groups began criticising the prominence of Holocaust content in comparison to other genocides (Moses 2012). Therefore, unsurprisingly, the history of the CMHR is one of dispute and of passionate memory competition, where it seems that "memories crowd each other out of the public sphere" (Rothberg 2009, 23) instead of informing each other. Of course, it is not the memories themselves that compete for recognition but the politics behind the decisions made to acknowledge some while discarding other historical narratives, which is why taking a closer look at how certain mnemonic content has been advanced is revealing. In the case of the CMHR, it was the Canadian-Ukrainian community in particular which demanded that more room be given to the Holodomor, a famine caused by the Soviet occupation of Ukraine in the early 1930s. Noteworthy in this regard is that Canada, unlike many other nation states, acknowledged the Holodomor as a genocide in 2008 (Ukrainian Canadian Congress 2008). This recognition lent weight to the demand for its memory to be featured in the museum and influenced decisions being made at the CMHR about which atrocities to accentuate. The museum's (former) CEO Stuart Murray responded to the growing issue of memory competition by saying that the CMHR was "not a genocide museum" but "a human rights museum in the sense of how we're [the CMHR] looking at some of these issues" (CNC News 2011). What he meant was that the CMHR aspires to be an "idea museum" and did not intend to become a memorial museum to genocide in general; therefore, not all instances of mass violence would be detailed. Instead, some cases, like the Holocaust and the genocides of the 1990s in Rwanda and Srebrenica, were chosen specially to prompt discussions about human rights and not primarily to be commemorated in the museum. This is a very important statement because it, first of all, illustrates the tension between memorialisation and activism that I have already noted and, moreover, suggests that the past, or, more precisely, genocides of the past, are not on display in their own right and to commemorate their victims but in order for lessons to be learned from them. I will provide more detail about how this plays out in the exhibitions themselves in the following, but before I delve into the exhibition's narrative and emplotment within the museum as a whole, I would like to elaborate a little more on these controversies.

When the debates about the issue of which genocides would be allotted how much space in the exhibitions did not cease, the CMHR revised its explanation that it was not a genocide museum and instead stated that it was relying on the list of genocides recognised by the Canadian Government and the United Nations. It was only to such cases that an exhibition – however large or small – would be granted (Hankivsky and Dhamoon 2013). This reasoning had immense consequences for the representation of the genocide committed on Canadian soil in the residential school system (Gray and Gardner 2016). Despite being recognised as a "cultural genocide" by the Canadian Truth and Reconciliation Commission in 2015, the CMHR has abstained from placing too much emphasis on this contested issue, only accounting for it in a small booth in the museum's largest gallery entitled "Canadian Journeys". This exhibit aims to show that "there have been steps and missteps on the road to greater rights for everyone in Canada. This panorama of experience reflects continuing efforts to achieve human rights for all" (CMHR/Galleries). According to this, the residential school system was simply one of the "missteps" of Canadian history, and, what is more, all of the "steps", whether good or bad, are framed as "human rights journeys". Employing the image of a journey evokes a sense of purpose for the greater goal of human rights, thereby attributing value to even the worst of incidents, such as Indigenous genocide and the ongoing kidnapping and murder of Indigenous women and girls across Canada (Baker 2019).

For this reason (amongst others) the curator of the exhibition on "Indigenous Perspectives", Tricia Logan, decided to leave the museum even before its opening, criticising that she "[...] was asked in July 2013 to remove the term genocide from the small exhibit on settler colonial genocide in Canada. [...] Atrocities against Indigenous peoples would remain in the museum, but I was no longer permitted to name them as genocide" (Logan 2014, 122). Such decisions seemed to still be in place during my visit in 2018, as I was surprised not to find more gallery space dedicated to the subject of the residential schools, nor any other particular notice of the genocide (for example in the form of a monument). For any museum in contemporary Canada but, of course, even more so for a dedicated human rights museum which claims to be operating in the service of *all* members of society, such decisions are at least questionable, if not outright scandalous. It has long been criticised how systematically "Indigenous knowledge systems, values and historical perspectives have been written out of the 'official' version of the building of the Canadian nation" (Donald 2009, 9). To have a human rights museum repeat the same patterns and authorise them once again due to its status raises serious concerns about curatorial decisions but even more so about the discursively structured regime of truth underlying curatorial processes.

In this context it is particularly pertinent to keep in mind the impact of decisions to acknowledge or not acknowledge certain atrocities as genocide. There is, of course, a judicial component to such decisions because the genocides committed have legal consequences as well as financial ones, the latter stemming from claims for reparations that are only considered to be justified once the crime has been recognised as a genocide. Moreover – and this seems especially important in regard to a museum dedicated to human rights and their advancement – it is in relations like those described above that the coloniality of knowledge determines not only which histories are told but also which lives are grievable and worth honouring – and therefore those which are not. It also influences decisions about what kinds of practices constitute genocidal violence, whether they have ceased or if they are still influencing the present (Glowacka 2019).[5] In this context, Pamela Palmater has unambiguously written that, even though "Canada may be described by the settler society as a postcolonial state, it is not postcolonial for Indigenous peoples", because for Indigenous peoples, "the colonial experience has never ended" (2015, 2–3). Therefore, as it stands, the explicit exclusion of a more detailed account of the settler-colonial genocide can only be explained as an expression of the many paradoxes of the human rights project and liberal democracy more generally – an aspect to which I will return in chapter 8.

A museum advocating for social change

Now, how is the critique of Canada's oblivion to or neglect of its own violent colonial history (and present) linked to the ways in which Holocaust memory is put on display at the CMHR, and how is it woven into the broader storyline of the

5 This is not the place to engage in the discussion about whether the settler colonialisation of the Americas brought about a massive genocide or whether to call the five-hundred-year history of violence something else (see, e.g., Cave 2011). Nevertheless, I would like to point out the power structures inherent in this debate, because, as Judith Butler puts it in her contemplation of precarious, "grievable" life, "specific lives cannot be apprehended as injured or lost if they are not fist apprehended as living. If certain lives do not qualify as lives or are, from the start, not conceived as lives within certain epistemological frames, then these lives are never lived nor lost in the full sense" (Butler 2009, 1). For a detailed account of the debate about "colonial politics of recognition" (Coulthard 2014) and "the colonial origins of the concept of genocide", see, e.g., the edited volume on issues of genocide by Moses (2008).

museum? Though this book is concerned with the forms and functions of Holocaust memorialisation, it was in relation to the museum's overall composition and to other aspects of the museum that I found that the Holocaust exhibition, even though it is just one gallery of many in the large museum, was of pivotal importance for the overarching narrative on human rights and their communication. I will therefore pause at various galleries during my tour of the museum and try to detail their content in order to make sense of their connection to the Holocaust gallery and its overall emplotment.

The CMHR describes its own dramaturgy as one descending from darkness to light (CMHR virtual tour 2021). Starting on the ground floor, the visitor slowly makes her way up, either taking ramps or elevators that eventually end in the Izzy Asper Tower of Hope overlooking the city of Winnipeg and its surroundings. The "Examining the Holocaust" gallery is located in the centre of the museum, at its heart (a location that had been suggested during the process of the museum's creation). To get there, visitors either start in a gallery space for temporary exhibitions or go to the first permanent exhibition right away, which is located in a large gallery entitled "What are Human Rights?". This first gallery serves to give a first impression of just how inexhaustible the subject of human rights is, providing diverse examples of human rights issues and human rights activists. I began my first tour of the museum in the temporary exhibition, which seemed, surprisingly, to link my research at the CMHR to my case study of the Johannesburg Holocaust & Genocide Centre. The exhibition at the CMHR, which ran from June 2018 until the end of August 2019, was titled "Mandela: Struggle for Freedom" and had been developed in partnership with South Africa's Apartheid Museum. The temporary exhibition was based on the premise that "Mandela continues to inspire struggles for freedom around the world", and in the interpretative framework of the CMHR, the struggle for freedom is simultaneously a struggle for human rights. What I found particularly striking about the exhibition was its effort to engage visitors by asking them questions like, "What would you do if you were imprisoned for 27 years?" At one point in the exhibition a letter was displayed which Mandela had written to his daughter while in prison. After reading the letter, visitors were encouraged to write their own letter to a loved one, almost suggesting that anyone of us could find ourselves imprisoned like Mandela, or could at least imagine what it must have been like. Later in the exhibition, visitors were also asked to design their own poster of resistance, and, at the end, a video collage showed people from across Canada speaking about Mandela. Interestingly, all of the people speaking in these videos concluded that "the future is in my hands". Therefore, in a sense, this temporary exhibition laid the foundations for the core objectives of the CMHR, which are to "foster an appreciation for the importance of human rights" and to encourage visitors to get involved in human rights causes. It is these same principles that were already enshrined in the bill on the partnership between the museum and the federal government, "A Call to Personal Action" (Thorsteinson 2008, 24).

In the first permanent gallery, where I went after visiting the Mandela exhibition, a long timeline on "The Global History of Human Rights" assembles one hundred "Selected Moments" in human rights history. The timeline dates back as far as ancient Rome and, like the much shorter timeline at the Memorium, ends with the establishment of the International Criminal Court as well as the most recent UN declarations and conventions. Leaving the gallery, there are two possible walkways. Visitors can either go into the exhibition on "Indigenous Perspectives", which was strikingly empty during my visits, or proceed straight to the gallery on "Canadian Journeys", which assembles seventy different stories of "journeys" towards "human rights for all". The "Indigenous Perspectives" exhibition features many "traditional" Indigenous exhibits and stories but only very few on the everyday lives of Indigenous peoples in contemporary Canada, let alone their experiences of racism. The first time that racism is mentioned as an issue is in the next gallery on "Canadian Journeys", which, amongst other things, provides details about anti-Black racism in Canada during the first half of the twentieth century. Though it openly addresses racist attitudes amongst many Canadians at the time, the niche on anti-Black racism perpetuates the impression that this is all a problem of the past. As proof of the pastness of racism and, moreover, of the contribution made by the CMHR to a more equal society, the museum displays a Canadian ten-dollar bill, which, since 2018, has pictured the Black business woman and Civil rights activist Viola Desmond on one side with the CMHR on the other.

From here, visitors walk up another ramp zigzagging through the museum and reach the aforementioned Garden of Contemplation to pause and reflect. The garden is followed by an interactive panel on "Protecting Rights in Canada", where visitors are not only given information on the evolution of the Canadian legal framework but are even allowed to participate in courtroom decisions on various rights issues. In this room, visitors are invited to vote on cases concerning human rights in Canada. Something similar takes place in a gallery at one of the CMHR's predecessors and the first museum of its kind in North America, which served as an inspiration to Israel and Gail Asper: the Simon Wiesenthal Museum of Tolerance (MOT) in Los Angeles (having visited the MOT two years prior to my visit to the CMHR, I immediately noticed the many resemblances, especially regarding the devices employed to engage visitors). As visitors then walk up the next ramp and towards the Holocaust gallery, the path becomes narrower, the lights are dimmed, and the ceiling seems to become oppressively low. This effect is underscored by the sudden onset of music mixed with distant sounds from busy streets and horse-drawn wagons passing by, evoking the feeling of going backwards in time to a city somewhere in the Germany of the 1930s. The dimmed lighting also brings to mind the distinction between dark and better times, and seems to be in accordance with the overall motto of the Holocaust exhibit, which is "The Fragility of Human Rights". As described above, the Holocaust gallery is the darkest place in the CMHR, and from here visitors slowly ascend towards the promising light of a better future, a vision that is "as shared as the sky", as it is expressed in an advertisement for the CMHR. I felt as if these curatorial and architectural means were reminding me that it is human rights which provide us with light, which have the power to lead us from darkness towards more hopeful futures.

I will go into more detail about the Holocaust exhibit itself in the next section, but first I would like to continue our walk through the museum in order to make tangible the overall emplotment of the Holocaust gallery. Unlike the room on "Indigenous Perspectives", which every visitor can easily pass without looking into it any further, as the walkway offers different choices on that level, entering the Holocaust gallery is inevitable (unless one takes the elevator and skips the floor on which "Examining the Holocaust" is located). Once visitors have engaged with the history of the Holocaust and made their way to the next room, which is on the same level as "Examining the Holocaust", they are met by a large display of the Universal Declaration of Human Rights. The display carries the title "The Human Rights Revolution" and opens the floor to the gallery on "Turning Points of Humanity", which is all of a sudden brightly lit. Monitors in the shape of open books provide information on various people and their continuous work for the realisation of the principles enshrined in the UDHR. The exhibit provides details about efforts being made for future conventions such as the ones on children's rights, women's rights and rights for disabled people, with an emphasis on the advocates of those specific rights, who "work tirelessly to make this great hope a reality". Less information is given on the circumstances that made such specific charters necessary despite the existence of the UDHR. The following gallery, called "Breaking the Silence", then accounts for some moments from recent history when it was not possible to protect human rights for all. At the entrance to this room, visitors are greeted by a life-sized bronze statue of a sorrowful child. The monument symbolises "Bitter Memories of Childhood" and is dedicated to the victims of the Ukrainian famine. The same hollow-eyed girl stands at the entrance to the National Holodomor Museum in Kyiv, Ukraine, and can also be found elsewhere in Canada, for example, in Manitoba's neighbouring province, Saskatchewan, where a large Ukrainian community found refuge and later erected the first memorial to the Holodomor in Canada (Holodomor Research and Education Consortium). Although it presents an overview of the four other genocides (beside the Holocaust) that have been recognised in Canada – the Armenian genocide, the Holodomor, and the genocides in Rwanda and Srebrenica – "Breaking the Silence" is, as its title suggests, more about the need to speak out against human rights violations than it is about historical accounts of the genocides or their memorialisation. On a large display, visitors are furthermore invited to choose an atrocity they want to learn more about, the first historical one being the Atlantic slave trade and the last the suppression of Afghan people by the Taliban. However different all these atrocities are from each other, there is an overall theme applied to each case that emphasises how individuals who "dare to break the silence about mass atrocities" have the power to "promote the human rights of everyone".

Fittingly, the next gallery on the new upper level is called "Action Counts" and presents Canadians who have taken action for human rights. At the same time, visitors are invited to play a game at an interactive table and explore possible ways to get involved in human rights causes (and, at the CMHR, such causes might be anything from the fight against genocide to speaking up against bullying). In the game at the centre of the "Action Counts" room, visitors play a character who has just found out about a food crisis in an Inuit community in the far north. They want to help and decide to host a benefit concert to raise money for the Inuit. In order to make the concert happen, visitors have to get their character to move around and talk to other characters, whose support they need to ensure the success of their efforts. They first go to City Hall to get a permit, then they consult the Elders' Council. Next, they go to the radio station to advertise the concert and, finally, they speak to their band and make further plans about whom to invite and so on. Thus, on level five of the CMHR, on our way towards the tower of hope, visitors have not only been encouraged numerous times to become activists for human rights but have also been presented with ways to get involved. Now, there are only two more galleries with permanent exhibitions left to see, one on "Rights Today" and the very last one called "Inspiring Change".

During my first visit, when I covered the entire museum, the rooms became emptier and emptier the higher up I walked, and upon entering the last room, I was greeted by surprised museum staff with the words "Oh wow, welcome, you made it to the top!" It took me about seven hours to get all the way up, so, presumably, most visitors who want to end their journey through the CMHR in the Izzy Asper Tower of Hope and enjoy the panoramic view simply take the elevator. This is what I did too each time I returned to the CMHR after my first visit.

"From darkness to light": The Holocaust at the CMHR

As mentioned above, the Canadian Museum for Human Rights – despite immense criticism – is home to one of the biggest exhibitions on the Holocaust in Canada (Moses 2012; Lehrer 2015), while more hotly contested issues closer to Canada's own history, like the genocide committed over the course of about one hundred years within the scope of the residential school system, are less prominent. So, rather than having a single exhibit to highlight the utter subjugation and killing of Indigenous peoples and detail its contemporary impact, the museum weaves such issues into broader narratives about a fight for justice. This leaves the Holocaust in a very prominent position within the museum, and in the following, I will take a closer look at the narrative employed to tell its story and also contemplate how it fits it into the overall storyline of the museum.

The "Examining the Holocaust" exhibition was curated by Clint Curle and Jeremy Maron, who are also participants in the ongoing scholarly debate about the role played by Holocaust memory at the CMHR. I was fortunate enough to meet with both of them and to be given a tour through the exhibit by Jeremy Maron. However, it would be possible for anyone to access the information that I am relating in this chapter, either at the museum itself or in the publications quoted.[6] I have already described the walkway into the gallery that proved to provide informative documentation of Holocaust history, similar to what can be found in the many Holocaust museums across the world. The same iconic photographs and objects are displayed, and, at first sight, I would have concluded that this exhibition could be situated anywhere, with no special connection to the overall framework of the CMHR. However, I did subsequently find narrative strategies that specifically reflect the CMHR's approach and agenda to stimulate human rights advocacy rather than to teach historical contents or to commemorate the victims of the Holocaust.

The exhibition is organised around the themes of the "Abuse of State Power", "Oppression" and "War and Genocide". The panels that detail aspects of German history leading up to the Holocaust are titled "An Unstable Democracy", "Distorting Democracy" and "Descent into Dictatorship". These panels address the larger question of how the Holocaust became possible within a "devel-

6 During my research at the CMHR I met with a couple of staff members and soon realised that all that they would tell me about their work could also be found in the publications by and on the museum. The only exception was a lengthy conversation with former Manager of Education Mireille Lamontagne, who was very open to my questions and took the time to think with me about the issues I raised, for which I am very grateful.

oped" democratic nation such as Germany, and at the same time, visitors are encouraged to reflect upon their own societies and the current human rights causes that might be at stake. The displays on Weimar Germany, the rise of Nazism and the first years of Nazi rule are then followed by a display entitled "Freedom Denied", followed by "Control of Daily Life", leading inevitably towards the most horrific part of this history: "Persecution".

In between the displays on German history and the evolution of Nazism's genocidal practices, there is a small theatre showing a movie about Canada's role during the Second World War and the consequences of Canadian antisemitism. Due to very strong antisemitic tendencies, so we learn in the movie, Canada was the country that granted the lowest number of Jewish refugees asylum among the Allied forces. The very informative movie concludes with the following statement: "As a nation, we must face our failures, now and then." In comparison to how the museum addresses or does not address other difficult and contested issues related to Canada's own history and present, I was almost surprised at how critical this short movie was. It might have been one of the highlights of the entire museum, as it dared to take a more dialectical perspective on just how tolerant Canada is and has always been.

Back in the exhibition, there are more panels informing visitors about the Roma genocide as well as the persecution of homosexuals and people with disabilities, all grouped under the title "Humanity Rejected". There is no mention of the victim group of so-called "asocials", nor of the Nazis' political opponents, including the large number of communists who were tortured and killed during the twelve years of Nazi rule. The last panel in "Examining the Holocaust" is about the term *genocide* and how it was coined, with the famous poem "If This is a Man" by Primo Levi emblazoned on the wall next to it. As I mentioned, this gallery is followed by the one titled "Turning Points of Humanity". This chronology – i.e., with the Holocaust coming first, followed by the coining of the term genocide (even though the term had actually already been outlined by Raphael Lemkin *before* the Holocaust) and, last but not least, the Universal Declaration of Human Rights – is underscored by the title of the panel on the UDHR, "The Human Rights Revolution". This title can be read as if it really was human rights that won the war against Nazi Germany and its collaborators, which frames the Second World War as having been, in essence, a war for human rights.

What is more, the overall framing of this gallery as one about the "fragility of human rights" implies that human rights existed prior to the UDHR. While it is true that there were events such as the 1789 Declaration of the Rights of Men as well as the institutionalisation of some minority rights, it is nevertheless incorrect to speak of human rights having existed at that time, so I suspect that the titles chosen for the exhibition and its panels are less about historical accuracy than about serving the overall storyline of the museum. Interesting in this context is how the curators describe the core conflict they had to solve during the curatorial process: "Many Holocaust education and commemoration initiatives face a challenging question: Should they relate the Holocaust to other atrocities and human rights violations, and/or explore human rights issues that go beyond the specificity of the Holocaust?" (Maron and Curle 2018, 1). In other words, they tried to find an approach to the Holocaust that would "balance the particularity of the Holocaust and the universality of human rights" (Maron and Curle 2018, 2). What is overt in these considerations and also mirrored in the exhibit is the conviction that the Holocaust is itself a human rights issue, that Holocaust history and memory are intrinsically linked to human rights. The question that needs to be juggled, so it seems, is one of comparison and universalisation but not about the relationship to human rights generally. It should, however, be argued that the human rights prism is just one possible perspective and interpretative frame when it comes to the Holocaust, probably the one that is currently applied the most, but nevertheless not the only way of understanding or making sense of this history and its memory.

The narrative of the Holocaust exhibit at the CMHR is not intended to stimulate ambiguous thought, though. Instead, it has been conceptualised to "bring to the fore aspects that can inspire consideration of broader human rights issues" (Maron and Curle 2018, 3). What these considerations might be and how the explicit link between the Holocaust and human rights is put to work can best be observed in the museum's app, which serves as a guide through the museum once it has been downloaded to a smartphone. In the section on the Holocaust, app users listen to a conversation between a man, a woman and Clint Curle (using headphones, it is actually possible to hear the conversation, which can otherwise be followed by scrolling and reading through the text). Curle explains to them what it is they are seeing in the exhibition as well as what they are supposed to learn from it: "As you look into this gallery, what you really see is the cost of human rights neglected: a really powerful lesson in the need for ongoing vigilance to guard against anti-Semitism, prejudice, persecution of minorities, and other human rights violations." Once again, the narrative upheld here suggests that the Holocaust took place because human rights were neglected. I will come back to this interpretation of the Shoah in chapters eight and nine, as it deserves further scrutiny. For now, if we turn back to the app, our attention is brought to the "questions" this gallery might prompt. A female voice comes in to ask, "What can I do to make sure this never happens again?" A male voice sceptically responds, "How can one person even make a difference?" The answer to these difficult questions is provided once more by Clint Curle, who says:

> The best defence against the repetition of something like the Holocaust is a culture of human rights, where individuals really internalize the values of human rights and see that each one of us has a responsibility to be vigilant [...]. When we shoulder this responsibility, that's the best thing we can do to make a future that we're proud to pass on [...].

What Curle tells any doubtful but motivated app users sounds familiar, as it entails the same emphasis on individual responsibility and the importance of civic engagement as the UNESCO and IHRA publications I discussed earlier. However, at the CMHR, the strategy used to motivate such behavioural changes is different to that of UNESCO und the IHRA in the sense that it relies on taking a strong emotive approach. This we can see clearly in the next slide of the app, which presents an interactive mood map. We are asked, "After visiting Examining the Holocaust, how do you feel?" The four options we are given in the mood map are "moved", "thoughtful", "inspired" and "surprised". These are the only choices, and all of them are positive. There is no option to feel sad, enraged, disgusted or terrified, or indeed any other negative emotion. Instead, the idea behind the mood map is that positive emotions spark action, whereas negative emotions are believed to render people inactive (Lehrer 2015). But as we learn if we continue to use the app, action is what the Holocaust gallery and its rooms are seeking to stimulate: once we enter the next room, which is dedicated to the "Turning Points of Humanity", the narrator of the app encourages us to "think about a time you did something to support human rights. [...] Have you volunteered for human rights groups or causes?" Both the male and female in the recording begin to think out loud: "Hmmm, let's see...", and remember that, yes, they had both already volunteered for different causes such as a "food bank" or "education rights for all kids". With these reflections, not on the history of the Holocaust but rather on our own commitment to human rights, we are leaving "Examining the Holocaust" behind and moving on – we might even say, progressing – towards a stronger human rights culture for which, so we are being told, we all have equal responsibility.

Making difficult knowledge consumable

While the Holocaust exhibition with its additional text and media is very straightforward in its message and general claims, the curators maintain that they have carefully balanced "the particular" of the Holocaust and "the universal of human rights" (Maron and Curle 2018, 1). In their reflections on their curatorial process, Maron and Curle explain how, at first, even before the CMHR became a national museum, the exhibit was planned as

> one that positioned the Holocaust as the primary catalyst for the United Nations' 1948 adoption of the Universal Declaration of Human Rights (UDHR). To simplify this preliminary narrative, the world gazed with horror upon the liberation of the Nazi death camps, and drafted the UDHR in response, as a manifestation of a promise of "Never Again." (Maron and Curle 2018, 5)

However, as they report, the CMHR later refrained from displaying such a direct link between the Holocaust and the Universal Declaration of Human Rights because this causality had been, first of all, criticised for not being historically accurate and, secondly, because understanding of the pitfalls of exploiting Holocaust history increased. Instead, "[t]he experts and stakeholders called on the CMHR to re-think its approach and uncover authentic human rights insights from within the Holocaust, rather than using it as a mechanism to set up a triumphant celebration of the UDHR" (Maron and Curle 2018, 6). This is a very interesting insight and seems to stand in stark contrast to my personal impression of the exhibition's narrative, which in my view did exactly what Maron and Curle claim that they tried to avoid: it tells – despite the detailed historical information provided – a very simple and teleological story that suggests that the UDHR was a "revolution" sparked by the Holocaust. What is more, framing the UDHR as a revolution looked to me as if it was the happy ending to the otherwise terrible story of the Holocaust. My reading of the exhibition's narrative cannot, of course, be detached from the overarching storyline of the CMHR. Even if the exhibit itself does not suggest a causal link between the Holocaust and the drafting of the UDHR, the museum circuit and the headlines or titles of the panels together with the digital guide do indicate such a link and, furthermore, explicitly marry it to the call for personal action that is omnipresent at the CMHR.

In this sense, the storyline prompts us to assume not only that we have institutionalised human rights because of the Holocaust but also that this was only made possible by the brave individuals who spoke out against injustices. Moreover, the human rights culture to which we aspire continues to depend on individuals who decide to advocate for human rights causes. In this vein, the CMHR really is not a memorial museum but a museum primarily concerned with the dissemination of ideas, including a behavioural ideal, and it is primarily for this purpose that histories are evoked. Even though some periods of history are studied in more depth, the end to which these pasts, especially atrocities, are being presented is to stimulate the emotions necessary to become actively involved in the name of a human rights culture rather than to foster critical thinking. I will return to this aspect of "difficult knowledge" as a "terrible gift" (Simon 2006) at the end of this chapter and will elaborate on it more in chapter 9, but for now I would like to point to the narrative strategy of employing a happy ending to a story that is otherwise difficult to bear – that is, happy endings make difficult knowledge consumable and retrospectively tame the past so that it does not leave a stain on the present or the future (Failler 2015).

Equal rights and equal duties

Paying attention to the overall emplotment as well as the specific narrative of the Holocaust exhibit at the CMHR revealed a trope that features prominently in the CMHR. That is, as I have argued above, an emphasis on individual responsibility coupled with a call for action, and the CMHR's goal is to not only to build a human rights culture but also to create "upstanders", a term that refers to anyone who stands up in the face of injustices and speaks out, anyone who "breaks the silence" and becomes an advocate for social change. As the CMHR was advised early on in the report on additional collaborators submitted to the federal government:

> The Advisory Committee recommends that the CMHR be socially responsible and progressive in its approach, while the individual visitor should come out of the museum motivated with a personal call to action [...]. The CMHR must take every opportunity to engage young Canadian men and women and especially Aboriginal youth in the scope and substance of human rights issues. Canadian youth [...] have a unique opportunity to become catalysts for change and a powerful force to promote human rights. (Thorsteinson 2008, v–viii)

My impression after spending many days at the CMHR, studying its exhibitions, publications and educational materials, was that it really put this advice into action. If anything, the visitor leaves the museum with a sense of duty, a feeling of responsibility for the wellbeing of others and humanity as a whole. What I find particularly noteworthy about the recommendation quoted above – and this reflects the account of the issues concerning Indigenous perspectives and knowledge given by the museum – is the advice to "engage Aboriginal youth" in particular. Why is that and what is the logic constructive of such a recommendation? In other words, why should "Aboriginal youth" in particular be motivated to get involved in human rights issues when it is their communities who still suffer the most from systemic inequality? These questions bring us to a core contradiction at the heart of the CMHR, which is in a sense brought about by the special role played by the Holocaust exhibit at the museum.

Whilst the curators of "Examining the Holocaust", Maron and Curle, made it clear that their aim was not to make the exhibit about redemption, the CMHR does convey the impression that human rights have redemptive power. Thus, in a sense, the same applies to the Holocaust gallery and its narrativisation, which cannot be viewed separately from the museum in which it is located. The museum as a whole strongly relies on the notion of "righting wrongs" throughout its exhibitions. This becomes plain to see when looking at the storyline within the CMHR and is especially pertinent in the imbalance between the injustices of the past (that are very present) and the acknowledgement of current-day injustices in Canada (which is rather scarce). As has been explained, one of the early debates about the CMHR was fuelled by existing claims to the land on which the museum was to be built and the lack of interest in these claims by the museum's stakeholders and the city of Winnipeg. However, the decision was made to carry out archaeological mitigation at the site where the museum was to be built to look for "buried cultural resources" (Quaternary Consultants LTD 2013, i). The archaeological work at the Forks was performed in 2008, and almost 400,000 artefacts were recovered. The artefacts were, according to former CMHR CEO Stuart Murray, "evidence that this site has long been a place for peaceful meeting [and] also supports Aboriginal oral history passed down through generations" (CMHR 2013). While the importance of the site had long been emphasised by Indigenous communities, who did not need further evidence but instead demanded that the museum take seriously what it had found at the Forks and build elsewhere, construction on the CMHR went ahead as planned. Some of the archaeological findings were later integrated into educational programmes as well as into the exhibitions, which prompted Murray to make the following promise: "The Canadian Museum for Human Rights will continue the tradition of respectful dialogue, discussion and learning. We will acknowledge the lessons of the past, examine what we have achieved by coming together, and what we have lost by standing apart. We will examine what it means to be human, simply human" (Murray qtd. in Bender 2013). This story sounds similar to the setting described at the beginning of James Clifford's famous text on museums as "contact zones", where museum staff and Aboriginal elders come together to learn about the sacred meanings of some of the objects held in the museum's collection. The CMHR proceeded in this very same way and consulted elders about the artefacts that had been found. However, it reserved itself the right to make the final decision about what to make of the meanings and how to include the stories of the artefacts in its overall storyline. As Murray says in the above quotation, the archaeological findings present "lessons of the past" and are, by this logic, part of history without any special impact on the present. A bronze of a moccasin footprint found at the Forks is, for example, prominently displayed at the entrance of the gallery on "Indigenous Perspectives". The story told about the footprint is related to the history of the site but bears no mention of the heated dispute over its present-day use. In Angela Failler's words,

> These gestures of inclusiveness reiterate a memory entrepreneurship approach through which images or signs of Indigeneity [...] become a kind of commodity that non-Indigenous Canadians are invited to consume as examples of our seemingly benign or even benevolent past and "reconciled" present relations with Indigenous peoples. [...] [W]hile the bronze moccasin print, for example, is not available to buy, its presence in the CMHR suggests to visitors that (for the price of admission to the museum) they too can be part of the museum's commitment to advancing human rights simply by viewing and appreciating artefacts of Indigenous culture. (Failler 2015, 4)

Failler's critique resonates with my impression of a strategy I want to call *exhibitionary atonement*, which suggests that it is possible to make up for past wrongs by simply putting them on public display. Here, the narrative of redemption comes in again because it supports the overall storyline about the victory of the present over a past that was dark and evil.[7]

Becoming an "upstander"

In order to paint a full picture, I would like to include a few more details about the educational materials that are designed to enrich the museum visit and put further emphasis on the CMHR's storyline. I have already explained the prominent position, right at the centre of the museum, in which the Holocaust gallery is located. The additional material for teachers planning to see this gallery with their students summarises the aim of such a visit as follows:

> The history of the 20th century world shows us that human rights can be denied, even in developed societies with elected governments. In order to prevent mass violations of human dignity and human rights such as the Holocaust, it is important to remain vigilant in the defense of human rights for all. We study the Holocaust to learn to recognize genocide and to take a stand against the attitudes that support it. (CMHR/Teacher Guide 2017)

The Holocaust also features prominently in another programme on the role of "othering", together with the genocide in Rwanda and "Indigenous experiences

---

7 I will carry out an in-depth, comparative analysis of forms of such exhibitionary atonement that I also found at the Memorium in chapter 8, which will follow my final case study on the Johannesburg Holocaust & Genocide Centre. I nonetheless wanted to mention it here already, as it leads to a clearer account of my overall assessment of the CMHR.

with colonisation in Canada" (the "Dignity and Rights" programme). Both programmes assume that by "learning about why and how extreme human rights abuses can be carried out", the learner will also discover what can be done "to prevent them from recurring". For me, what is most interesting about these objectives and how they are formulated is the tacit prescription of answers. The answer to the question of what we could do to prevent atrocities from happening is given throughout the museum and its pedagogical materials and might be most apparent in the summary of the intended "enduring understandings" in the gallery on "Turning Points for Humanity":

> In December 1948 the Universal Declaration of Human Rights (UDHR) was adopted by the United Nations. It stirred the countries of the world to aspire to the ideal that rights belong equally to each and every human being. Its thirty articles express humanity's highest hope and have inspired people and governments to strive to make this great hope a reality.

If we join in to champion human rights, the goal of preventing "human rights abuses" will finally be reached. In order to underscore this point, many stories of so-called "upstanders", of people who have advocated for human rights, are told throughout the museum. They include Nelson Mandela, Viola Desmond and Raul Wallenberg. The museum defines the term as follows: "An upstander is a person who recognizes injustice, knows their personal strengths and uses those strengths to create change" (CMHR/Be an Upstander). In the accompanying educational materials, learners are called upon to "use [their] personal strength to create change" as well as to reflect on the people around them who might be considered "upstanders". In a virtual programme available on the CMHR's homepage, visitors are invited to choose a person close to them and explain why this person (a neighbour, family member or friend) is an upstander. The sentence to be completed is: "My... is an upstander in my life because they used their personal strength of..." The options that the programme provides to fill in the blanks are "organisation", "education", "communication", "kindness", "honesty", "perseverance", "optimism" and, lastly, "helpfulness". Similar to the mood map described earlier, there is no single option available to pick supposedly negative emotions like anger as the engine behind taking action. Did Nelson Mandela risk his life in the fight against apartheid out of "optimism", and did Viola Desmond go the difficult road of taking racist Canadians to court because she was aware of her "perseverance"? Did Raul Wallenberg choose to help Jews during the Holocaust out of sheer "helpfulness"?

This programme is similar in its message to the interactive game in the gallery "Action Counts", which encourages visitors to help an Inuit community out of their food crisis, as it relies on and prescribes the same emotive approach as the mood map. Both the games and the exercise described above are revealing of what Didier Fassin (2012) has called "humanitarian reason": a mode that moralises what ought to be regarded as a broader political issue, a structural problem that might require more action than some individuals showing benevolence (Robinson 2020). Acts of charity are presented as the virtuous reaction to systemic inequality. Nowhere in the museum do we learn that such a choice of action is just one option of many and, as much as feeling inspired by the trauma of others is admirable, it is far from being the most common cause of (political) activism. We do not learn about the many actions that have been taken out of exasperation for having to experience gross injustices, about those that have resulted from despair and the feeling of sheer helplessness, especially during times of genocide. Nor do we learn about political opposition as a driving force behind activism. Instead of raising money for impoverished Indigenous communities, we could also join or become allies of the Idle No More movement, which calls for an "Indigenous revolution" and was launched in opposition to the conservative Canadian government and its "dismantling of environmental protection laws" – the same government which decided that the CMHR should become a national museum. But supporting causes such as Idle No More would mean radically questioning all that contemporary Canada is based on, to call out its colonial conditions instead of celebrating it as a guardian of human rights and democracy.

In the juxtaposition of these different emotions and reasons for activism in the name of social change, it becomes plain to see that the lessons conveyed throughout the CMHR follow a specific agenda that puts forward an ideal of active citizenship that is compliant with the current order and does not question its foundations. Power relations and domination are not considered to be structures in democratic societies but wrongs that exclusively feature amongst authoritarian forms of government or in the distant past. Here, the memorialisation of the Holocaust as the event preceding and prompting the "Human Rights Revolution" plays an important part in the overarching story told at the CMHR: the CMHR ends our journey through the museum by telling us: "Now it's up to you to create change." What this change might entail, who will benefit from it and where its limits might lie, however, remains open. This is not because the museum encourages different approaches to such change, but rather because it makes it very clear what vision it supports and what attributes it demands of its visitors to enable them to put their "personal strength" into action.

7 The South African Holocaust & Genocide Centre: Safeguarding Democracy

In 2017, I first learned that South Africa not only had three Holocaust museums but had also been extending the inclusion of the topic in its national school curriculum since 2007 – a curriculum with the aim of placing a stronger emphasis on human rights education (Tibbitts and Keet 2017; Gilbert 2019). The topic of the Holocaust, though it had already played a part in earlier versions of the post-apartheid curriculum, was given a prominent place in the revised national curriculum for history, because, according to Brenda Gouws, a "synergy" (2019, 48) was assumed to exist between Holocaust education and the purpose of the new curriculum, to "establish a society based on democratic values, social justice and fundamental human rights" (Department of Basic Education 2011, 3). South Africa's Minister of Education Angie Motshekga explained the decision to cover the subject of the Holocaust in the reformed curriculum as reflecting an intention to "promote knowledge in the local context, while being sensitive to global imperatives" (Department of Basic Education 2012). It was the latter statement in particular that prompted me to wonder what this meant and to which "global imperatives" exactly Motshekga was referring. I wanted to learn more about the conditions under which Holocaust memory came to be institutionalised in South Africa and to find out more about its political implications. As I began asking myself these questions, decolonisation movements such as #RhodesMustFall and #FeesMustFall were enjoying great support all over South Africa (and beyond), calling among other things for the decolonisation of curricula in schools and universities (Ngcaweni and Ngobeni 2018). Where in this field of tension can Holocaust memorialisation and education be located? What significance does the case study of the Holocaust have for South Africans, and how does it intersect with other teaching, especially on human rights?

Post-apartheid South Africa is often praised for its progressive constitution, its embrace of a human rights agenda and its efforts to bring about reconciliation. Yet the same constitution and reconciliatory agenda is also frequently criticised for being modelled on Western democracies, for its neoliberal underpinnings and lack of transformative power (Dladla 2018; Modiri 2019). On the one hand, there is a discursively constructed national as well as global narrative which turned South Africa into the poster child of successful transitional justice. This narrative emphasises the well-known Truth and Reconciliation Commission (TRC) of 1996 that prevented mass vengeance and has become a shining example of how to deal with a difficult past in order to prevent further conflict and create

https://doi.org/10.1515/9783110788044-009

social harmony (Scott 2020, Ch. 2).[1] Testament to just how strong this narrative is even today is one of the most recent TRCs, held in Canada in 2016 to grapple with the colonial residential school system, which was modelled explicitly on the South African commission. The Canadian TRC was accompanied by events like the exhibition on Nelson Mandela at the brand-new Canadian Museum for Human Rights (see chapter 6). This perception of Mandela and, more generally, that the anti-apartheid struggle was a struggle for constitutional democracy is especially present in the global North, i. e., from South Africa's liberal elites to Canada and Europe (Madlingozi 2017, 2018). What is more, the implementation of a new legal system and human rights mechanisms during the post-apartheid era, like the Human Rights Commission and the Constitutional Court, is presented as having allowed the former racial state to transform into a stable democracy within just a few years. In all this, historic figures from that struggle such as Nelson Mandela and Archbishop Desmond Tutu have become international icons of peace, symbolising the transformation of the racist apartheid state into a republic with a highly commended constitution as well as the culture of human rights it sets out to both secure and advance. Interestingly enough, as I will show in the course of this chapter, efforts to implement Holocaust memory in the post-apartheid curriculum as well as in the broader mnemonic landscape of the new republic are intrinsically linked to this narrative.

On the other hand, however, the storyline of the emergence of a new "Rainbow Nation" is also a very contested one, especially amongst many younger South Africans who are still experiencing the many repercussions of apartheid and the injustices of more recent politics resulting from the neoliberal rationale to which the immediate post-apartheid period gave rise (Dladla 2018). While during the transition phase various international players (such as human rights NGOs and policymakers from the global North) as well as numerous new local civil society organisations were involved in shaping the new state, "South Africa increasingly signed, ratified or acceded to various human rights instruments and

---

1 In her comparison of South Africa's TRC and the Nuremberg Tribunal, Joan Scott makes an interesting observation, noting how the idea for the TRC "explicitly rejected" the Nuremberg Principles because it did not want to focus on legal proceedings in order to put perpetrators on trial but instead emphasised a notion of forgiveness and healing through truth. Scott explains this decision with the fact that, unlike Nazi Germany, which had been defeated in a war, in the transitioning South Africa there were no clear winners, as many important institutions were still "in the hands of the oppressor" (Scott 2020, 31). I cannot go into further detail about the historical context here, but my comparative analysis of mnemonic narratives about the Holocaust and human rights at the Memorium and the JHGC will certainly take this observation into consideration.

standards and committed itself legally and morally to the promotion, protection and attainment of human rights measured against international and regional benchmarks" (Tibbitts and Keet 2017, 90). Despite these commitments, structures of the old apartheid system did not cease to exist but instead, as some scholars and activists claim, were transformed along with the many other Institutions into a form of "neo-apartheid constitutionalism" (Madlingozi 2017, 123). Legal scholar Tshepo Madlingozi observes how "the majority of black people is not simultaneous with the dominant society made up of white people and the black elites" and therefore coins the term "neo-apartheid constitutionalism" in an attempt to point out the extent to which "systemic racism continues today" (2017, 123). Although under the new 1996 constitution all South Africans are now equals, Mogobe Ramose draws our attention to the crucial fact that the contemporary South African state never made the effort to reverse the order established in the unjust wars of colonisation but instead chose the road of amnesty and forgiveness – a significant choice, as he argues:

> Abolish apartheid, so the reasoning went, then all shall be fine. In this way, the question of freedom in South Africa was reduced to the problem of the constitutional recognition of the "civil rights" of the conquered peoples of South Africa. Thus, an all-inclusive constitution, recognising the "civil rights" of all the peoples of South Africa, was deemed to be the solution to the apartheid problem. On this reasoning, it was unnecessary to question the morality and political legitimacy of the "right of conquest" because South Africa belonged to all who lived in it. (Ramose 2007, para 4)

As a result, while the image of the state increasingly emphasised equality, "inequalities could increase within the now supposedly free civil society" (Gordon 2008, 225) as it became even more difficult to address these injustices as such, because the legal and social system of the new South Africa supposedly served all its citizens equally. The consequence of this is that, despite the "lived experiences" of many Black South Africans, especially within the economic sector and in relation to land entitlement, and in stark contrast to the proclaimed human rights culture, the "ontological structure of colonial-apartheid [...] remains in place" (Madlingozi 2017, 124). On a similar note, philosopher Ndumiso Dladla explains that the subsequent and

> [...] somewhat idealised falling away of the category of race does not subtract from the unjustly gained privilege and power of the beneficiaries of racism who acquired that power and privilege on the basis of the discourse and politics of race. Nor does it restore land, freedom, justice, dignity and equality to the victims of racism who were dispossessed and conquered on the basis of appeals to race. The effect of this approach is ultimately to leave the effects of an unjust history undisturbed [...]. (Dladla 2017, 104)

Inherent in both Ramose's and Dladla's observations is the quest for historical justice and also for memory. Both disapprove of how easy it was and still is for the many people who had benefitted from apartheid and its racist structures to move on and not be held to account, neither by the judiciary nor by losing privilege or entitlement.

But how are such continuing injustices and criticism of them related to Holocaust memory and education, which aims to bring about social justice and equality – an endeavour that seems to stand in contrast to upholding a system of neo-apartheid? In regard to the education sector more broadly, Tibbitts and Keet have pointed out how the interplay between national and international neoliberal policies increasingly demanded that not only a strong human rights agenda be implemented in the curriculum but also a stronger link of "schooling with economic development" (2017, 89). Does such a link, and neoliberal rationality more generally, influence the ways in which the Holocaust is memorialised and taught in post-apartheid South Africa? And more specifically, how is it put on display and employed at the Johannesburg Holocaust & Genocide Centre (JHGC)? These questions form the backdrop to my study of the museum and its biography in this chapter, and I will only address them in more detail and in relation to the overarching topic of this book in chapter 8, where I will also connect them to the other two case studies of the Memorium Nuremberg Trials and the Canadian Museum for Human Rights.

Memory entrepreneurship for the protection of human rights

Forms of Holocaust memorialisation emerged in South Africa long before the end of formal apartheid, soon after the end of World War II, when Jewish survivors of the Shoah moved to South Africa and brought to the small Jewish communities already living there their lived experiences of what had happened in Europe (Nates 2018, 207). From then on, memorial services took place regularly, and a few small memorials dedicated to the Jewish victims of the Holocaust were erected. Throughout the forty-six years of apartheid, commemorations remained almost exclusively within the Jewish community. Moreover, as Shirli Gilbert points out, "[t]he largely unquestioned linkage of these histories [Nazism and apartheid], rooted in their shared origins in racist ideology, has led to the widespread assumption that the Holocaust could only have been taught after apartheid's demise" (2019, 351). However, as Gilbert explains further, Nazism and the Holocaust did appear in textbooks during the apartheid era, though without drawing any connection between the racist ideology of the Nazi state and its similarities with South Africa.

Nonetheless, it was only when the system of apartheid officially came to an end and the first democratic elections were held in 1994 that advocacy for Holocaust education began outside the Jewish community (Nates 2010). One important organisation in this process was the newly established non-profit Foundation for Tolerance Education that started promoting the value of educating youth about the Holocaust. Even more impactful was a travelling exhibition that was shown across South Africa and parts of Namibia in 1994 and 1995, and organised in partnership with the Anne Frank House in Amsterdam, titled "Anne Frank in Our World". The Anne Frank exhibition placed the history of the Holocaust "alongside" that of apartheid and thus became, according to two of the most important local activists and practitioners of Holocaust memory, Richard Freedman and Tali Nates, a turning point for Holocaust education in South Africa (Freedman 2012). That was because it transformed the Holocaust into a case study that could be used to address broader issues such as "prejudice and abuse of power" more easily than by turning to the painful history and reality of apartheid (Nates 2018, 208). These projects then also led to the establishment of the first Holocaust Centre, opened in Cape Town in 1999.

When the first substantial changes to the old apartheid school curriculum were made, they were, as mentioned above, marked by a dedication to human rights (Keet and Carrim 2002). Since 2004, human-rights-related topics have increasingly become an organising principle within the new curriculum, something which can, according to Tibbitts and Keet, be seen as a "barometer of a society's values" (2017, 91). Historian Shirli Gilbert has published an extensive review of the different units on the Second World War, Nazism and the Holocaust and has come to the same conclusion, finding that the perspective of "human rights is a key [...] in most textbooks".[2] She also determines that the "Holocaust specifically is allocated far more space in post-apartheid textbooks than it was previously, and it is presented within an unambiguous framework of human rights" (Gilbert 2019, 370).

In-depth study of the Holocaust as part and parcel of a larger human rights framework was eventually introduced to the curriculum for grade 9 and 11 learners in 2007 because it was considered to further support the human rights framework. Holocaust education has since been included in history and the life sciences with the aim of teaching learners to "act in the interest of a society that respects democratic values" (Department of Basic Education 2011). This envis-

2 Her study includes a review of textbooks and their portrayal of Nazism and the Holocaust during the apartheid era as well as in the post-1994 years.

aged outcome of the lessons learned from the Holocaust provides some insight into the aforementioned "global imperatives" to which the Minister of Education, Motshekga, had referred when providing reasons for including the Holocaust in the curriculum.[3] While famous anti-apartheid activists and politicians of the new republic like Desmond Tutu and Ahmed Kathrada have frequently referred to the Holocaust and the impact learning about it had had on them (Mikel-Arieli 2019), the actual implementation of its memory and education was primarily the result of a different line of argument, one that was more concerned with the universal human rights agenda than the ways in which teaching about the Holocaust might help to make sense of local experiences of racial power dynamics and the global scale of racist ideology. Taking into consideration the efforts made by both international and national education policymakers to strengthen human rights education in South Africa, this might not seem surprising. However, this is certainly noteworthy in the overall context of this book, as it also testifies to the importance of global policies and programmes on the Holocaust, such as those introduced in chapter 4.

Along with the change in the curriculum, the South African Holocaust & Genocide Foundation (SAHGF) was also founded in 2007. Eager to contribute to the broader acknowledgment of Holocaust history and memory, the SAHGF made it its main task to support the curriculum and help educators and learners alike to better understand the history of the Holocaust as well as its relevance for contemporary South Africa and the world at large. This is still the task of the last of three Holocaust and genocide centres, which was opened in Johannesburg in 2019: the Johannesburg Holocaust & Genocide Centre (JHGC). In order to better grasp the rationale underpinning these memory endeavours, I would like to briefly recall a milestone that was productive of the global intertwinement of Holocaust memory and the human rights project, and that seems to have influenced South Africa's curricular reform as well: two years before South Africa's change in curriculum, the proclamation of International Holocaust Remembrance Day had reaffirmed and institutionalised a perspective that was being disseminated from the 1990s onwards, which is that Holocaust memory and education strengthen human rights. The acknowledgement of the importance but also utility of Holocaust memory, as it was first institutionalised by the UN General Assembly and soon after by the South African Ministry of Education, adds a further dimension to the international demands referred to by Motshekga and more-

3 For more on teachers' and learners' experiences with the promotion of social justice through the case study of the Holocaust, see an interesting study on this topic conducted by Gaston et al. (2018), which focuses on the SAHGF's programmes for teachers.

over indicate how closely local memory entrepreneurship is entangled with global memory politics. It is necessary to keep these global developments in mind when trying to comprehend why the founder of the JHGC, Tali Nates, views the inclusion of the Holocaust in the South African curriculum as a "commitment to protecting and educating about human rights" (2018, 209).[4]

When the JHGC was founded in 2008, it was not yet a museum or a centre with its own building but nonetheless started its work soon after by running an "outreach education programme" directed at schools and other educational programmes for different age groups (Nates 2018, 211). The SAHGF can be understood as the umbrella organisation for the three independent centres in Cape Town, Durban and Johannesburg. It coordinates Holocaust education in all of the country's nine provinces and tries to ensure some degree of coherence of content. The SAHGF is furthermore in partnership with the United Nations Information Centre to coordinate the annual commemorative events on 27 January. In all of these projects, the JHGC is the only one of the three centres that explicitly addresses a genocide other than the Holocaust and the only one that has partnered with a government body, namely the City of Johannesburg. Nonetheless, as Nates reflects, in all three cases most of the funding has always come "from individuals, foundations and corporations, mainly from the Jewish community in South Africa" (2018, 211). It was the City of Johannesburg, though, which provided the JHGC with the site for its own museum space, into which it moved in 2016. The building was designed by architect Lewis Levin and inspired by conversations with survivors of the Holocaust as well as the 1994 genocide in Rwanda, and is therefore "full of symbolism", such as railway tracks that represent both the Holocaust and core colonial infrastructure (May 2018). The JHGC thus finally became a proper *centre*, able to host exhibitions, events and memorial services, and to embark on educational projects on a broader scale. Since 2016, when a preliminary exhibition on the Holocaust and the genocide in Rwanda was installed, the JHGC has run programmes for learners who come to the centre to get additional information about Holocaust history. It took another three years before the final JHGC was opened in 2019.

---

4 In chapters 8 and 9, I will return to the issue of "global imperatives" and the democratic values to be learned from studying the Holocaust, as they are also relevant to my other two case studies on the Mermorium and the CMHR. But let us linger for a moment at the JHGC and its work.

Challenges and opportunities of learning about genocide

In April 2019, the Republic of South Africa celebrated the twenty-fifth anniversary of its first democratic elections, which had marked the official end to the racist apartheid system in 1994. The month that led up to the historic first elections, March, has since been declared Human Rights Month in order to "remind South Africans about the sacrifices that accompanied the struggle for the attainment of democracy in South Africa" (South African Government 2019). Furthermore, the official statement about those years explains the reasoning behind the public holiday on 21 March, which commemorates the victims of the Sharpeville Massacre in 1960[5] and is officially known as Human Rights Day:

> Our Constitution is hailed as one of the most progressive in the world. The Constitution is the ultimate protector of our Human Rights, which were previously denied to the majority of our people under Apartheid. We commemorate Human Rights Day to reinforce our commitment to the Bill of Rights as enshrined in our Constitution (South African Government 2019).

The Johannesburg Holocaust & Genocide Centre officially opened its doors to the public just before Human Rights Day, thus adding another event to the schedule of the 2019 Human Rights Month. This was done deliberately, because the linkage between the creation of a human rights culture and education about Holocaust history and its implications for today is very strong in South Africa, as the biography of the centre has already shown. Moreover, Shirli Gilbert has found that "Nazi Germany is portrayed as an example of a failed democracy" in South African textbooks and is as such usually "implicitly or explicitly contrasted with South Africa" (2019, 370). This is an interesting assessment which indicates yet another layer inherent to the Holocaust-human rights nexus: that of nation-building and its demarcation from "undemocratic" regimes – those in the past as well as in the present. The narrative of the JHGC taps into the same knowledge, though its perspective on contemporary South Africa is to some degree more critical than the one found by Gilbert in the textbooks.

5 On 21 March 1960, a large demonstration, organised by the Pan African Congress, was held in front of the police station in Sharpeville. The protest was part of a nationwide campaign against pass laws, which commanded that every non-white South African carry a passbook with them when outside their designated area. The peaceful protesters were met by armed police forces and, in the course of the demonstration, sixty-nine people were shot dead and about 180 more severely wounded. This horrifying event, soon to be known as the Sharpeville Massacre, was covered by news across the world and is seen as a turning point in the history of the anti-apartheid struggle (South African history online).

As explained above, the JHGC is one of three institutions in South Africa committed to addressing the history of the Holocaust, engaging in dialogue about the meaning this history still holds today and also serving as a memorial to its victims. Despite its inclusion in the national curriculum and references to human rights and other "global imperatives", it is hardly self-explanatory why Holocaust education is considered relevant in or for South Africa. The SAHGF identifies the reasons for it as follows: "[Teaching the Holocaust] can be very rewarding as it provides an excellent opportunity to introduce and discuss moral and ethical values and human rights issues" (2013). Furthermore, founder Tali Nates describes the mandate of the JHGC as follows:

> The JHGC serves as a memorial to the victims of the Holocaust and genocide with a particular emphasis on the 6 million Jews who were killed in the Holocaust, all victims of Nazi Germany, and the more than 800,000 Tutsi and moderate Hutu victims of the genocide in Rwanda. It teaches about the consequences of prejudice, racism, antisemitism, xenophobia and homophobia, and the dangers of indifference, apathy, and silence to freedom and democracy. (Nates 2018, 214)

At an event with other museum directors hosted by the UN, Nates furthermore explained how the JHGC seeks to "explore the connections between genocide and contemporary human rights violations" in order to urge visitors "to reflect on the consequences of prejudice, of discrimination" (2020). In this vein, the JHGC focuses on "lessons for humanity", which, at least at first sight, sound very similar to the lessons called for by UNESCO and the IHRA as well as at the two other museums I have investigated. But are they?

Towards making "never again" a reality

The JHGC addresses "lessons for humanity" through memory education while considering itself a centre for dialogue rather than a conventional museum. Even though it focuses on both the genocide in Rwanda and the Holocaust, most of the programmes it offers to high schools and most of the additional events hosted by the centre cover the Holocaust in more depth, granting it a more prominent position than the 1994 genocide in Rwanda – unless requested to do otherwise by the schools. The section on Rwanda in the exhibition is also much smaller than the part dedicated to the Holocaust. However, both sections are woven into one overall plot, which constitutes the narrative of the JHGC.

There are two possible ways to enter the JHGC: either through the parking lot located underneath the building and then by taking the stairs or elevator to the ground floor; or, on special occasions or when large groups arrive, by using the entrance from the road into the centre's spacious forecourt, which also includes a café and gift shop. By taking the latter, the visitor always remains on the same level. The ground floor houses the permanent exhibition as well as two seminar rooms that are frequented by school groups. Once visitors have entered the actual exhibition space, they have to walk through it in its entirety, as there are no short cuts out. However, it should be mentioned that the JHGC is much smaller than the larger CMHR in particular, and visitors can therefore easily cover the entire exhibition within about two hours and walk out of the gallery to use one of the all-gender restrooms in just a minute or two. The upstairs level has some space for temporary exhibitions that is also used for larger events, as was the case at the centre's opening, which I was fortunate enough to attend. Next to this multifunctional space is a small resource centre as well as the offices used by the centre's staff. The brick building's many windows let in a great deal of natural light. In some areas, the lighting represents an aspect which the JHGC wants to emphasise – that is, how most instances of genocide happen in broad daylight and under the eyes of many ordinary people. Drawing on this, the centre's exhibits and educational programmes pose questions about "Moral Choices" and encourage visitors to reflect on being a bystander as well as on ways to become an "upstander" – a term and related idea that I encountered at the Canadian Museum for Human Rights as well.

On this note, a very famous and oft-cited word of warning from Primo Levi – who is also quoted with a different poem at the CMHR – greets visitors in the hall through which they enter the exhibition space: "It happened, therefore it can happen again: This is the core of what we have to say. It can happen, and it can happen everywhere." These words seem to caution us and draw our attention to the fact that genocide might not just occur again, but could also happen where we least expect it, maybe even where we least expect it. In line with this idea, the permanent exhibition, which opened in 2019, has been constructed around the well-known imperative that was first articulated after the end of the Second World War and the Holocaust: "never again". However, at the JHGC, "never again" is not underscored by an exclamation mark but instead ends on a more sceptical note, with a question mark. Asking "Never again?" instead of exclaiming it emphasises how the promise of an end to war and genocide has not been kept while mass atrocities have continued to happen and still occur today. The foundations for the successful prevention of mass atrocities have been laid, and visitors learn right at the beginning of the exhibition about how the United Nations adopted the Convention on the Prevention and Punishment of the Crime of Genocide in 1948. However, the large text on the wall of the first gallery reminds us that "[d]espite acceptance by International Law in 1948 that genocide should be prevented, it remains a challenge for the world today." This reminder is placed right next to a large photograph of displaced Rwandans during the 1994 genocide. Other twentieth-century genocides that preceded the Holocaust, namely the genocide in Namibia committed by the German colonial forces against the Herero and Nama, and the Armenian genocide are mentioned at the beginning of the permanent exhibit, too. Thus, in a way, it seemed to me that the statement that genocide continues to happen and might happen everywhere was "the core of what we have to say" for the JHGC, albeit with the important additional massage that it is we who can make "never again" a reality.

The mention of the genocides which precedes the Holocaust serves as a point of reference for important aspects of the exhibition, explaining that many practices of racial segregation and "race science" were not newly invented by the Nazis but had been tried out before, and providing information about the use of the term *genocide* itself. The first information boards are on "Genocide: The Story of a Word" and detail the history of Raphael Lemkin and his struggle to persuade the UN to recognise the crime for which he had found a name. Lemkin was determined to develop a definition and a term that would grasp the horrific crime of intentionally destroying a "national, ethnical, racial or religious group" (Genocide Convention) after he learned about the mass atrocities committed against the Armenians. As a lawyer, his aim was to include genocide prevention in international law – a commitment that only succeeded after the Holocaust, though not as fully as Lemkin had intended.[6]

The displays at the JHGC continue with "In Search of a Word" and "The Birth of a Word", emphasising the importance of being able to *name* the crime committed for the greater goal of preventing it in the future. The exhibit then points us to the Nuremberg trials, where, so we learn, the word "genocide" was used for the first time in a courtroom setting "to describe mass murder". It is, however, important to note that, even though it was occasionally referred to as genocide, the atrocities committed by the Nazis against Jews and other minorities were prosecuted in Nuremberg as *crimes against humanity* and were not defined as genocide (Schabas 2007, 2009). Lemkin was present at the trials precisely because he was *unsatisfied* with the court's proceedings, which paid no attention to the genocidal practices taking place in Nazi Germany before the outbreak of the war in September 1939, but instead addressed the crimes against humanity

6 For more information on Raphael Lemkin, his life, motivations and struggles, as well as the controversy regarding colonial crimes and their recognition as genocide, see, for example, the thoroughly researched book *East West Street* by Philippe Sands (2016); and Frieze (2013).

as war-related crimes only.[7] In this sense, the interpretation of the history of the word as being central to the JHGC can be regarded as a very optimistic one that reassembles the narrative at the Memorium as well as the overarching tale of the rule of law successfully taking off at Nuremberg that is regularly evoked as the founding moment of the Holocaust-human rights nexus.

In the same entrance room to the JHGC's permanent exhibit there are four more boards that are differentiated from the "Story of a Word" by colour. They serve to establish a connection between the history that took place in the West and in South Africa. Two boards refer to South Africa during the Second World War in order to demonstrate that the history that is about to unfold throughout the exhibition was not as detached from South African history as most visitors might assume. Another display shows the famous picture of Eleanor Roosevelt holding the newly proclaimed Universal Declaration of Human Rights that also features at the CMHR. But unlike the CMHR, which presented the declaration as the beginning of a revolution, the JHGC has taken a more nuanced approach. Along with some brief information about the adoption of the UDHR, we are reminded that South Africa, which introduced apartheid the very same year as the UDHR was declared, was one of eight countries which abstained from the vote and only signed the declaration many years later, in 1998. The visitor therefore learns that the path towards a human rights culture, though it might have begun in 1948, was not an easy one, and that it remained possible to violate human rights and establish racist regimes despite their institutionalisation. At the same time, the new, post-1994 South Africa made sure to quickly join the international community of human rights advocates by signing the UDHR soon after its first democratic elections. Thus, even though it is only one display, to me it seemed to have an important function at the beginning of the exhibition as it links the history of the Holocaust and its aftermath to that of South Africa and, moreover, demarcates apartheid South Africa, which did not respect human rights, from the new republic that has human rights woven into its national fabric.

From the introductory gallery on genocide, we proceed into the first room about Holocaust history, to which I will return in the next subchapter. There

7 Legal scholar W. Schabas describes the relationship between Nuremberg and the Genocide Convention as follows: "[T]he recognition of genocide as an international crime by the General Assembly of the United Nations [...] can be understood as a reaction to the IMT's Nuremberg judgment. It was Nuremberg's failure to recognize the international criminality of atrocities committed in peacetime that prompted the first initiatives codifying the crime of genocide. Had Nuremberg recognized the reach of international criminal law into peacetime atrocities, we might never have seen a genocide convention" (Schabas 2007, 36).

are two more aspects I would like to foreground in this section on the emplotment of the Holocaust-human rights nexus at the JHGC: firstly, the transition within the exhibit from Holocaust content to the genocide in Rwanda and, secondly, the *Garden of Reflection* that comes at the end of the exhibition space.

At the conclusion to the segment on the Holocaust, the exhibition quite suddenly takes us from Europe back to Africa, with an entire wall covered by a map of the African continent. The colours of the exhibition space change from darker black and blue colours to a shade of orange. However unexpected this change in topic might appear at first, it nevertheless relates back to the first gallery, which also includes a colour photograph from Rwanda and evokes the image of the reddish African soil. South Africa, at the very southern tip of the large map, is pictured in a darker colour than the rest of the map, and so is Rwanda. This use of visual means suggests a link between two seemingly unrelated, even contrasting places and their histories: the first democratic elections in South Africa and the outbreak of genocide in Rwanda both taking place in the same month, April 1994, and the two countries being only about a four-hour flight from each other. The rhetorical device used here is similar to the one deployed at the outset of the exhibition, where we are reminded of the concurrence of the international acknowledgment of human rights and the imposition of the racist system of apartheid. These two aspects of an interconnected world history also relate back to the Holocaust, at least as far as the JHGC proposes when we look ahead towards two large glass boards on the wall. These display the portraits and quotations of two genocide survivors, who are both in close contact with the JHGC: Irene Klass, who survived the Holocaust as a child and moved to South Africa in 1950, and Silvester Sendacyeye, who survived the genocide in Rwanda and has been living in South Africa since the year 2000. The two survivors face each other as if in conversation, which Klass begins by saying: "I thought that when the world learned what had happened to us it could never happen again. But it did…". To this, Sendacyeye seems to respond directly, being quoted as follows: "[…] and a genocide happened yet again to us here in Rwanda in full view of the world." This powerful dialogue between the older *white* woman and the young Black man – an aspect that will not go unnoticed by any South African visitor, given the meaning of skin colour so deeply inscribed into both South African history and contemporaneity – is a very effective means to remind us of the unrealised promise of "never again" with which the exhibition began. It also underlines a message important to the centre, which is that becoming a victim of genocide is not a matter of race or skin colour but could happen to anyone anywhere. Whether this could also be read as a declaration of the importance of the JHGC and its work itself was something that provided much food for thought and that I will return to in my comparison of the JHGC and the other two museums in chapter 8.

The exhibition space dedicated to Rwanda is notably smaller than the one that hosts the Holocaust exhibit and begins with a film that provides some overall information on the events. This information is supported by a more detailed timeline, though the historical account of the time prior to the genocide is not very detailed. This might come as a surprise, given the many voices which suggest Rwanda's colonial past, first under German and later under Belgian rule, was somewhat constitutive of the genocide. The exhibit does hint at the colonial conditions prior to the genocide: "After WWI, Belgium took control of Rwanda [...]. Thinking that Rwanda was made up of separate 'races,' they favoured Tutsi, who were given privileged positions, power and wealth." However, there is no further mention either in the exhibition or in any additional educational materials of this important fact about the separation into the supposedly superior and inferior "races" of Tutsi and Hutu being an invention of external colonial rule. This absence of engagement with colonialism and its consequences, whether in regard to Nazi Germany, Rwanda or South Africa, struck me as odd and kept me thinking, especially because there also appeared to be a parallel to the CMHR and its lack of critical reflection on the settler-colonial genocide that took place in Canada. I will therefore return to this exhibitionary void, this gap, in my later discussion of my empirical findings.

At the JHGC, instead of looking at the impact external Western interventions had on the occurrence of the genocide, the exhibit emphasises the lack of engagement from the international community, in particular the withdrawal of UN peacekeeping forces. A quotation from the former head of the Red Cross in Rwanda serves as the headline to the displays on this issue: "Everybody knew, every day, live, what was happening... Who moved? Nobody." These failures are detailed and accompanied by accounts of "Post-Genocide Apologies", as the title reads. Furthermore, we learn about "bystanders" as well as "upstanders" like the Canadian Lieutenant-General who remained with just a few of his "men" in Rwanda even after the UN had given the order to reduce forces, saving the lives of "over 30000 Tutsi". We also learn that Kofi Annan, who would become the UN Secretary General in 1997 and help the Task Force on Holocaust Education and Remembrance to international importance, was also the official who, in 1994, "signed the order to reduce UNAMIR's forces". In conclusion, a display entitled "Warning Signs" reads: "The genocide did not happen suddenly. There were many convincing warnings. Although international decision makers did not know everything, they knew enough to understand that disaster lay ahead." In a sense, the overall exhibit then returns to where it began: the issue of *calling* atrocities genocide. Some information is given about the international refusal to officially recognise that what was happening in Rwanda was in fact genocide. In this way, the emphasis from the beginning is underscored once again and weight added to the overall emplotment presented by the JHGC, namely through the detailed account of urgently needed but long denied international intervention in Rwanda and in the face of genocide more generally. Interestingly, pointing to alternatives to this narrative, international relations scholar Olivia Rutazibwa notes the following, which I would like to quote here in full:

> As a teenage, second-generation Rwandan immigrant in Belgium, I was more personally affected than fellow classmates by the hypocrisy of the international community: the preaching of respect for human rights, followed by their omission during one hundred days of mass murder before the eyes of the world. It felt like there was more to the story than "good intentions versus regrettable outcomes". [...] I realised that I [...] had operated on an assumption that external involvement in the affairs of the "developing world", if well intentioned and effective, was desirable, indispensable even. Letting go of this assumption [...] I reconsidered the conventional narrative that attributes the genocide against the Tutsi in Rwanda to non-intervention, and came to see that the (post)colonial run-up to genocide was a story of too much intervention, even in the name of democracy. (Rutazibwa 2019, 65–66)

Rutazibwa suggests a more complicated perspective on international humanitarian and peacekeeping interventions, one that does not presuppose that such actions are always desirable if well-intentioned, i.e., supportive of democracy and human rights. Instead, she proposes a view of such interventions which scrutinises the underlying rationale of international involvement in the "developing world" and casts doubt on the optimistic perspective that we also find displayed at the JHGC, which includes very general approval of all sorts of engagement, from individual action against injustice to national and supranational interventions carried out in the name of democracy.

The centre's storyline is underscored once more at the very end of the exhibition when we enter a small garden that provides a space for reflection. On the walls is another large board, which displays the following quotation from an unknown survivor of Sachsenhausen concentration camp: "I have told you this story not to weaken you but to strengthen you. Now it is up to you!" The quotation is also displayed in Rwanda's most dominant language, Kinyarwanda, and in Hebrew, though in no South African language other than English. The main message is that stories of genocide, however difficult to bear, have the potential to make us stronger. This is a powerful ending to the exhibit on the Holocaust and the genocide in Rwanda, and it once again reminds us that we are responsible for making "never again" a reality. The quotation simultaneously urges us to be attentive to "Today's Challenges", because even though we cannot undo the atrocities of the past, it may well be in our hands to prevent violence in the future:

> As a centre of memory and education in South Africa, the [...] JHGC is dedicated to promoting awareness of the racism, xenophobia and hate speech that still plague our society today. [...] We invite you to commit to creating a caring and just society in which human rights and diversity are respected and valued. What can you do to make a difference in your own family, your school, or your community?

Images of xenophobic attacks that have taken place in recent years throughout South Africa instantly point to the urgency of the activism envisioned by the JHGC and propose a field in which we could engage.

The walk through the exhibition ends in the same hall in which it started, and visitors might pass the Primo Levi quotation again which relates back to the caution extended on the board about "Today's Challenges": genocide happened and could happen again, anywhere and to anybody. Thus, a visit to the JHGC begins with a warning and ends on a similar note of caution, constantly reminding us that there is still so much to be done on the way to a more "caring and just society". Like in the CMHR, visitors are called upon "to make a difference", with the encouragement of the unknown survivor ("now it is up to you!") still ringing in their ears. Like at the CMHR, the desired outcome of a visit to the JHGC therefore seems to be oriented towards activism, and the JHGC contributes to motivating "upstanders", even if the storyline disseminated in the museum has a different emphasis and is far from being as superficial as that of the CMHR. In regard to its overarching emplotment, the JHGC shares more similarities with the Memorium, as both museums foreground the importance of the rule of law as well as international commitment to its fundamental principles. How is Holocaust memory is embedded in this broader narrative?

The JHGC as a memorial to the Holocaust

The founder of the JHGC, Tali Nates, is a historian by training and herself a second-generation Holocaust survivor. Her father and uncle were amongst the Jews saved from persecution by Oskar Schindler,[8] and her dedication to Holocaust

8 Oskar Schindler is well-known from Steven Spielberg's movie *Schindler's List*. Born in 1908, his middle-class Catholic family belonged to the German-speaking community in the Sudetenland, where, as a young man, he joined a political party which strongly supported Nazi Germany. After the outbreak of the Second World War, Schindler moved to the Polish city of Krakow and took over a run-down enamelware factory that had previously belonged to a now dispossessed

memory and education is therefore deeply connected to her family's history. In a statement given to the *South African Jewish Report* newspaper, Nates explained that the JHGC serves to "show you history", while "the rest is up to you" (2015). This sounds very similar to the quotation from the survivor of Sachsenhausen concentration camp and, of course, does not mention the powerful means employed by museum exhibitions and their didactics. I personally found the Holocaust exhibition at the JHGC to be one of the best I have seen so far, as it is not only very nuanced but also emphasises aspects that I know are often disregarded, at least in the German context. These include a detailed account of Jewish life in Europe *before* the Shoah as well as some honesty about the knowledge that most Germans had, or could have had, about the Holocaust, had they cared to know. This being said, I will now give just a brief presentation of the exhibition space and then spend more time on the educational material produced by the JHGC, as I find it to be more insightful in regard to the overall topic discussed here.

The centre's exhibition combines collections of photos, testimony and films with multimedia exhibits and some unique artefacts from the time of the Holocaust, many of which were donated to the JHGC by survivors living in Johannesburg. The museum's display was designed by Clive van den Berg, who also contributed to the famous memorial space at Freedom Park in Tshwane,[9] and realised by curator Lauren Segal (Sassen 2020), while its historical content was assembled by Tali Nates and Chaya Hermann. It takes an approach towards Holocaust history that is not chronological but thematic and places emphasis on aspects such as the choices people had about whether or not to support Nazism and the Holocaust. In drawers which can be opened as well as in audio material and on multiple tablets, visitors can decide for themselves which facet of Holocaust history to learn more about, while the exhibition space provides overall information on the abuses of state power, the development towards genocide, and, in a small room, about the mass killings carried out by so-called *Einsatzgruppen* and at killing centres.[10] Accounts of the persecution of Jews and other minorities

---

Jew. While also being a beneficiary of Nazi rule, Schindler later became famous for saving over one hundred Jews who had worked in his factory before being deported to death camps, foremost to Auschwitz. For more on his life and engagement saving Jews from the Nazis see, for example, the detailed information about him and his wife provided by Yad Vashem (https://www.yadvashem.org/righteous/stories/schindler.html (accessed 10 March 2021).

9 The city of Tshwane, the South African capital, was formerly known as Pretoria.

10 On "Einsatzgruppen", please see Footnote 59 in chapter 5. In reference to the wording preferred at the JHGC I am here using "killing centre" instead of the more common term "extermination camp".

are linked to issues of *othering* and *scapegoating*, which can be seen as the particular approach taken by the JHGC to victims and perpetrators alike, which focuses on the victimisation of innocent people being a result of the personal inadequacies of individuals unable to deal with their suppressed frustration and misconduct, who therefore indulge in victim blaming. Dirk Moses argues that the problem with "this view of victim-construction is that it's religious rather than political. It's a secularised theology about the origins of evil: groups are victims of prejudice that arise within evil people" (2021). Nowhere at the JHGC is it expressed in this way, but the gist of Moses' assessment fits the narrative of the Holocaust exhibition in the sense that throughout we are reminded of our option, even in the most difficult times, to withstand evil and not partake in the *scapegoating* of others.[11] This aspect of the storyline is underscored by the pedagogical material of the centre, to which I will now turn.

From "moral dilemmas" to "activist behaviour"

Unlike the Memorium or the CMHR, the JHGC welcomes fewer individual visitors and instead primarily opens its doors to school groups which come to the centre to deepen their understanding of Holocaust history and its relevance in the present. Richard Freedman, former head of the South African Holocaust & Genocide Foundation (SAHGF) established in 2008 and also one of the presidents of the Federation of International Human Rights Museums, praised Holocaust education in South Africa for its "potential [...] to challenge conceptions of racial prejudice, and the abuses of extreme power" (2012). Moreover, as Tracey Petersen notes, "Holocaust education was claimed by the newly democratic state as a vehicle of reconciliation" (2015, i), because, as Freedman argues, "The study of the past provides a framework for confronting the many forms of prejudice which, even today, remain latent challenges within South African society" (2012, 2).

---

11 I agree with Dirk Moses' view on the apolitical nature of the scapegoat approach that risks not looking closely enough at Nazi ideology and its political dimensions beyond the individual, and I also find his emphasis on choices to be a very necessary one, at least in certain contexts. Especially in Germany, the tendency to deny individual responsibility by means of the narrative of not having had any choices about how to act or to what extent one should participate is very strong. It is therefore necessary to remind Germans of the many choices made in favour of Nazism, antisemitic violence and the widespread Nazi ideology in general. There is thus a fine line between overemphasising the rather apolitical explanation to the often-asked question "Why the Germans, why the Jews?" and issuing the necessary reminder of how many people decided to support the murderous regime and its policies.

Generally, as Freedman explains, Holocaust education in South Africa – a country which is geopolitically far removed from the actual historic events but which has its own "difficult" past – is perceived as an "entry point" or a "catalyst" that is helpful in introducing difficult issues closer to South Africa's own history.

As explained before, the JHGC as part of the SAHGF sees it as one of its main tasks to support the national curriculum through programmes tailored to teachers or in various programmes for learners. According to the homepage of the JHGC, all of its programmes "relate to human rights awareness and draw on lessons from the Holocaust and the 1994 genocide in Rwanda [...]." The programmes, as it continues, have "all been specifically developed to teach about the consequences of prejudice, racism and discrimination, and to promote an understanding of the dangers of indifference, apathy and silence." (JHGC/Learner Groups)

I will now introduce some of the JHGC's educational work and analyse the ways in which it contributes to the centre's overall narrative. I will look for additional aspects that might not feature within the exhibition space but that also help to construct this narrative. Most of the regular programmes for learners begin in one of the seminar rooms, where the participants are handed small workbooks in which they are asked to provide some information about themselves and about what they would consider to be their identity, and to note down things they noticed during their visit.[12] An introductory film on the Holocaust is also shown in the seminar room before the groups head into the exhibition for a guided tour.[13] Depending on the programme chosen by the teachers, learners then engage with different issues relating to the overall topic of the Holocaust and human rights. The pedagogy relies on the assumption that

12 Tracey Petersen makes an interesting point in her dissertation on the Cape Town Holocaust and Genocide Centre: its teaching on identity, according to Petersen quoting Bekerman and Zembylas (2015), is not "considering how teaching and learning about identity, be it their own or of historical persons or peoples, might 'perpetuate the dominant binary divisions of the world,' and a view of an 'essentialised identity.' This is of particular relevance when considering the centrality of an acceptance of essentialised identity and identities to the functioning of the apartheid state, and the implications this has for teaching, and learning, in post-apartheid South Africa" (2015, 283). A similar observation is made by Wendy Brown (2006) in her discussions of the Simon Wiesenthal Museum of Tolerance. To a certain degree, this criticism can also be applied to the JHGC, though it seems to have a less of a focus on identity than in other programmes run by the SAHGF.

13 I followed many of these programmes and also guided some groups through the exhibit myself. My accounts are therefore not strictly derived from an outsider's perspective, and I am grateful for the chance to partake in the work of the JHGC in such a way.

> The Holocaust, as a case-study of human rights abuse [...] has the potential to draw out personal attitudes and prejudices such as xenophobia which otherwise remain repressed. [...] It remains the goal of the SAHGF to utilize the study of Holocaust History to produce learners who are motivated and empowered to recognize their potential to be effective agents of positive change, and will choose not to be bystanders in the face of injustice. (SAHGF 2013)

In this vein, learners are challenged throughout the modules to reflect on their own experiences of discrimination and their own discriminatory actions as well as the choices they might have made that could have resulted in passively letting discrimination happen instead of standing up against it. Small workshop units on “Moral Choices” and “Dilemmas” discuss examples from the time of the Holocaust, such as the story of a survivor who, while prisoner in a concentration camp, lost his hat and therefore stole another inmate’s one, because without their hats prisoners were not allowed to attend roll call – or, more precisely, because if a prisoner appeared at roll call without a hat, he would be severely punished. The learners are then asked to discuss the decision to steal from and endanger another inmate in order to save one’s own life. At the same time, they are encouraged to reflect on their own behaviour towards others and think about difficult choices they might have had to make in the past. In this way, the module aims to teach learners to be aware of the effects that their behaviour might have on those around them. The head of the JHGC Tali Nates sums up the goal of the centre’s education programmes by saying that it hopes to motivate visitors “to move from bystander to activist behaviour” (2018, 214).

In this sense, the JHGC not only contributes to human rights education but also to citizenship education. In the eyes of the JHCG, desirable citizens are prudent, sensitive to the threats of prejudice and aware of the importance of democratic values such as tolerance and respect for human rights. As the SAHGF’s *Educator’s Manual* explains: “Learning about the Holocaust remains relevant to all citizens of the world, as it alerts us to the warning signs such as institutionalised prejudice, acts of ethnic cleansing and gross human rights violations, that emerge in societies moving towards genocide and urge us to take action” (SAHGF 2013, 17). This statement expresses the core of the lessons disseminated at the JHGC, both in the education programmes and in the exhibition: we need to be attentive to the world around us and recognise the “warning signs” early enough to be able to intervene. The educational material, however, adds another layer to this message, addressing those South Africans who might need encouragement to realise their agency and claim their own rights in order to then be able to contribute to society’s wellbeing. Here, unlike at the CMHR, the motivation is less about generating activist behaviour aimed at engaging in acts of charity or showing benevolence (as was suggested in the CMHR’s game “Action Counts”) and more about empowering learners to see their own potential as members of civil society. The is particularly the case with the Change Makers programme, which was developed at the 2016 *Salzburg Global Seminar* (an education policymakers' think tank based in Austria) and is carried out in partnership with members of Aegis Trust in Rwanda.[14] In this project, educators from the JHGC and the Kigali Genocide Memorial in Rwanda go to other African countries to foster skills amongst facilitators and learners that, like in the programmes in Johannesburg, will enable them to "become active upstanders and leaders who will promote pluralism and tackle extremism in their societies" (JHGC/Programme Menu). The programme, which lasts three to four days, can also be booked by local South African schools. According to the "Programme Menu" of the JHGC, during Change Makers, "learners will be taught critical thinking and leadership skills to resist violence and to challenge the ideas of extremism by becoming upstanders and change makers within their communities". Many of these cross-African programmes are supported by European political and cultural foundations such as the progressive German Rosa Luxemburg Foundation and the more conservative Konrad Adenauer Foundation. Other supporters include the UN and UNESCO, especially in the case of the Change Makers programme, which seems to be of special interest to global NGOs and institutions alike.

Lessons for humanity

Having introduced the JHGC, its exhibition and educational materials, I would now like to sum up the "lessons for humanity" that visitors take away from a visit to the centre and briefly discuss how they are connected to present-day issues in South African society. Once again, in the words of Tali Nates:

> The inclusion of the Holocaust in the national curriculum represents a commitment to protecting and educating about human rights. [...] The Department of Education in South Africa believes that the inclusion of Holocaust history in its compulsory national curriculum is vitally important for the understanding of human rights, peace and democracy. (Nates 2018, 4)

---

14 The Aegis Trust is a British NGO that was founded in 2000 to help open the UK's first Holocaust centre. It soon expanded its scope beyond the UK and, according to its mission "of a world without genocide or mass atrocities", supports memory work and peace education across the globe, with Rwanda one of the first post-genocide societies to seek support from Aegis. For more information see the Trust's website: https://www.aegistrust.org/what-we-do/our-starting-point/ (accessed 5 March 2021).

Or, as Education Minister Motshekga puts it: “History encourages civic responsibility and critical thinking – these are key values needed in a democratic society. The study of History creates a platform for constructive and informed debates about peace, human rights, and democratic values” (2015). From the perspective of the SHGF and its Johannesburg Centre, the response to my initial concern regarding Holocaust memory and education in South Africa would be twofold: firstly, since South Africa’s post-1994 constitution is dedicated to the advancement and protection of human rights, the country’s schools need to make an effort to teach human rights; secondly, the Holocaust is a powerful lesson from which to learn about the consequences of neglecting human rights and can therefore encourage every member of society to be more cautious, more tolerant and less silent in the face of injustice.

What the JHGC teaches is therefore the importance of civic engagement for human rights, peace and democracy. Its educational initiatives fall into two categories of human rights education (HRE) as identified by Monisha Bajaj: HRE for global citizenship and HRE for coexistence. Both concepts are based on the underlying ideology of “HR as a new political order” as well as “HRE as healing and reconciliation” (Bajaj 2011, 491). The first category “seeks to provide learners with membership to an international community through fostering knowledge and skills related to universal values and standards” (Bajaj 2011, 489). This aim aligns with the quotation from the *Educator’s Manual* cited above, which stated how important learning about the Holocaust is “for all citizens of the world” (SAHGF 2013). Furthermore, we have seen that the advancement of universal values is omnipresent at the JHGC, featuring prominently in the exhibit as well as in the additional educational material. However, I find the aspect of coexistence to be equally important to the teaching of the JHGC, though it is not spelled out quite so explicitly. This is because the entire narrative about equal responsibility for a “caring and just society” is underpinned by the notion of a reconciled South African society – a South Africa that, despite its current problems, has left apartheid behind and committed to fostering human rights and realising equality for all. The xenophobia described by the centre is one of these new challenges, which include the challenges of “Black-on-Black violence” instead of just incidents sparked by white supremacy as in the past. In a way, this example seems to prove what the JHGC has been stressing all along, that is, how everyone, despite having different socio-economic background, ethnicities, skin colours, genders or other possible positionalities, is prone to prejudice that might turn into a more radical form of hatred of *others*, even into genocide. At the same time, this view means that anybody can become the target of othering or scapegoating.

Still, the JHGC is mindful of the complicated nature of its teaching, as Nates' deliberations show: "The inclusion of the study of the Holocaust and expanding the teaching to the case studies of Namibia and Rwanda, serve as an opportunity to develop a deeper understanding of genocide and how it relates to colonial atrocities" (2018, 205). However, by turning to these cases from the past, colonial conditions are only addressed in the past tense, and as I briefly explained in regard to Rwanda, the impact of colonialism is not represented with as much nuance as it could be. Nor is the prevailing impact of colonialism and of apartheid structures in particular confronted within the JHGC – a topic which should be part of any education programme that aims to advance human rights and, more generally, a better future for all in South Africa today. While the vague (or non-existent) ways in which colonialism, apartheid and white supremacy are addressed at the JHGC might be a result of the common confusion about racism being nothing more than "prejudice" held by individuals, in the specific South African context it also serves as a means to avoid addressing the ongoing violence of white supremacy as something inherent to the political system, instead rendering it a problem of subjects rather than of society. What is more – and I will return to this aspect in the following chapter, as it also concerns the other two case studies – I could not shake off the feeling that the particular narrative about shared responsibility for a better South Africa, coupled with the warning about the trap of othering into which we all might fall, can only be fully understood in light of the aforementioned *exhibitionary atonement*. In the context of the JHGC, I mean by this the elevation of teaching "lessons for humanity" to a higher good, fighting for which is on such a morally superior level that it redeems those people of their guilt who were once beneficiaries of the (old) apartheid system (against which they did not fight) – as if the struggle for human rights has the power to make them innocent again, to render their wrongdoings towards the parents of those whom they teach today (figuratively speaking) irrelevant in the face of the new and shared effort to safeguard democracy.

Only once during my research at the JHGC was this subject bought up: Irene Klass, who not only features prominently within the exhibition but also still comes (or did so in 2018 and 2019) to the centre to speak to learners about her experiences during the Holocaust, was asked by a student if she, after arriving in South Africa as a young woman in the 1950s, fought against apartheid. She did not. And while in her specific case, as a traumatised child survivor having to make a new home far from anything she had ever known, one might forgive her inaction, most of the *white* staff at the JHGC were equally silent in the face of the racist system of apartheid, from which they nonetheless benefited simply because they were *white*. However, this subject is seldom even mentioned, and only once did two of the centre's frequent volunteers talk to me about this after I openly spoke about being the (great-)grandchild of bystanders as well as Nazi perpetrators. This aspect did not cease to make me uncomfortable as it appeared to be hypocrisy at best, but at the same time, it is only against such a background that it makes sense to me why, on the one hand, a better South Africa, even a better world for all, is presented as the main aim of the JHCG while, on the other, urgent matters such as the ongoing economic apartheid (Madlingozi 2017) or the struggle for the redistribution of land are not addressed at all, thereby mostly avoiding looking through a decolonial lens.

As it stands, the JHGC's approach has more to do with the universal approach taken by UNESCO and the IHRA towards past, present and future than it does with actually embedding its message within the specific South African context. This is a pity, especially because, in other aspects, the exhibition at the JHGC does indeed contest the universal narrative present in UNESCO's and the IHRA's teachings. Even though the objectives of education on the Holocaust and other genocides are in many aspects similar to those formulated by these supranational bodies, the prominent tale of the successful and linear evolution of a global conscience that is sensitive to the lessons for humanity, for example, is, as mentioned above, presented in a more complex way in the JHGC's exhibition: it crucially points out not only that the UN adopted the Universal Declaration of Human Rights the same year that the system of apartheid was introduced in South Africa but also that the regime which implemented racial segregation based on the idea of white supremacy, leading to decades of violent domination over the non-white population, was backed by an international community that, for many years, was mostly indifferent to it (Gurney 2000). To make visible the synchronicity of the institutionalisation of international human rights on the one hand and the establishment of yet another inhumane colonial regime on the other, the JHGC emphasises this contradiction in some of the first panels at the beginning of the exhibition. So, it does indeed try to balance the particular and the universal (as the CMHR also claims to do), not only of the Holocaust and the genocide in Rwanda, but also that of its South African context. These critical reflections are, unfortunately, more nuanced in regard to the past than to the present, as its vision of possible futures is circumscribed by the hegemonic discourse of liberal democracy as our last utopia.

8 Memory as a Means of Government

> Humanity does not gradually progress from combat to combat until it finally arrives at universal reciprocity, where the rule of law finally replaces warfare; humanity installs each of its violences in a system of rules and thus proceeds from domination to domination. (Foucault 1977, 151)

In this quotation, Foucault argues against the dominant idea of history as progress and, moreover, takes a stance against an episteme which presents histories of violence (or "warfare") as humanity's point of departure, from which we are gradually moving further and further away. However, he does not just reject a teleological understanding of history but also claims that humanity, instead of becoming more peaceful and law-abiding over time, continually installs new systems of violence and domination. As will have already become apparent, Foucault thereby casts doubt on the fundamental logic underpinning human rights museology and its forms of Holocaust memorialisation that suggest the opposite, as human rights museums – at least the three discussed here – are based on the assumption that humanity indeed does move forwards. On our path towards eternal harmony, we are leaving violent pasts behind, all the sooner when we actively learn from them. In this story of perpetual progress, the Holocaust is framed as "the archetypal collapse of democracy into genocide from which human rights lessons can be drawn" (Moses 2012, 233). What is more, this story relies on the framing of democracy and human rights as the gatekeepers of a better future, because liberal democracy has, as we have learned in all three museums, proved to be the only form of government that successfully deals with "intolerance" and "ignorance" – attitudes that supposedly still threaten it.

Thus, throughout my case studies, it has become clear that what connects Holocaust memory with human rights and vice versa is a multilayered complex of memory politics. These politics, by employing historical narratives, often point to universal ideals such as a "human rights culture" (CMHR, JHGC) and global citizenship (UNESCO; IHRA). And since respect for human rights does not come "naturally", it needs to be established and constantly nurtured by various structures and a multiplicity of means – many of which I have already described in the previous chapters. In chapter 4, I made the point that formalised Holocaust memory education has become a subgenre of human rights education (HRE). In contrast to my assessment, Anja Mihr emphasises the difference between the two in an article on the intersections between Holocaust education and HRE:

https://doi.org/10.1515/9783110788044-010

> Holocaust education focuses on the past and the history of World War II. It is about learning to empathize with the victims of crimes against humanity that can result in a moral imperative. [...] Holocaust education programs deal with specific issues and target a specific, conflict-affected or historically connected audience [...], whereas human rights education targets society and citizens in general anywhere in the world. (Mihr 2015, 525)

She evaluates Holocaust education as a format which is designed for a specific "audience" and which focuses on a very specific historical case, whereas human rights education is less definite and more open in terms of its content and objectives. In line with the hypothesis which started off my research, I would like to oppose Mihr's claim as I find that many Holocaust education programmes – especially when interwoven with HRE – do target "society and citizens in general anywhere in the world". As stated in the introduction to this book, I am suggesting that a public memory which is conditioned by the Holocaust-human rights nexus has become a technique of government that produces a certain type of citizen-subject and aims to disseminate this ideal globally. To be more precise: what I am seeking to demonstrate in these final chapters is how an ideal type of the global citizen-subject is constructed that I propose calling *the historically aware human rights advocate*. This citizen-subject is produced precisely at the intersections between Holocaust and HRE programmes that transcend the particularity of the Holocaust and turn it into a universally applicable narrative, because Holocaust education is, contrary to Mihr's conclusion, *not* just concerned with specific historical aspects, nor is it primarily tailored towards any distinct audience. Instead, it is designed to function in Europe, but equally in America, Asia and on the African continent.

The idea that learning from the past, especially from the Holocaust, will stimulate activist behaviour and transform people into "upstanders" (CMHR; JHGC) for democracy and human rights is not necessarily a feature of Holocaust memory work; rather, it must be actively evoked and written into the storylines of museums. It is on these techniques and mechanisms which shape the narratives and construct museums' particular emplotment within the story of progress that I will focus in the following. Therefore, as its title suggests, in this chapter I will elaborate more on why I claim that memory is a means of government and how this function plays out. For this purpose, I will further analyse the findings from my three case studies and discuss them in relation to the educational endeavours for global citizenship education (GCE) that I introduced in chapter 4, and extract the normative ideas of what makes a *good* global citizen, which are will implicit, though not accounted for, in the empirical material. These ideals have become clear in my assessments of the different memory institutions around the world that are taking part in the ongoing construction of the Holocaust-human rights nexus by acknowledging their own roles as "practitioners of humanity" (Ong 2006, 198). Jennifer Carter evaluates this process of combining memory and human rights in museum spaces optimistically when she writes that "museums [...] embrace the dual discourses of memory and rights while giving concrete representation to what is inherent in 'the abstract universalism of human rights'" (2017, 9). According to Carter, there is a fruitful interplay between two related discourses, whereby one adds meaning to the other by translating the universal back into particular stories of violence and suffering. In this way, she argues, human rights discourse becomes more tangible for the public, which means that museums are contributing not only to the commemoration of victims but also to their universal recognition within a larger frame of "human suffering". Levy and Sznaider have spoken in this regard about a "globalized horizon of experience" (2002, 103) which allows people around the globe to evoke Holocaust memory in a similar way, requiring compassion for the suffering of others combined with the will to reduce their pain. Most scholarly work on human rights museums identifies three core accomplishments to which they strive to contribute, namely reparation, reconciliation and justice (Carter 2017; Perla 2021). In this scenario, empathy and compassion are elicited to reduce historical distance and increase knowledge and reflexivity, which will lead, so it is hoped, to a sense of life-altering perspectives and active responsibility (Carter 2017).

By discussing the case studies in a more interpretative manner, this chapter proposes another key function of human rights museums (especially those that address the Holocaust), namely the dissemination of the normative concept of citizenship outlined above and thus the shaping, or "programming", of behaviour. In this vein, I claim that museums convey "consensualized historical narratives" (Friedrich 2014, 31) in order to summon the past as a pedagogical device for the production of citizenry. The ideal of the willingness to participate in the reduction of other people's pain and suffering is assumed to be a vital quality of the historically aware global citizen and, moreover, part and parcel of what Didier Fassin (2012) calls "humanitarian reason" – a mode of government that depoliticises the political because it relies on moral arguments to help others to reduce their suffering without addressing the political roots or causes of such suffering. The way in which this plays out was, for example, evident at the CMHR, where we were encouraged, while playing a game, to help starving Inuit by organising a benefit concert without raising any questions about why it is that an Inuit community in the north of Canada is experiencing a life-threatening food crisis in the first place.

The Holocaust in human rights museums revisited

I discussed the extent to which individual freedom (not freedom in the sense of liberation) has become a central tenet in current neoliberal politics in chapter 2. What I want to stress here once more, however, is that this notion of freedom is not limited to economic freedom but entails all possible life choices, spanning from decisions concerning health and lifestyle to choices about what goods to consume and which educational programmes to take part in (Rose 2017). In chapter 4, I argued that museums fit well within this machinery of choices and stipulated aspirations, and also introduced human rights museology and the global educational programmes underpinning it. The museums that are modelled as social enterprises seem to contribute especially effectively to neoliberal rationality while simultaneously flourishing as businesses. As Haitham Eid explains, social entrepreneurship can help museums "do good" in their communities while doing well financially, because a social enterprise is "a business with primarily social objectives whose surpluses are principally reinvested for that purpose in the business or in the community, rather than being driven by the need to maximise profit for shareholders and owners" (2020, 47). In a broader sense, museums see their engagement with human rights issues as a "public service", and this underscores the tacit image of museums as institutions devoid of any particular political or financial interests. In a similar vein, as mentioned above in regard to South Africa's revised national curriculum (Tibbitts and Keet 2017), education in general is expected to benefit the economy – an expectation that does not seem to be in conflict with human rights lessons. However, in this chapter I am not just going to argue that human rights sell[1] but will also demonstrate how investing in human rights is not primarily a kind of business plan or merely an altruistic endeavour; rather, it is a highly political venture, which needs to be grasped as such.

In a society that is free – in the sense that it requires its members to choose responsibly to augment their own goals and best fulfil their hopes – everyone is also *free* to choose whether to engage with history and, if so, to choose what particular historical content to engage with. Therefore, every visitor and volunteer at a Holocaust exhibition has either personally decided to be there or, if the visit has been arranged by a teacher, as is often the case with school groups, is at least able to choose how intensively they wish to participate. So, given the in-

---

1 Even though the important aspect of funding should not be neglected in an overall analysis of human rights museums.

crease in visitors at Holocaust related memorial sites, more and more people around the world are actively choosing to concern themselves with this difficult knowledge (Bajohr et al. 2020).[2] Why? In an attempt to get closer to answering this complex question and explain how Holocaust memory has come to occupy the space it currently does, I will now revisit my case studies in Germany, Canada and South Africa to compare and contrast their content with the global education programmes introduced in chapter 4. In more theoretical terms, I will identify memory's "affiliations between individual aspirations and governmental objectives" (Rose 2017, 307), which I was able to establish during my research.

Framing the past as "lessons"

To some extent, my research has led me to be sceptical of the very concept of memory that is dominantly referred to and researched, even while I continue to use it. This scepticism relates to a particular dominant conception of memory because the history of the global North has come to represent the entirety of "history". This has been carried out through the use of Euro-modernity as a singular noun and by authorising only one "modernity" with its singular linearity of historical progress. I already elaborated on this in sections 2 and 3 of chapter 2 but would now like to relate it to my empirical material and my overall hypothesis. As I have explained, the idea of memory can be divorced neither from the notion of history nor from its corresponding temporality, and the ways in which it is conceptualised therefore relate back to the same Euro-modern tradition of thought, activating the "historical operation" which demarcates the past from the present and the future, and establishing the relationship between them (de Certeau 1988; Scott 2020). This double erasure of both the plurality of histories as well as of time itself has an impact on how we think about the past and on how it is most often represented, that is, as a closed entity different to our present or future. In my understanding, this is a core paradox of dominant memory politics, which became apparent in the museums I examined and can also be seen in the educational materials of UNESCO and the IHRA: the idea that the past, even if we occasionally recall it through mnemonic practices, is over and behind us; that it is something we might turn to for educational purposes (in the widest sense) but that otherwise does not have any repercussions in the pre-

2 It should be noted in this regard that "dark tourism" is a phenomenon that does not manifest itself exclusively at Holocaust-related sites but applies to other places of catastrophe and violence as well (from Chernobyl to the killing fields of Cambodia) (Martini and Buda 2020).

sent, let alone any impact on the future. The emplotment of Holocaust memory into the story of progress towards the rule of law and a human rights culture that I have outlined above has an important function in all this, firstly, because it helps to draw a clear line between past and present, and, secondly, as I will explain in the following, because it serves to conceal the intimate link between coloniality and modernity.

All three museums, the Memorium Nuremberg Trials, the Canadian Museum for Human Rights and the Johannesburg Holocaust & Genocide Centre rely on the notion of turning to the past in order to learn from it – though to different degrees – and in this way contribute to the framing of history as "lessons". This conceptualisation is omnipresent in the work of UNESCO and the IHRA, which relentlessly promote the value of learning from the past and the lessons Holocaust history provides for the "international community".[3] (In this context I would like to once again make mention of the poem by Primo Levi which features so prominently in the main hall of the JHGC and cautions us to not forget that what has happened in the past may happen again to anyone at any time in the future.) In this sense, Holocaust memory not only holds important lessons for us but is also a compelling warning sign which will eventually attract our attention and convince us of the need to further engage with its content. At the Memorium, visitors learn about the importance of the international legal mechanisms which make it possible to react appropriately in the face of crimes against humanity and which paved the way for the establishment of an important pillar of the international community: the International Criminal Court. In both examples, conceptualising the past as a lesson allows us to perceive history as an ensemble of instructive cases from which we can learn for the future and which is once again underpinned by the idea of progress, which offers the prospect of receiving redemption or atonement for wrongdoings rather than having to take continuous responsibility for new interhuman relations.

I mentioned this aspect in the case studies when I suggested thinking about certain narrative devices as a means of *exhibitionary atonement*. If we recall the CMHR and its rather superficial participation in the debate over the genocide committed on Canadian soil against the Indigenous population (which some claim is ongoing, as there is still no drinking water on some reserves, and Indigenous women are still being murdered in shockingly high numbers), the framing

---

3 The term or concept "international community" is yet another signifier without any clear definition which is closely linked to the ideal of global citizenship and the rule of law. Therefore, the international community in the sense in which, e.g., UNESCO evokes it consists of democracies alone and therefore also has the function of distinguishing between the (morally) superior members of the community and its outsiders (Ellis 2009).

of history as lessons indeed seems to hold the promise of righting wrongs. That is because turning to an even more horrific crime than the Indigenous genocide – and the Holocaust is perceived as such – will teach us everything we need to know in order to build a better future, which, after all, is supposed to be "a vision as shared as the sky" (CMHR commercial 2017). At the JHGC, I observed a similar tendency towards (re)gaining a position of innocence by assuming the morally superior role of teacher of human rights. This position, made possible by the storyline, which emplots the Holocaust in such a way that it elevates memory education to the level of practice best suited to teaching the values of democracy, seems to redeem even those who have been indifferent to or even complicit with apartheid in the past (and who maybe still benefit from its continuing structures), because they have now taken up a much greater fight in the name of all humanity. How else would it, in the age of neo-apartheid, be possible to have a majority of *white* instructors teach Black youth about the dangers of prejudice without making any mention of their own involvement in apartheid structures? In this way, the case study of the Holocaust might open the door to further engagement with South Africa's past as well as with Canada's settler-colonial genocide, and yet it simultaneously seems to offer a way out, an alibi almost, which makes it possible to *not* address one's own relationship with structural racism and its everyday violence in the past and present. While in the cases of the CMHR and the JHGC it is the museums themselves which stimulate exhibitionary atonement, I did not find this to be the case at the Memorium. This might be due to the Memorium's dedication to "documentation", which prevents it from employing narrative devices that support the museum's overall emplotment within a universal narrative or making nominal references to the present and future. However, the Memorium cannot be separated from the German society in which it is situated, where the wish to be innocent and guilty at the same time is ubiquitous, as the examples of Heiko Maas and the newspaper coverage of the Memorium's opening have shown.

We therefore need to be aware that, as Hodgkin and Radstone put it, "our understanding of the past has strategic, political, and ethical consequences", and "contests over the meaning of the past are also contests over the meaning of the present and over ways of taking the past forward" (2003, 5). I would add that it is not only the "contests over the past" that point to politics about the present or the future but also any presumed "consensus" about the need for memorialisation, which also serves to meet certain ends. By emphasising this once more, I hope to underline how powerful the linkage between Holocaust memory and the moral economy of human rights is due to the way that it juxtaposes the evil past of the Holocaust with the desirable present and future of a "human rights culture". In contrast to the Holocaust, the flaws of our present time and its political conditions are less stark. What is more, public memory relies on certain bodies of knowledge which provide the basis for not only how to memorialise and teach past events but also how to determine which lives are considered *grievable* (Butler 2009) and worth learning lessons from and which are not. Simultaneously, the narrative that suggests that all evils are in the past (Bevernage 2015) tends to present the past as a sealed container which we might open in order to learn from its contents, but not as part of our present and future realities. While it is true that the Holocaust ended with the defeat of Nazi Germany, the difficult knowledge of it not only continued to influence and still impacts the lives of the survivors and their descendants but could, on a meta level, also cast doubt on the beliefs and ideals cherished at the three museums rather than support them (Dean and Failler 2019; Simon 2006).[4] The same applies in an even more concrete way to Indigenous knowledges and the colonial conditions that still render them less relevant than the dominant singular version of modernity and its progress. In this context, the power-knowledge nexus determines the dominant understanding within society of the impact of settler colonialism and apartheid as phenomena that belong solely to the past and not to the Canadian or South African present. Such an understanding is the necessary foundation for the calls to action cited earlier that are directed at Aboriginal youth in Canada or at the South Africans who, in the words of Tshepo Madlingozi, are not "simultaneous with the dominant society made up of white people and the black elite" (2017, 123).

Once again, the Memorium is a slightly more complicated case, because it only rarely makes explicit mention of any teachings that it intends to convey. One lesson is nevertheless overt at the Memorium, and that is the importance of the rule of law, which, as I believe, is only as cogent as it is because of Holocaust memory and its entanglement with human rights discourse. What I mean is that it is only because the Nuremberg trials are remembered as a response to the Holocaust in global memory that the story "From Nuremberg to The Hague" can unfold the significance of its storyline (Sznaider 2008). Therefore, in all the museums I studied, the past is not only considered to be of value for contemporary educational enterprises, but its teachings moreover present aspirational horizons of hope for the future, to which visitors will almost automatically subscribe if they internalise the lesson's message as intended.

4 The question of the disruptive power of difficult knowledge, especially of Holocaust memory, will be the subject of discussion in chapter 9.

Memory and its futures

If we primarily turn to Holocaust memory for the lessons it can teach us, then what exactly do these lessons entail and why have they become so prominent? The three museums each emphasise slightly different moral imperatives of our current global order: the rule of law (Memorium), the value of liberal democracy and an international community committed to its protection (JHGC) and, of course, human rights and the importance of engaging for its causes (all three of them, but especially the CMHR). In their work, all three museums exhibit difficult histories of war and genocide but nonetheless draw somewhat hopeful conclusions. In this regard, Joan W. Scott reminds us that

> [t]here is an unresolvable tension in the very word history between moral imperatives and political practicalities: the "lessons of history", after all, not only expose errors that demand correction, evils that require repudiation, but also remind us of human imperfection, of the necessary compromises of politics, and the impossibility of securing peace on earth. (2020, 3)

Her observation is particularly interesting with regard to the Holocaust, which has, on the one hand, come to represent the universal prototype of evil but, on the other, has also gained prominence as the most (in)famous case study from which we can learn for the future. This dual role of standing in as a proxy for all the violence of which humans are capable while also serving as a lesson on how to be a better person and create a better world only takes effect if the memory of the Holocaust is deprived of its ability to deeply unsettle those who engage with it. But serving as an instructive case for a better world, memory first of all needs to be freed from the notion of "impossibility" and "human imperfection", because its primary function is to remind us of how the present has overcome these terrible wrongs – and it may even show us the path towards perfection. It is thus pivotal to many of the contemporary attempts made by memory politics to avoid the tension described in the passage quoted above by means of taming or consensualising the past. In the case of the Holocaust, this is carried out by weaving its history and memory into a broader narrative of progress towards human rights and a global democratic order.

Despite the difficult knowledge intrinsic to Holocaust memory, it is increasingly being turned to for its supposed bridging abilities, as it has had a capacity to contribute to historical dialogue and mediate possible conflicts. This potential ascribed to Holocaust memory will supposedly allow it to help build social cohesion and eventually bring peace. In this way, its memory is not only concerned with the specific past of the Holocaust but also implies a particular vision for the future which is derived from the lessons of history. At first glance, it might seem that there is nothing problematic about this practice at all, but it soon becomes clear that suggesting that there is just one right answer to the Holocaust (and, as a matter of fact, to all histories of violence) can also become a means to prescribe and thereby limit political imagination, a tool of governing about which we, in the light of continuing racial and colonial power dynamics, should be especially concerned.

From the outset, I intended this book to be about the impact of global memory politics on imaginaries of the present and the future. In the section above, I have already mentioned the issue of the future, which I claim is at least partially envisioned though retrospective politics. Or, in other words, in the constellation of Holocaust memory and human rights on which I have been focusing, looking back at the past is simultaneously a gesture towards the future. However, this is not confined to the Holocaust-human rights nexus but is integral to historical operations in general, because the "operation of history [...] is meant, after all, to provide moral cover for what are always more complex and troubling political realities, realities that defy the easy distinctions between the past and the present in order to provide an opening to the future" (Scott 2020, 59). According to Michel de Certeau, on whose writings Scott relies in the quotation above, such future politics are the main aim of the historical operation which distinguishes past from present in order to legitimise the visions of the future being proposed. In this context, relying on the memory of past atrocities as a point of reference from which to define a better world has become a common trope in national as well as international politics. In my research, this became most apparent at the CMHR. Following de Certeau (1988) and Scott (2020), who emphasise the moral imperative of history, I want to suggest that the reason for the increase in human rights museums that memorialise the Holocaust is precisely the future that these institutions and their discursively constructed narratives have in mind. Accordingly, public memory of the Holocaust has a future-determining ability that is especially pertinent in the institutionalised lessons to be learned from its history. While at the JHGC, visitors are called upon to take action for democracy by authorities like Holocaust survivors, whose statements and poems are present throughout the exhibition, the CMHR advertises the horizons of hope which it would like to help achieve much more explicitly – in its publicity strategies, its app, and in the exhibitions themselves. Moreover, all three museums run education programmes which work with cases of individual suffering and link them back to learners' own experiences. These lessons are subsequently utilised to evoke moral sentiment in order to ensure more humane conduct (Fassin 2012) – and hence, by taking long detours through historical disasters, they pave the way for emotionally charged future politics. In this way, the leap to the future is inseparable from a revived memory and needs to be scrutinised alongside the images of the past that appear to be at the heart of any representation of history. However, memory politics, "the invocation of history", as Scott asserts, are "always driven by some implicit or explicit political aim in which 'history' is at once a transcendent force (moving inexorably towards a better future) *and* the record of human action, accomplishment, [...] or the capacity for evil" (2020, 96).

It is at the juncture where Holocaust memory meets normative human rights politics aimed towards the future that the ways in which this specific form of memorialisation is based on governmental rationale becomes most overt. In the setting of museums that function as sites of governmentality, memory works most effectively as a technology for disseminating specific future visions and authorising measures taken in the name of those visions. This is, firstly, because the discursive convergence of Holocaust memory with the human rights project has the capacity to produce a specific type of citizen-subject that not only devotes itself to the safeguarding of a human rights culture but moreover accepts human rights and liberal democracy as the best that we can hope for. What is more, the version of Western liberal democracy that is advocated throughout the examples considered here is presented to us as the only acceptable response to the past and the only aspirational political order. Equating the Nazis' specific crimes with a barbaric past protects a moral vision of liberal democracy as the embodiment of the progressive flow of history (Scott 2020, 27). Such memory politics not only strengthen the idea that the liberal democratic nation state, together with supranational bodies such as the United Nations, is humanity's highest achievement but also treats ethno-nationalism and racism as the exclusive problem of undemocratic states, disregarding the colonial and racist past and present of European states, the US, Canada, New Zealand and Australia. Present-day injustices are thereby constantly being relegated to the past, which leads to the portrayal of the Western political order with its core principles as the only one worth aspiring to (Bevernage 2016; Brown 2004). For this reason, as already explained in chapter 2, Samuel Moyn cautions us against a way of thinking that presumes that there is a causal link between the history of the Holocaust and the current future-oriented politics of universal human rights, writing, "One of the worst outcomes of the imaginative linkage of the Holocaust and human rights is that it allows people to believe that the sole alternative to a humanitarian and human rights framework is genocidal violence or, at best, immoral complacency" (2014, 97). However, as Moyn continues, "the alternative to our contemporary humanitarian culture of human rights is not doing nothing. It is doing something else – and perhaps something better" (2014, 97). One of the governmental objectives to which memory risks contributing is precisely making such a different future unimaginable – an important aspect to which I will return at the end of this chapter.

The ideal of the historically aware human rights activist

In the theoretical account I gave of how studies of governmentality probe all calculated and rational activities, as well as the mentalities they create, we saw the aim to influence the conduct of "people, individuals, or groups" (Foucault 2007, 102). Education and programmes of empowerment which motivate citizen-subjects to actively participate in the shaping of their lives and society as a whole are important features of the conglomerate of techniques of government that exists in contemporary democratic societies. Accordingly, democratic discourse relies on a concept of citizenship that distinguishes between "subjects" and "citizens". In *The Will to Empower*, Barbara Cruikshank persuasively argues that individuals in a democracy are transformed into "self-governing citizens" through what she calls "technologies of citizenship" (1999, 67). That is, citizens are "made" by discourse in a certain way and are encouraged to actively participate in the "collective interest" of their society (Cruikshank 1999, 19). For this reason, as already explained in chapter 2, subjects and citizens alike are constantly being urged by various actors, institutions and programmes to become more engaged in society, either to empower themselves (which is usually demanded of subjects) or to empower others (mainly a task assigned to citizens). Neoliberal democratic rationality thus targets not only the economy but all spheres of politics and the everyday lives of governmental subjects. It promotes individuals' ability to care for themselves and, if possible, voluntarily care for others as well.

To a certain degree, the reader will already have noticed an intention to influence behaviour that is present throughout the case studies. All of the myriad texts on the Holocaust and human rights education published by the UN (especially UNESCO) and the IHRA as well as their partner organisations sound very much the same. A similar sentiment can furthermore be found in the museums I studied, especially the CMHR and the JHGC. While the International Holocaust Remembrance Alliance (IHRA) promises "behavioural changes" and explicitly refers to building "global citizenship" in its educational programmes, the museums emphatically disseminate the ideal of creating "upstanders". These global citizens are formed when encounters with the Holocaust touch the "hearts and minds" of students. In a UNESCO publication, this logic is summarised as follows: "The concrete horrors and inhumanity of the Holocaust marked the antithesis of the Global Citizenship that the world needed to cultivate for the future" (Stevick 2018, 4). Even though the idea of "the citizen" and "citizenship" are ever-present in the communications of these institutions, they do not give any explanation of the implications or underpinnings of these concepts. This is especially noticeable in light of Barbara Cruikshank's argument that in democratic discourse one does not become a "citizen" simply by holding legal citizenship but by being actively formed by various means that are again linked to power relations. In what follows, and in order to bring my argument home, I will extend my previous considerations concerning institutions of memory and their programmes in two ways by explaining them both in regard to the techniques of citizenship and in terms of the neoliberal rationale that is often concealed in their ideological underpinnings. In this way, I will make tangible the relationship between contemporary – presumably depoliticised – human rights discourse on Holocaust memory and how it formulates the kind of citizenship it desires.

On empathy and activism

In chapter 4, I provided an overview of influential publications on human rights and citizenship education which are designed to help form "clear-thinking and enlightened citizens" and aim to train "citizens aware of the human and political issues at stake in their society or nation" (UNESCO 1998). While all the publications by UNESCO and the IHRA agree that such an ideal citizen-subject necessarily needs to be equipped with ethical and moral qualities, it is institutions such as the museums I analysed which serve to develop these qualities in their visitors. In UNESCO's and the IHRA's programmes as well as in those of the museums, a "sense of belonging" and a feeling of responsibility for a "common humanity" is evoked through engagement with the history of the Holocaust. As I argued at the outset of this book, the model of looking back at (selected) pasts and linking them with the present and future is ubiquitous in current memory politics. Human rights museology adds an emotive approach to this topic, stimulating empathy and thereby aiming to foster activism. A clear example of this emotive approach in memory work is the didactically mediated invocation of affect by means of ending texts with accounts of extreme atrocities such as genocide.

The CMHR and the JHGC in particular take an emotive angle to address ethical and moral issues throughout their exhibits and educational programmes, which serves the same overall purpose of urging their visitors to "exercise and defend their democratic rights and responsibilities in society" (Kerr 2013, 3). For example, the quotation displayed in three languages on the wall of the JHGC's Garden of Reflection, which was put there "to strengthen" us, can be understood in this sense: we will only realise our full potential as citizens if we accept the burden of history that will eventually make us stronger. The reason why it will supposedly strengthen us is that it will provide us with the moral mindset which will prepare us for our sometimes difficult task as active participants in society, as people who stand up for human rights against all odds. Another clear example of the attempt to engage visitors emotionally is the aforementioned mood map at the CMHR, which presents us with four possible emotions that we might feel after our visit to the gallery on the Holocaust: "moved", "thoughtful", "inspired" and "surprised". As I have already pointed out, all of these "moods" are positive ones that are believed to lead towards human rights activism (see chapter 6). What is more, throughout the CMHR, there is an emphasis on human suffering, to which human rights and people who advocate for them are presented as the best answer. Moralising language calls for compassion and aims to stimulate the affects necessary to recognise the virtues of democracy and humanitarianism, which are derived largely from the memory of genocide – in the specific example of the mood map, the Holocaust. Unlike the Memorium, which does not present any objects in its exhibition, the other two museums, especially the JHGC, present many personal objects throughout their exhibitions. At the JHGC, all of these items once belonged to survivors who later lived in Johannesburg and donated their very personal memory objects to the centre. Examples include a violin and a doll that were kept by their owners during – or rather, despite – the Holocaust, and in the section on Rwanda, a powerful installation of clothes worn by victims of the genocide form just one of several examples of such an emotive curatorial approach. The emphasis on the need for the rule of law omnipresent at the Memorium as well as the particular narrative of the JHGC, where the genocide in Rwanda is presented as only having happened because the international community stood by and watched instead of intervening, add yet another component to the issue of and the interplay between personal concern and global responsibility, to which I will turn in the third subsection of chapter 8.

Moral sentiments have become a central pillar of current memory politics and politics more generally – they underlie political discourses and legitimise political action carried out in the name of humanity and human wellbeing (Fassin 2012). Thus, moral sentiments are combinations of affects and values such as the empathy and tolerance mentioned above (Feldman and Ticktin 2010). Generally speaking, moral sentiments are understood as emotions that point us to the misfortunes of others and make us want to alleviate them. In this regard,

> [e]mpathy has been identified as a key emotion for facilitating and swaying public debate on social justice issues [...]. However, the idea of empathetic imagination, and the way it is often uncritically embedded in liberal discourse as a "feel good" concession, has been strongly criticized as a way of reasserting existing power relations when socially privileged subjects choose to confer or withhold empathy. (Smith and Campbell 2015, 454)

There are thus several ways to understand the complicated emotion that is empathy, from feeling compassion for the discursive other's suffering to the ability to learn how this supposed *other* thinks and feels (Zabalueva 2018, 241). In this sense, and this became apparent both at the CMHR and the JHGC, "empathy and compassion are inevitably bound up with the ongoing ethics of privilege" (Pedwell 2014, 15). That is because, according to Pedwell, empathy in the transnational or more universal context is always situated at the intersection of neoliberalism and coloniality, as feelings of empathy and compassion are commodified and can become a source of profit for those demonstrating empathy and compassion towards others, as some of the previously cited scholars have argued in regard to human rights museology more generally. It therefore seems that empathy, in the realm of citizenship ideals, is primarily an emotion to be fostered amongst citizens, not subjects, as it is the former who enjoy the privilege of performing actions that arise from empathy. The example of the "Action Counts" game at the CMHR, which urges us to perform an act of charity for Inuit that is rooted in both neoliberal and colonial logic, shows this clearly.

In all this, it is assumed that Holocaust memory will guarantee the development of empathy, which is why it often serves as a point of departure, a case study from which we can learn about the need to care for others. Yet in the specific constellation of memory discussed here, we also find a set of moral sentiments that are directed at an opponent (someone or something to whom we do not grant empathy). This antithesis to the global citizen's own cherished ideals is often a rather abstract one, namely antisemitism or, more generally, hatred. In this mode, the emotions evoked serve to condemn certain groups of people, entire nation states or ideologies that can all be framed as threats to the safety of humanity. In this way, empathy with the victims of genocide not only serves the cause of humanitarian activism but also speaks directly to individuals who might not yet have decided on the "right" path for themselves because, for example, they are still allowing themselves to harbour an aversion against supposed "others". They therefore need to be empowered to gather the strength they will need to choose the path of tolerance and compassion instead. What is interesting in this regard is how the CMHR and the JHGC seem to focus on precisely these two different components of the endeavour to encourage moral excellence amongst their visitors, and especially amongst the groups of learners who participate in their programmes: the CMHR, with its high admission charge and a digital guide that requires people to have smartphones onto which to download it, has citizens in mind who are in a position to play an active part in their society by helping others. The JHGC does present supporting those in need as a virtue as well, but its programmes tend to address subjects who have not yet fully developed their potential as citizens and thus still need to be "empowered". Here, it is the educators at the centre who take on the role of empowerment assistants, whereas at the CMHR, the visitors themselves are called upon to act as such assistants to those who might require it.[5] In both versions of empowerment, either of oneself or others, "the once critical approach to issues of oppression and discrimination" has been substituted by a version of the concept employed "by mainstream development agencies [such as UNESCO], albeit more to improve productivity within the status quo than to foster social transformation." (Rai 2007). These more mainstream ideas about citizen empowerment, which do not acknowledge that power relations and domination are structures of democratic societies as well as of authoritarian forms of government, help to depoliticise the concept instead of fortifying agency for political change. Depoliticisation in general is a common feature of retrospective politics at their juncture with human rights because the human rights project has a strong tendency to depoliticise the fields in which it engages, especially fields of conflict (Bevernage 2018; Madlingozi 2015). As Wendy Brown reminds us:

> The Human Rights discourse not only promulgates a politics that it dissimulates through the rubric of tolerance, it also promulgates a discourse of depoliticization that is itself a means by which the politics of tolerance – the operations of tolerance as a discourse of normativity and power – are dissimulated [...]. The process [...] produces a more generic depoliticization of conflicts and of scenes of inequality and domination. (Brown 2006, 142)

The importance of Brown's critique is clear, especially where Holocaust education and the human rights project are fused, as is the case in the UNESCO policy guide *Education on the Holocaust and preventing genocide* (2017) and in some museum spaces. The guide emphasises the "contribution" made by Holocaust education to global citizenship education throughout its pages, while museums, especially the CMHR and the JHGC, put its ideas into practice. It is assumed that teaching students about the history of Nazi Germany and the Holocaust in particular will motivate them to reflect upon the prejudices and stereotypes they might hold and to ideally *unlearn* them (Antweiler 2019). This approach tends to render highly political issues, such as structural racism, as problems resulting from individual misbehaviour – a problem of tolerant vs. intolerant people, not a problem of the political order itself. In the following, I will investigate how this kind of depoliticisation and individualisation of conflict and structural oppression, which we have seen in most of the material I have analysed, is linked to neoliberal rationale and memory's ability to function as a tool of government.

---

5 Even though in the chapter on the CMHR as well as in the subchapter above I also discussed the museum's mission to engage Indigenous youth in human rights causes, which is an endeavour to empower subjects rather than call upon citizens, the museum's overall plot nonetheless gives rise to the analysis presented here (due to the examples given above).

Individual responsibility for the wellbeing of humanity

The moralisation of political life discussed above replaces political responsibility for systemic change with moral responsibility for suffering individuals. In doing so, it risks depoliticising inequality, conflict and violence by making them a problem of the individual subject and not of the political discourse that produces subjects and their experience of inequality in the first place (Scott 1992; Çubukçu 2017). In all the publications I have examined as well as at the museums, this notion of the responsible neoliberal subject is overt. It is marked by responsibility shifting from politically structured society to the individual that takes care of itself.

In the case of the Memorium, the tendency to individualise Nazi crimes can be found at the tribunal itself, in the accounts presented by Chief Prosecutor Jackson and in the later statements given by prosecutor Ferencze. The twenty-four defendants at the initial trial were presented as embodiments of evil, who had "used their power of state to attack the foundations of world peace" and were therefore to "pay for it personally" (Jackson 1946, 88 – 89). Ferencze also used terms such as "ignorance" and "arrogance" to describe the attitudes of the *Einsatzgruppen* that led to the atrocities which were to be tried. Nazi ideology and the immense support it received throughout Germany (and beyond) was by no means the subject matter of the hearings, leaving a void in the narrative that is sustained in the Memorium's exhibit, which also primarily focuses on individuals (as a reminder, the key protagonists of the exhibition are the perpetrators, the lawyers and the judges). The CMHR, which propagates a perspective of reconciliation, does not place much focus on the reasons for conflict or genocide nor on who perpetrated it. Instead, the large museum emphasises how individuals can contribute to preventing or solving conflicts in order to achieve social harmony, thereby remaining strictly in the realm of benevolence and charitable actions. The JHGC addresses its visitors using similarly moralising language, though it also stresses the importance of international engagement, for example, on the level of states, supranational organisations and NGOs. In the narrative presented by the JHGC, it is individuals and the international community who together bear responsibility for the wellbeing of humanity. However, what the JHGC does just as much as the CMHR is employ the motif of equal rights and equal duties as well as the search for personal attitudes and prejudice, which otherwise might not come to the fore and could remain 'uncorrectable'. The emphasis on individual responsibility culminates in an activity with which the JHGC ends all its programmes for leaners: the Butterfly Project. This activity asks the students to "reflect on the lessons they have learned" and to leave "a message of courage for others" on a designated wall prominent within the centre's main hall.

Such means, which leave visitors and students alike with the feeling that the world's destiny is in their hands, primarily paint issues of oppression and social justice as the duty of the individuals working on them towards a common goal in the same manner as they might try to live a healthy life. While we should, of course, all be held accountable for our actions, especially when they concern other people, such a perspective nonetheless leaves the fundamental asymmetric structures of the political order itself unchallenged. This tendency to individualise and thus depoliticise conflict and structures of oppression that was also present at the Nuremberg Trials, was already embedded within the Universal Declaration on Human Rights as well as UNESCO's founding document (and all its subsequent programmes), as I argued before. In this vein, what is being advocated by the memory authorities of UNESCO and the IHRA as well as the human rights museums in this study is active citizenship, but always within the frame and language of (neo)liberal democracy and its human rights agenda. To emphasise this once more: this kind of attempt to engage others and oneself in such a manner might be neither a bad nor a good thing, but it is certainly political and, furthermore, a very consequential perception of the world(s) we live in, as Jessica Whyte explains: "as individuals are made responsible for fulfilling their own needs, the language of equal rights serves to block redistribution, progressive taxation, social welfare, affirmative action, and reparations for slavery and colonialism" (2017, 3). In a society that supposedly grants equal rights to everyone, racism and other forms of discrimination and oppression are portrayed as problems that are not inherent to the system but simply a matter of individual misconduct.

This clearly illustrates what Cruikshank (1999) points out: that active citizenship is conceptualised as the solution to society's ills, such as xenophobia or the rather abstract threat of "extremism", because it is presented as the cure for these undesirable attitudes. Rather like Vanessa Andreotti's (2012, 2017) more general assessment of global citizenship education, this variant of what Andreotti calls the "uncomplicated single story" remains on society's surface and only promotes "quick fixes" instead of the complex engagement with the past and the present or with the ideas about the future it proposes. I therefore contend that, in the context of (global) citizenship education, the morally charged message is that genocide in general and the Holocaust in particular have very simple causes: the hatred, prejudice and intolerance harboured by individuals. The neoliberal preference for rational, responsible subjects persists even when the topic is genocide. Of course, genocide is not just carried out because too many members of a group hold too much of a grudge against supposed others. The Holocaust did not just happen because too many Germans were intolerant. Merely focusing on individual responsibility ignores the role played by Nazi ideology, the nation state and the international community. Instead, we are asked to take responsibility for ourselves and others, to educate and to receive education so that, in due course, everybody will accept their obligations as members of society and be enabled to enjoy their equal rights.

However, the matter is more complicated, as we can see, for example, when we consider how often racism is confused with "prejudice". The widely used prejudice approach primarily targets racism on the individual level, framing it as an "attitude" or a "belief" instead of as a political system (Bonilla-Silva 2015, 73). In opposition to the racism-as-prejudice approach, scholars like Charles W. Mills (1997) and Eduardo Bonilla-Silva (2015) not only point out that there is more than just one racism – there are "variations in how racial regimes are organized" (Bonilla-Silva 2015, 76). They moreover argue that prejudice alone cannot uphold racial domination and emphasise that, while non-*whites* can indeed exhibit prejudiced behaviour, they cannot be racist in the sense that they are "commanding a racial structure", as in the case of global white supremacy (Bonilla-Silva 2015, 76). Ndumiso Dladla, referencing anti-apartheid activist and prominent thinker of Black Consciousness Steve Biko, explains this differentiation by pointing out that "the enjoyment of power over the lives of one's racial-others is a necessary addition to discrimination for an instance or situation to be genuinely racist" (2017). He adds that, while non-*whites* indeed hold positions of power which allow them to discriminate against supposed others, there is a significant difference between "historical power" and the sort of power that might come momentarily with "political connections, money or property" (Dladla 2017). Only the former, as he continues in the same paragraph, can create prevailing racist structures, because it is a position which "includes the [...] power over the very enterprise and discipline of historical writing and representation [...] to create institutions of historical production, as well as representative academics, cultural producers and public figures who authorise one's version of the account of the past" (Dladla 2017). This observation is pivotal in the context of my argument here and emphasises an aspect that cannot be stressed enough: the writing of history, and hence the creation of public memory, is a highly political enterprise that cannot be separated from existing power structures and their continuous reiteration. Therefore, for memory to *not* function in this vein, it requires an awareness of these entanglements as well as active reflection on the historical narratives that are being promulgated – especially if they are at odds with the political realities they are meant to address (Scott 2020).

To a degree, the teachings of all the materials and sites examined here contribute to critical assessments of our present world(s), as they also point to present-day injustices as issues that need to be tackled, problems that need to be overcome. But they differ in one very important aspect, which is quite clear in the question of individual responsibility: the less biased and less discriminatory attitudes and "behavioural changes" which Holocaust memory education aims to bring about can only be realised against the backdrop of understanding all matters of inequality as problems of prejudice and will therefore inevitably remain within the realm of "soft reforms" instead of more substantial social and political change (Stein and Andreotti 2021). And one of the key things hindering more thorough change is precisely this neoliberal rationale, which solely addresses the individual, both as a problem and a solution, and in which the memory education endeavours that I discuss here are also rooted – even though, according to South African philosopher Mogobe Ramose, and with special relevance to the case studies of the CMHR and the JHGC, "justice demands the restoration of the humanity of the indigenous conquered peoples through the reversal of the dehumanising consequences of colonialization" (2007, para 16). Here, I am prompted to ask: Who bears responsibility for abolishing colonial conditions and what would that entail? In other words: are the lessons of the Holocaust that hold the promise of a better future able to respond to the fundamental contradictions generated by colonisation and apartheid and, in the case of Germany, the many repercussions of National Socialist ideology? In the context of global and local memory practices and teaching about the Holocaust and human rights that are – as I tried to show in chapter 4 – primarily derived from a very universalised narrative authorised in the global North, can these practices and teachings be tailored specifically to particular South African, or Canadian, or German circumstances, or indeed to any other situation? A reversal of the colonial conditions which still structure our global order might call for different lessons to be learned from the past than the ones conveyed by UNESCO, the IHRA and in human rights museums, lessons that do not endorse the neoliberal trend towards individualisation or cherish a single global morality derived from Enlightenment ideals and Western democratic discourse.

The duty to engage: Politics of memory for the global citizen

At the core of the democratic discourse just described is the formulation of multiple responsibilities that involve the individual citizen-subject, nations and the so-called international community. These are, to name just a few, the duty to behave according to the law (Teitel 2016), to remember and truthfully face the past (Meral 2012; David 2020) and, on the supranational level, the responsibility to protect (R2P) the international democratic order. According to the R2P mission, what must be protected is democracy itself – with all its norms and achievements, and most of all, its human rights framework (Welsh 2012; Singh and Kim 2017). That human rights matter has been proclaimed as consensus across the political divide and is not limited to specific geographical locations, whilst awareness of their importance is often derived from a historical consciousness. In this vein, despite political differences, politicians, organisations and local practitioners around the globe are uttering warnings about hatred and intolerance that follow a similar rationale of retrospective politics and that employ the memory of the Holocaust to morally underpin their appeals to responsible citizen-subjects. In their 2020 volume, social scientists Sarah Gensburger and Sandrine Lefranc (2020) also find that certain importance is being attributed to memory education in schools, which is believed to influence the behaviour of individuals as future citizens. They quote former French Minister of Education Najat Vallaud-Belkacem, who emphasised that (French) republican citizenship is based on shared memory and a refusal of fatalism (Gensburger and Lefranc 2020, 23). On a similar note, German politician Heiko Maas has demanded the introduction of Holocaust education for refugees as a means of educating them about democracy. In this sense, the practice of memory education is productive of the aforementioned hierarchy between the historically literate citizen and subjects who still need to understand or learn to internalise democratic values; memory politics thus have the power to distinguish between desirable and less desirable members of society, and even of the international community (Barkan and Karn 2006; David 2020). In this way, as I would like to show in the following, the constellation of memory described in this book has become a technique used to exercise power that can be apprehended most clearly through the issue of democratic duties.

Despite the many advocates of tolerance, according to Freedom House, a US-based, non-governmental organisation that conducts research on the current state of democracy, respect for human rights and political freedom has been in decline for more than a decade (Freedom House 2019). Historians Gilbert and Alba (2019) as well as sociologists Gensburger and Lefranc (2020) assess the efficacy of memory policies in preventing an increase of intolerance as being rather low, since "[a]cts of intolerance, violence and racism have indeed increased significantly, both in number and intensity" whether in the European Union or the US (Gensburger and Lefranc 2020, 34). Of course, there are many different reasons for this decline, such as the rise of authoritarian regimes, which are now "banning opposition groups", and a more general "breakdown of the rule of law" (Freedom House 2019) or, as Wendy Brown, for example, argues, neoliberalism and its systematic dismantling of all aspects of social life (2006; 2015). The years of Donald Trump's presidency in the United States even gave rise to the concept of the "post-human rights" age, which aims to grasp the decline of human rights enforcement architecture and humanitarian efforts more generally. The Covid-19 pandemic only compounded this worrying trend further and made it even more complicated, with people in Germany (and some other European countries) protesting against the obligation to wear masks or keep their physical distance to others by displaying signs with yellow stars that, instead of "Jew" – like during the Holocaust – now have "German" written on them. Others who have "resisted" the measures taken to slow down the pandemic have compared themselves to well-known victims of the Nazi regime like Sophie Scholl and Anne Frank (Hasselbach 2020). If it were only a few outsiders or "misfits" trivialising Nazi-era persecution, there would be no need to mention them here, but the movement is quite large and growing, which seems to suggest (though this needs to be closely monitored in the future) that Holocaust memory has become such a common argument that it now serves more as an empty signifier than as the warning sign against hatred that it is often used as, and that it is therefore being utilised even by the political far right.[6] This argument has been put forwards about other achievements of liberalism more generally (for example free speech), whose content and meaning are being transformed by neoliberal rationality and are now available even to the right in their fight against the very values liberal thought used to embody (Brown 2015). Thus, it could be argued that the programmes I have described in this book are now needed more than ever and should be strengthened, despite some questionable ideas inherent in their teachings. Is it nonetheless useful in this situation to emphasise their political nature and ability to exercise power and (re)introduce hierarchies?

One reason to answer this question in the affirmative is that policymakers are still responding to reports like "Freedom in the World 2019" or the pessimistic rendering of our time as a post-human-rights era not with critical inquiries into what is causing the increase in antidemocratic tendencies but by making recourse to long-standing "soft-reform" programmes. Another even more important reason is that liberal democratic discourse, despite the various contestations of both its ideological underpinnings as well as its core features, continues to rely on the future-oriented notion that it is the only political system that can create and sustain the conditions for a better life. However, from early on, the discursively produced public memory of Europe's rise from the ashes of the Second

6 This observation is very topical and primarily based on media reports rather than on scholarly evidence. Moreover, it is a recent phenomenon, which is why I have not described it in the most nuanced terms here. Allow me to nevertheless point to this development as it complicates this matter and adds weight to its topicality.

World War and its commitment to preventing crimes against humanity has usually excluded European colonialism and its dehumanising practices, portraying European powers as guardians of "civilization" instead (Whyte 2017). In a similar vein, the process behind the creation of the UDHR served, as I argued in chapter 3, not only to create a universally applicable set of rights but also to undermine more radical approaches to the re-ordering of the world after two world wars and at the dawn of (formal) decolonisation. This began at the Nuremberg Tribunal, where – as we learn in all three museums, but especially at the Memorium and the JHGC – history itself was on trial and the object of judgement, with the death sentences passed amounting to symbolic proof that justice had been delivered, with the imperative of "never again" promising that evil had been recognised and eliminated (Sznaider 2008; Scott 2020). Thus, the framing of liberal democratic discourse as the best possible aspiration for everybody's future, whatever their geopolitical location or status within society, is, as we have seen in the case studies, often presented in comparison with the past or, more specifically, in comparison with times and events in the past that are denounced as having been bad or wrong and which should thus be prevented from ever occurring again. The imperative of "never again", which still needs to be realised, could be read as confirmation of the importance of the museums as well as the global educational programmes of the IHRA and UNESCO – adding to their relevance and moral authority regardless of their contradictions and entanglements with governmental rationality. In this way, the past becomes the legitimising argument for actions taken in the present because they are presented as the only options to safeguard us against repeating past wrongs. As a consequence, neoliberal rationale is not identified as intrinsic to the problems that need to be challenged because the focus on past wrongs often works to conceal what might be new forms of injustice resulting from the flaws within democratic discourse, which therefore cannot be alleviated by it. What is more, those who position themselves on "the right side of history" are not only authorised to educate those who are not yet on the same page but even have the power to speak to not-yet-historically-aware subjects from a position of moral superiority, and sometimes even to sanction them.

A duty to remember

Even though it played a role before, the attacks of 11 September 2001 led to a marked increase in human rights discourse, which was further undergirded by the intensification of demands to secure the global Northern democratic order and all its institutions. Levy and Sznaider have observed how, on the one hand, "[t]errorism challenges the political salience of human rights principles and frequently causes the state to revert to one of its founding imperatives: the provision of security for its citizens." Yet at the same time, as they continue, "[i]n a world where citizenship and solidarity are based on global interdependencies, human rights are supposed to provide the glue that binds people together" (Levy and Sznaider 2010, 142). In this way, human rights discourse (along with an increase in anti-Muslim racism) has gained force, and in order to sustain the (neo)liberal democratic hegemony, various means have since been employed in what has come to be called the "war on terror". These means range from military action to educational programmes, which are included because, according to the 9/11 Commission Report issued in 2004, "education that teaches tolerance, the dignity and value of each individual, and respect for different beliefs is a key element in any global strategy to eliminate Islamist terrorism" (National Commission on Terrorist Attacks upon the United States 2004, 113). What is referred to as "Islamist terrorism" in this quotation is implicitly linked to an understanding of Islam as a "backwards" ideology. This line of thought is also present in the justifications formulated by Heiko Maas for Germany taking a role in the Security Council and educating (Muslim) refugees about the history of Nazism. Both of these claims are backed up by one of the most powerful moral arguments in existence: the memory of the Holocaust.

In a similar vein, former and current UN Secretary-Generals Kofi Annan and António Guterres also drew on the memory of genocide, though not on a specific one, when they launched the campaign to prevent future genocides (Annan 2004) and the "Call for Action" to reduce human suffering (Guterres 2020) respectively. The human rights museums also all switched, though to different degrees, from advocating peaceful activism on the part of individuals to advocating military intervention in the face of mass violence. At the JHGC, this is quite explicit in regard to Rwanda, while the CMHR in its Holocaust exhibition discusses why the Allied forces did not bomb Auschwitz to put an end to its factory of death, and the Memorium postulates the (occasional) need for intervention (humanitarian or even military) as a means for launching transitional justice mechanisms and ensuring legal proceedings. All of the examples mentioned in the museums are different, require different questions and prompt different answers, but in all of these contexts, the combination of moral sentiments and the idea of the responsibility to protect democracy strongly underpins the idea of learning from difficult pasts in order to not only behave in line with democratic values but, more than that, to champion humanist activism by all means, even if it involves a so-called humanitarian war. As becomes clear, the continuous construction of the notion of a shared humanity that needs to be protected from its undemocratic others strongly relies on the memory of past atrocities. Thus, many memory policies rely on the emotional impact of the programmes that are implemented and therefore "focus on innocent children and humiliated women, privileging their unique stories, and exposing their helplessness and tears" (Gensburger and Lefranc 2020, 15).

This discourse on peace and security has been accompanied by a different way of perceiving and protecting humanity – a vision of which is inherent in all the examples of memory politics discussed here: the idea that remembrance will contribute to global security. Talal Asad makes an intriguing point by taking a quick look at the historical origins of humanitarianism:

> Compassion and charity are as old as human history, but helping human beings who are suffering – especially suffering due to human [sic!] – has taken on new forms in modern times without entirely displacing older ones. In scope, humanitarianism tends to be global; ideologically it is linked in one way or another to the progressive emancipation of humanity, and emotionally it builds into "crimes against humanity". (Asad 2015, 402)

In a way, Asad expresses what I tried to show at the beginning of chapter 8 but also gestures in a much broader direction, which helps us to understand how closely notions of a shared humanity, the dedication to humanity's wellbeing and the memory of genocide are entangled. Only if we remember the past with its many failures, so the message seems to go, can we really grasp the merit of humanitarian action – both military and peaceful.[7]

Accordingly, Holocaust memory that relies on the condemnation of crimes against humanity has not only been globalised but has also become a common tool in human rights and peace-building policies across the globe. As argued in chapter 4, global Holocaust education is envisioned as an important pedagogical tool for shaping future generations into "global citizens" who are ready to support human rights causes, stand up for themselves and encourage others to do the same. It therefore has to do with and influences international relations and the global political economy, but often primarily operates as a technocratic pedagogical endeavour that takes place in schools or museums and that is undertaken by teachers and community educators. Therefore, the forms of pedagogy fostered by UNESCO and the IHRA that are realised in different ways in the museums promote "the will to empower" (Cruikshank 1999) the subject-citizen and aim to make citizens take responsibility for any unproductive behaviour, such as denigrating others, by reminding them of the mass crimes of the past.

---

7 The reading of memory politics as a part of humanitarian interventions has the potential to become another research project of its own, towards which I can at this stage however only vaguely point.

Rather than teach us about the origins and the rise of fascism and National Socialism, the lessons from the Holocaust are supposed to teach us to behave more humanely than our forebears did. In this regard, Jean-Luc Nancy makes a fascinating observation about the Universal Declaration of Human Rights: "In a sense, the Declaration is part of the general movement that, somehow nebulously, fosters the condemnation of 'fascism' and what this word would, over a long period, ignominiously signify. However, any questioning of the underlying reasons for the rise of fascisms is relegated to the background, if not even further" (Nancy 2014, 17). It seems, then, as if the global educational materials that I have analysed here fall in line with the absence of any thorough examination attempting to understand the "barbarous acts which have outraged the conscience of mankind" (UDHR). Instead, the UDHR and the materials I have looked at all focus on prevention. The UDHR in its preambles states very clearly how it intends to utilise the power of the rule of law to obviate the need for "men [sic!]" to make recourse, "as a last resort, to rebellion [...]". In a similar vein, all the publications, exhibitions and educational programmes I looked at share the intention of making recourse to Holocaust memory to strengthen the rule of law, which ought to protect human rights, in order to avoid any threats to the current global order. The UDHR has paved the way for today's global citizens, who are expected to fulfil their democratic obligation, namely the duty to remember, because in order to be aware of the historical threat of "tyranny", it is important to develop an understanding of our even greater shared duty to support the cause of human rights, which will eventually lead to global harmony. The universal claim that human rights are "the highest aspiration of the common people" (UDHR), despite the UDHR's emphasis on the importance of a jurisdiction, primarily operates on the moral level, and the moral realm does not need to provide explanations for past wrongdoings or for contemporary injustices because its virtuous cause is placed above all else – justifying all means.

This is, of course, a giant interpretative leap, as neither the museums nor the global education programmes claim, for example, that all aspects of the so-called war on terror are legitimate (as a matter of fact, it is not mentioned at any of the museums I studied). However, as I have tried to argue from the beginning, all of the mnemonic practices and technologies of memorialisation that I examined in my case studies need to be viewed in their wider political contexts as well as in light of the discourses and rationalities constitutive of these settings. The operation of history always implies moral imperatives that, even if they are not apparent or spelled out explicitly at all times, influence means of (institutionalised) memorialisation in the sense that they provide meaning to its forms of narrativisation and authorise the versions of the future inherent in all memory politics. I tried to make this clear in regard to the Memorium when I argued that this museum is closely linked to, if not dependent on, the universalised storyline of Holocaust memory, even though the museum does not address the Holocaust itself. In that particular case, as in the broader political ones discussed above, my claim is that the storylines employed only become effective or, put differently, only unfold their meaning because of certain bodies of knowledge that circulate within democratic discourse about the utility of the Holocaust as a point of reference for more peaceful times or about the existence of a constant threat to democracy emanating from "undemocratic" forces. The interdependence of these discourses, as I have shown, constitutes the dominant regime of truth, which posits the Holocaust as both a warning sign and a lesson at once, helping us to stay alert and identify the "enemy" while also urging us to unlearn undemocratic beliefs.

The duty to engage

Above, I discussed the emotions that memory education strives for and the techniques it uses to evoke affect, primarily at the human rights museums that I have investigated. But why is the affective mode of Holocaust memory so desirable in the context of governmental means? On the one hand, it can be linked to Joan W. Scott's observation about the lofty position achieved by positioning oneself "on the right side of history" (2020, 1). But another important connection can be made here that forms part of the techniques of the self and the shaping of people's wishes for themselves. This is because governmentality is most effective when it "impinges" on the relationship the subjects have to themselves in the sense that they aim to attach value to their being and conduct (Burchell 1991, 119). Being a citizen is proposed as a desirable identity for each member of a society. Therefore, self-identifying as a citizen who is on "equal footing with one's co-citizens" and taking action on this basis appears to be fulfilling (Burchell 1991, 121). However, assuming the identity of citizen, as I argued earlier, is not about simply holding a passport but entails a sort of political engagement which also makes the citizen a member of the political community. Now, as a member of any imagined community, what could be more desirable than to feel needed by and be engaged in the endeavour to secure and enhance humanity's greatest achievements? At least this is what the museums tell us: that it is in *our* hands that the future of the world lies, that it is *we* who need to make the right choices and try hard to be "upstanders" in order to actively participate in the journey towards the final realisation of a future vision that is "as shared as the sky" (CMHR) and therefore independent of any geopolitical realities. The duty to remember therefore goes hand in hand with the duty to engage, as we are constantly reminded in the field of human rights memory education.

The knowledge on which many practitioners in the field of memory activism and Holocaust education around the world rely is, as I have shown, produced and authorised by supranational bodies such as UNESCO and the IHRA. As Kaiser and Storeide note: "promoting international norms for Holocaust remembrance and education has taken place in a governance system that at least loosely connects norm entrepreneurs across multiple levels from the national to the European and global" (2018, 806). With this in mind, their charters, even though they are not legally binding, need to be understood in their norm-setting function, which operates by emphasising a sense of purpose rather than through the use of coercion. Moreover, Kaiser and Storeide's observation is particularly interesting in regard to the colonial conditions of the knowledge exchange taking place in the realm of global memory education, which needs to be scrutinised for the special role assigned to "norm entrepreneurs". It becomes clear that it is not only Holocaust historians and experts in pedagogy who are shaping commemorative and educational settings but also those who specialise in the dissemination of particular norms and values. Or, in other words: by looking at the knowledge of Holocaust memory education produced by bodies such as UNESCO and the IHRA, it becomes clear to which extent Holocaust memory has become fused with civic education in order to meet the goal of a standardised global morality.

It is in this constellation that general guidelines are produced and, moreover, a small number of local actors are given the opportunity to be educated by academics and memory practitioners in the global North and thus to become experts who then advise local initiatives on best practice.[8] Similar observations have been made by Joanne Coysh (2017; 2018) with regard to human rights education, which is the umbrella under which Holocaust education is promoted. The new experts then advise local initiatives on best practice. Coysh argues – and I agree with her – that human rights education has been drawn "further into the global political structures and policy-making framework" (2018, 55) and has thereby increasingly become an instrument of power. She refers to the Foucauldian notion of the power-knowledge nexus, and her argument may also be relevant to my attempted critical assessment of memory as a means of global governmentality, because the conveyers of Holocaust history, by linking its memory with human rights programmes, become experts in tolerance, anti-prejudice

---

8 Memory authorities such as Israel's Yad Vashem and the United States Holocaust Memorial Museum offer regular training for practitioners in the field of Holocaust memory education from across the globe.

and democratic conduct more generally. This affords them a morally superior position and sets them apart from others in their communities who supposedly still need to internalise the lessons of the Holocaust.

In the South African case, Holocaust education is supposed to be provided to the impoverished, not-yet-citizens who are thought to be particularly prone to harbouring partisanship such as xenophobic attitudes. The reason for this is that, as former SAHGF head Richard Freedman puts it, “the study of the past provides a framework for confronting the many forms of prejudice which, even today, remain latent challenges within South African society” (2012, 2). This recurring idea of learning from history to safeguard a better future puts those who do not engage with Holocaust history and its lessons in the difficult position of being viewed as potentially ignorant, not only about the past but also about the ways in which to foster wellbeing in the present and future. In Germany, this applies primarily to refugees, who are often accused of not yet having internalised the values of democratic Germany and who might therefore become a threat to civil peace. Antisemitism and misogyny are often evoked in the context of this discourse as the undesirable attitudes which refugees (especially from the Middle East or Arab countries) are bringing (back) to a society that has evolved out of such intolerant behaviour (Castro Varela and Ülker 2020). Thus, instances of antisemitism which involve refugees almost always prompt calls for Holocaust education (Messerschmidt and Fereidooni 2019; Mendel and Messerschmidt 2017). The Memorium indirectly addresses such issues with its programmes, which are supposed to strengthen respect for the rule of law, and also contributes on a more abstract level to the image of Germany as a nation state which has, despite some setbacks in the immediate postwar era, gradually come to embrace democracy and human rights – at least this is how president Frank-Walter Steinmeier put it in his keynote speech on the occasion of the seventy-fifth anniversary of the Nuremberg Tribunal. At the same time, the Memorium and German memory politics more generally speak to German citizens who have already learned their lessons from history and call on all historically literate citizens to prove how much they have atoned for their family’s and nation’s past by participating in efforts to further stimulate the progressive direction of history.[9] In Can-

9 It should be noted in this regard how the dual focus on historic guilt and contemporary innocence (albeit an oversimplification of German political realities) excludes all those Germans from the narrative whose families do not have a perpetrator or bystander background – be it Germans whose families only immigrated to either Germany after the Second World War or those whose families were persecuted by the Nazis (Amjahid 2021). Interestingly enough, while Germans long emphasised their families’ innocence, imagining their grandparents as saviours of

ada, the people that Holocaust memory education and its human rights agenda aim to reach are primarily those citizens who are not yet engaged enough in the sense that they do not volunteer for human rights causes or engage in charity. Simultaneously, the idea of empowerment, of being encouraged to learn more about one's democratic rights (and duties) addresses, as it was put in the government report on the CMHR, "Aboriginal youth" (Thorsteinson 2008, 36).

In this respect, Holocaust memory might become as much "a mechanism of exclusion" as a vehicle for achieving more ethical behaviour (Goldberg 2015, 15). Furthermore, the relationship between experts on norms and morality and not-yet-experts, between the dispensers and recipients of human rights, is not that different to the old colonial teacher-student dichotomy which Steve Biko claimed was constitutive of the settlers' mentality and behaviour towards conquered Indigenous people. In this context, hierarchy is introduced and perpetuated through education because, according to Biko, "the student must constantly turn to him [the settler] for guidance and promotion" (2017, 104). Thus, even today, in the constellation described here, those who have been historically and structurally classified as not yet having fully developed their potential as (global) citizens are the targets of a process of globally inspired memorialisation which is endorsed through historical pedagogy. This practice seems to suggest that those subjects (as opposed to citizens) do not yet understand the core values of democracy well enough and are instead in need of educational intervention, i.e., in the form of Holocaust education – even though they may have their own potent experiences and histories that can teach them about democracy and human rights, such as apartheid in South Africa, the Canadian genocide and the very recent experiences of war from which refugees might have fled to Germany. Instead of including such experience in their teaching, the "experts" from the global North risk perpetuating the colonial gaze upon the "unambitious students" of the South (both abroad as well as "at home") who are unwilling to accept the gift of morality and democracy.

In this way, other knowledges and experiences of, for example, colonial violence and oppression under apartheid, as well as other imaginings of change, are passed over as less relevant if they are not articulated in the international language of human rights, within which Holocaust memory has become important vocabulary. This form of memory education teaches about the "conduct of conduct" (Foucault 2007, 102) expected from German citizens, from Canadian and the South African citizen-subjects alike, and can supposedly be applied to

the Jews or as resistance fighters, the German public narrative has increasingly turned to an emphasis on guilt, as the example of Heiko Maas shows.

any other society as well. Heiko Maas, the former German foreign minister who entered politics after finding out about the questionable role his family played under National Socialism, can, for example, be seen as the prototype of such an ideal, as a citizen activated by memory. He rose to the lofty moral position of responsible advocate for peace and human rights, which eventually made it possible for him to demand that others also learn about the Holocaust in order to unlearn their prejudices.

All of this is part of a depoliticised discourse that emphasises the global citizen's responsibility to contribute to a world striving for peace and more humane conditions, morally underpinned by the memory of the Holocaust. As Talal Asad reminds us, this kind of narrative of "the birth of universal benevolence as a specifically modern virtue, the moral imperative to reduce suffering [...] is not unfamiliar" (2015, para 3). But he also points out the different manifestations of this imperative as it changes in different societal contexts: "They are diverse in the sense that they may evince horror at what they see or remorse at what they have done; they may express a feeling of inadequacy at the thought that they are unable to prevent some terrible suffering or of complacency at supporting a virtuous cause from a position of security" (Asad 2015, para 3). As my research has revealed, Holocaust memory, when fused with human rights discourse, grants this "position of security" from which to teach others about history, and even more importantly, about the right responses to it. The position of educator is already one of power, and, as I have shown in the theoretical chapters and throughout my case studies, it is intrinsically linked to the establishment and upholding of any power-knowledge nexus. In her mediation on "what it means to be human", Sylvia Wynter writes,

> Empire's most powerful apparatus is the education system. It initiates us into a culture and knowledge system that instructs us to want to be of a specific ethnoclass of humanity. [...] The tragedy of this is that whilst this particular idea of being optimally human holds us together [...] it can do so only in terms of the "us" and "the not us". (Wynter 1994, 44)

I have discussed above how this distinction between the binding "us" and the "not us", or the not-yet us, plays out in the memory politics constituted by the Holocaust-human rights nexus. But choices about which histories and realities of human suffering are suitable as "lessons" and how they are framed as such also determine the possible ways in which the future might unfold that are derived from those lessons of history. In this sense, memory not only has the potential to influence citizen-subjects and their conduct in the present but also to shape their future aspirations, which makes memory as a means of government even more powerful.

Governing the future

Throughout this book, I have sought to comprehend how Holocaust memory, at its juncture with the human rights project, is productive of political rationale and how its memory politics materialise and help to shape understandings of and visions for the world(s) in which we live. Therefore, asking how "operations of history" work as politics of memory, means asking how past and present are differentiated in order to create a different (and better) future. This is because, as I have argued above, the invocation of memories of a specific past comprises an implicit political claim and makes use of the idea of history as a transcendent force directed towards a better future. Jean Améry once stated that the "[f]uture is obviously a concept of value" (1970, 92). The act of constructing the future, in turn, finds expression in human rights policies in particular, which for their part cannot function without making recourse to the past. What is more, as Lewis R. Gordon has argued, within this logic only some people and their ways of life – that is, the "civilized democrats" (2019) – are regarded as belonging to the future, whilst all others are relegated to a past not worth preserving. Here, the coloniality of knowledge not only determines which lives are mourned and what pasts and whose pasts are framed as lessons but also which stories are safeguarded for their value in upholding modernity's single story and projecting it into the future. As I have come to understand through my research, memory can give legitimacy to this very problematic rationale, but not because it – rightly – condemns certain pasts, but rather predominantly due to its future-determining abilities. By this I mean that any public memory of the past that is even partially agreed on not only focuses on historical events but is always concerned with the future as well. It is dedicated to the future in the sense that it envisions or even prescribes certain ways of feeling, of living, of treating other people and, indeed, of being in the world more generally.

Memory has become essential to the practice of governing the souls of citizens and subjects alike, to shaping their desires, their hopes for themselves and others, as well as their aversions. Taking a detour through the past provides access to the affects and values which are aspired to and advocated for across the political spectrum, whilst the vocabulary of suffering, compassion and tolerance is used to describe our present and to justify the choices made for the future. However, the educational focus on the Holocaust, which declares that helping to shape a better future is its aim, begs the question of whether there is a similar awareness of apartheid or the subjugation of First Nations and whether similar efforts are being made to meet the need to discuss their continued effects – which after all are not yet in the past but being felt now, taking place on South African and Canadian soil respectively. It does seem that the digression to the

Holocaust, while serving as a door-opener to engagement with today's human rights issues, also risks displacing more difficult local or otherwise alternative memories, such as the memory of Germany's colonial atrocities, with another, more remote, memory. In the German case, it is of course more complicated, as the Holocaust is far from being the memory of some faraway place and is ingrained in society. Nevertheless, contemporary memory discourse, even in Germany, has created a feeling of distance to this history because of the clear-cut distinction between a bad past and a reconciled present. The aforementioned danger therefore needs to be kept in mind in regard to all three museum cases as well as global memory politics in general due to its aforementioned potential to create a sense of redemption that might result from the notion of "righting wrongs", which strongly features within the knowledge disseminated through the Holocaust-human rights nexus and the notion of history as progress more generally.

Presenting human rights – which already exist institutionally and only seem to need more people to respect them in order to fully succeed – as the virtuous response to the Holocaust and as a beacon of hope for the future of the world implies the victory of the good present over a murderous past. This narrative therefore allows us to treat the past and its failures as a closed entity instead of thinking about it as something that is simultaneously behind and before us in the form of a "terrible gift" (Simon 2006). However, acknowledging the "terrible gift" of difficult knowledge calls for, as Roger Simon puts it,

> forms of remembrance that help open up existing relations to continual critique and the difficult (and often conflicted) work of repair, renewal and re-invention of desirable institutions. This work can be supported by taking on the pedagogical possibilities and risks inherent in the recognition of and response to the incommensurable character of the historical experience of others. (2006, 187)

This means that taking seriously the memory and enduring impact of histories of violence demands "a sensibility that disavows timeless meanings recognizing instead the need for a critical consciousness of one's historically contingent relations to others in space and time" (Simon 2006, 187). The same applies to Indigenous knowledges and the colonial conditions that still render them less relevant than the one dominant single story of progress. Believing that the impact of settler colonialism and apartheid is something in the past but not, e.g., in Canada's or South Africa's present, or that Germany has healed its Nazi past, is the necessary foundation for the aforementioned call to action directed at every global citizen. In a world not impacted by its histories, where there is no structural inequality but only individual misdeeds, everyone bears equal responsibility for the wellbeing of themselves and of others. Human rights are there for everyone to claim, and we all share the duty to respect them, as the logic goes. In the assumption that it is the best political order that can exist, democratic discourse positions the idea of liberal democracy as an antidote to all forms of discrimination such as racism, antisemitism, sexism, homophobia and transphobia. This implies that, in a properly functioning democracy, these forms of discrimination and any other forms of inequality cease to exist. Such a juxtaposition is paradoxical, though, because it is precisely within democratic spaces that these dissimilarities can flourish. Condemning them is thus a feeble argument that externalises such attitudes as undemocratic, thereby suggesting that racism and other forms of systemic injustice are somehow imposed on democracy from the outside. As Ferit Güven puts it:

> To the extent that differences arising from class conflict, racial injustice, radical political opposition, and economic crises are suppressed, democracy can be successful. Democratic systems incorporate these differences only at the level of "political opinion". Hence, the real differences are reduced to differences of the ideas of different subjects and thereby rendered in a sense "private". (Güven 2015, 11)

What he writes can be related back to the problem already discussed of relegating responsibility for social justice and equality to the individual and thereby making these issues "private" and hence apolitical matters. This view furthermore perpetuates the teacher-student relationship known all too well from the colonial sphere: "real" democrats educate those who they claim are responsible for all undemocratic behaviour and impose the values, worldviews and "proper" democratic way of life onto their students by various means. In its fusion with the human rights project, global Holocaust memory risks functioning as precisely one of those means employed to provide lessons in "good democratic conduct" and to ensure the production of the "voluntarily compliant citizen" (Cruikshank 1999, 19). Once again in the words of Güven: "While the Western liberal discourse recognises that democracy cannot easily be spread by force and from outside, this very recognition affirms the possibility and even necessity that the nondemocratic (or insufficiently democratic) regimes will be able to achieve democracy in the future by an internal development" (Güven 2015, 2). This "internal development" is supported from both inside and outside by the lessons of history implied in Holocaust memory at its juncture with human rights. Güven goes on to claim that democracy (both as a policy discourse and a body of knowledge) is, in that sense, a form of domination in that it "functions as a tool to colonise the future of thinking as well as the political imagination" as it is presented as something without any alternative: "One cannot think of an alternative to democracy because democracy occupies the space of thinking the alternative, it occupies the possibility of any alternative, 'alternatively' as such"

(Güven 2015, 3–4). What Güven describes sounds similar to Frantz Fanon's criticism of the limitation of "human possibility" as well as Quijano's assessment of a colonisation of the imaginary, which they identified as being at the core of the Euro-modern project. Samuel Moyn (2014) voices a similar concern in his specific coupling of human rights and Holocaust memory, which not only hinders alternative imaginings but even risks rendering them dangerous and prone to slipping into violence. These observations are clearly pertinent to the topic of this book, because they first of all point to a regime of truth surrounding democracy and the right way to live and to govern societies that underpins many public memory endeavours. Secondly, they gesture in a similar direction to Luis Eslava's (2018) finding that tolerance and democracy education function as a form of indirect rule precisely because they perpetuate the coloniality of knowing, of being, and of envisioning the future. In doing so, the constellation of memory I have referred to in this book also helps to limit alternative visions for the future.

The human rights project and its humanitarianism are grounded in suppositions about the individualism of life itself without any possibility of wider political change. Humanitarianism in general and memory work in particular, when based on human rights, claim the right to intervene and to speak on behalf of those who are suffering and voiceless, and to teach those not-yet-citizens how to become "better". Humanitarian government has replaced anti-capitalist and anti-racist politics by defending the principles of human rights that rely on the depoliticisation of conflict, while the deployment of representations of the past helps to carve out the often oversimplified prototypes of good and evil. It is in this realm, I argue, that memory is a means of government aimed at what Michel Foucault has called the "conduct of conduct" of individuals and even entire populations for the purpose of keeping the global colonial matrix of power intact.

Yet despite this overall pessimistic assessment, I would like to close this section with a question: in the field of tension described above, are the predefined lessons that ought to be learned from the past for the future too tangled up with global governmantality and its single story, or is it still possible to apply them pluriversally? I ask this question because I do not want to conclude that one form of memory is better or more legitimate than another, or that one lesson is more relevant; rather, I would like to suggest that we gain an understanding of how memory politics risk contributing to the project of colonising the political imagination, even where their aim is to contribute to a more just world. That the very same memory, however, also has the potential to contribute to very different horizons of hope, will be the subject of my final chapter.

9 The Museum of Doubt: A Thought Experiment

> The choice that we have is not between remembering and forgetting; because forgetting can't be done by an act of will, it is not something we can choose to do. The choice is between different ways of remembering [...]. Memory does not always bear fruit and may even lead us astray. If we treat the past as holy, we exclude it from the world of meaning and prevent it from teaching lessons that might apply to other times and places, to other agents of history. (Todorov 2003, 311)

This chapter is, as its title suggests, a thought experiment more than a strictly analytical chapter. It is dedicated to an aspect of Holocaust memory that has so far only been mentioned in passing, which the quotation above sums up beautifully: the potential of memory to stir disobedience. In all of the materials and spaces which I have examined for this study, it was not only the "fruit" that Holocaust memory is supposed to "bear" which was clearly defined but often even the motivations for memorialisation. These unambiguous lessons could, however, be contradicted by pointing to the capacity of memory to "lead us astray". Thus, if we choose "different ways of remembering", if we allow memory to take us to unexpected places and into unfamiliar times, it has the power to create new relations and to offer alternative lessons – a view which I would now like to propose in regard to Holocaust memory.

In 1988, Holocaust survivor and historian Yehuda Elkana published an article in the Israeli newspaper *Ha'aretz,* in which he shared his thoughts on the state of Holocaust memory and "the need to forget", writing, "It may be that it is important for the world at large to remember. I am not even sure about that, but in any case, it is not our problem. Every nation, including the Germans, will decide their own way and on the basis of their own criteria, whether they want to remember or not" (Elkana 1988, para 4). In his article, Elkana criticises the use of politically motivated references to the Shoah to justify present policies. He emphasises the need for Holocaust education but finds that it is only appropriate "in the right political setting". He does not explain what he means by this, but he does point out that the lessons of the Holocaust can be interpreted in different ways, and that these interpretations relate back to the "political setting" in which they are evoked. This point is crucial because the conditions of today's uniform memory education need to be understood in the context of global governmentality, which only allows one specific interpretation of history instead of the various forms of memory so hopefully proposed by Todorov in the quotation above. This dominant version of memory education proved Elkana wrong about memory being a separate matter for "every nation", for it transformed into a "universal frame of reference" (Fracapane and Haß 2014, 10), neither had his

https://doi.org/10.1515/9783110788044-011

call to carefully consider the political context been heard. Instead, the standardised modes of memorialisation and their future-oriented teachings raised Holocaust memory to a position of exclusiveness that differentiates it from "the world of meaning" (Todorov 2003, 311). Some (like Dirk Moses in 2021), even argue that the memory of the Holocaust is being treated as something holy and protected as such. Still, as I have learned during and through my research, "the Holocaust spills over into non-Western spaces" and ensures "[...] that the metropolitan and colonial memorial landscapes are much more deeply imbricated with each other [...]" than public discourse on Holocaust memory often suggests (Phillips Casteel 2019, 261). However, I do not want to simply reiterate insights into the relationality of memory (Rothberg 2009) here, nor point once again to anti-colonial thinkers and how they make sense of the Holocaust (Césaire 2000). Instead, I would like to explore the possibilities of Holocaust memory being rewired, reconnected "to the world of meaning" – a concept which I propose from now on to use in the plural as *worlds* of meaning – in ways that are not just hegemonial. Thus, memory might put forward different knowledges and alternative horizons of hope than the ones examined in the previous chapters.

Moreover, in a rather unorthodox manner, this last section before my overall conclusion is an attempt to respond to one of the most frequent questions I was asked during my research: if you are so critical of dominant memory politics, then what is *your* suggestion? And even though I at first did not dare to even imagine myself responding to this challenge, I increasingly began pondering it myself, revisiting the writings of those who had already offered alternative, less agreeable approaches to Holocaust memory. These accounts, so I began to realise, could point me towards what could be done in addition to or even instead of the current practices of memorialisation that I found to be so deeply entangled with governmental techniques. I let my mind wander in this direction, because even though I saw the dominant memory politics which I encountered during my research in a rather critical way, I was nonetheless convinced that Holocaust memory does indeed have the potential to help make this world a better place – if we allow ourselves to think beyond the one particular "fruit" we want it to bear, beyond absolute lessons and answers, and instead become more sceptical, earnestly doubtful again. Similarly, I would like to explore how this alternative mode of memorialisation might be realised within a museum space. The question of how to make the museum – an institution historically bound up with the emergence of the European nation state and its eighteenth-century notion of the public sphere – relevant to the global conditions that shape the direction it takes is central to many contemporary museums' missions to decolonise. Inspired by this critical juncture in the historical trajectory of the museum's role and prompted by my own findings, this last chapter therefore gestures towards a visionary (and perhaps unrealistic) museum in a democracy still to come (Derrida 2005).

I approach these multiple yet interlinked issues through an imaginary place which I want to call *the Museum of Doubt*. This museum attempts to emphasise gaps[1] and cracks, as Georges Didi-Huberman (2012) identifies them in his intriguing volume *Images in Spite of All*. Such openings are inherent in each museum, like the gap between objects and interpretations, or the gap between image and language that serves to create a sense of distance in order to produce "objective" knowledge and to divide "us" from "others". Cracks and tears are moreover intrinsic to all objects but not represented as such and instead concealed in order for the objects to appear cohesive, as is the rupture between the present and the past – a rupture which tends to be inhabited by difficult issues and attempts to tame them. By emphasising gaps and other potential pathways within the museum, I also want to underscore the value of a decolonial agenda and ask how we are to rethink and rework the vexed relationship between what are often contested histories, local citizens and global publics on the one hand, and the existing tensions between the commonly expected narrative form of an exhibition and the expectations of its audiences on the other. Accordingly, I will explore how a museum might dislocate and reinvent its spaces and memorial practices in uneven contexts when the aim to generate certainty and bring about closure is less opaque, and where the freedom required for objects and histories to travel, to lay open their cracks, and hence to pluriversify is less restricted. Yet this chapter is not so much about a general utopian vision for the museum as it is about different possibilities of engaging with the Holocaust which could be fostered by or in the Museum of Doubt. For the purpose of outlining such alternative approaches to Holocaust memory (Karn 2012) in our current times and their political order, I would like to turn to various thinkers, some but not all of them survivors of the Holocaust or their descendants, to derive from their ideas the notion of uncertainty and doubt, which "my" museum foregrounds.

From doubt to certainty and back to doubt again

The feeling of rupture caused by the enormity of the Holocaust did not last – at least at the level of public memory. And while Walter Benjamin claimed that history disintegrates into images not stories and, due to the disruptive constella-

1 I would like to thank my colleague Olga Zabalueva for making me aware of the gaps.

tions of these images, can never be fully historicised (Khatib 2017), the power that narrativising the past can nonetheless unfold has become clear in my case studies. This is because narrative not only determines which pictures are framed and eventually become constitutive of the storyline but also how to describe them to those who cannot see them. In regard to Saul Friedländer's *Nazi Germany and the Jews*, Hayden White (2016) comes to the conclusion that Friedländer, unlike many other Holocaust historians and memory entrepreneurs, attempts to create throughout his writings effects of "estrangement" and "disbelievability" in order to interrupt any "stability of the narrative" (White 2016, 55). Moreover, according to White, in Friedländer's writing "[t]he events of the Holocaust are not emplotted in order to suggest a discernible trajectory from the beginning to end that would allow some sense of satisfactory moral or ethical closure for the whole" (2016, 55). I would like to emphasise this observation once more, as it outlines a way of engaging with the Holocaust that is quite different from those that I have described and analysed in this book. The most obvious difference probably lies in the renunciation of a "moral or ethical closure" to the story of the Holocaust, most often delivered through a "stable", coherent narrative. In this sense, the foregrounding of rupture, instability and scepticism in response to genocide can be read in contrast to the consolidation of the post-war world in the name of liberal democracy underpinned by the legacy of the Enlightenment. Whereas the first approach complicates the single story about the worlds we inhabit, the latter, as we have seen, led to the rise of moral Holocaust remembrance in the name of human rights. Therefore, the questions that initially prompted the research that went into this book remain at its end: Do present-day memorialisations of the Holocaust still invite the feeling of being unsettled by its difficult knowledge, and, if not, why not? Or put differently, how did it become possible to draw lessons from this history that do not teach us to keep on asking questions but instead tend to convince us that the right answers have already been found?

I thus began pondering what happens to difficult histories once they are institutionally memorialised, say, in a museum or within a specific educational framework. Still, even though I might have found some of the answers to these questions during my research process – at least about *how* memory of the Holocaust came to be emplotted within the human rights paradigm, and to some degree also why this particular storyline is favoured over a less integrable account – my discomfort with the ways in which the Holocaust is sought out for reassurance did not cease but only increased further. Didi-Huberman, talking specifically about so-called authentic sites of Holocaust memory (in his example Auschwitz), notes the paradoxical transformation of a "place of barbarism" into a site of "culture" to which the process of museumisation has led (2017, 23).

Achille Mbembe writes about a similar paradox in regard to the figure of the slave and how its impact is rendered less troublesome once it is placed in a museum (2017b, 206–209). In the broadest sense, Mbembe argues that, once it is in a museum, once it has been turned into a public good and thus made consumable, the slave and all the histories and difficult knowledges connected to this figure lose their sting. Roger Simon, who himself curated exhibitions that intended to emphasise the *unconsumabilty* of the Holocaust, asserts in relation to the problem of public memory that

> truly public history [is] a history that gathers us together in that it relates and separates at the same time. On these terms, a public history is not about a common understanding of historical events and their significance. Rather, it proceeds from a relatively durable set of referents regarding the past, which provide the basis for conversations that render history as meaningful, setting terms for our understanding of current social life and its future possibilities. (Simon 2006, 188)

What I find most remarkable about his vision for a "truly public history" is the idea that it brings us closer together while at the same time also separating us. This would entail an acknowledgment of multiple histories or at least of different perspectives on the Holocaust, for example, or on slavery – an acknowledgement that dominant memory discourse does not grant. Instead, as has been discussed by scholars like Dan Diner (1996) and Natan Sznaider (2008), public memory (or history) most often aims to first reconcile potentially conflicting narratives about the past in order to then achieve reconciliation on the level of society and even beyond. However, this way of unifying different, even oppositional perspectives on difficult pasts necessarily neglects the voices of those who do not want to reconcile and move on towards a shared future, because "no single beneficiary can be said to be capable of rendering the full meaning and significance of this testament [the history of the Holocaust]. The legacy made from this inheritance will always be in need of renewal and will forever be incomplete" (Simon 2006, 195).

In this sense, Simon suggests that we understand Holocaust memory not simply as a burden that might continue to cause conflict but, in a more optimistic sense, as a "terrible gift". By this he means that inherent in Holocaust memory is knowledge which is "difficult to bear" and which thus, as I would add, leaves us with a sense of uncertainty, a feeling of puzzlement and confusion with regard to "sometimes long-held beliefs about the world and our place within it" (Dean and Failler 2019, 5). This uncertainty ultimately relates to the notion of doubt that I would like to evoke in my imaginary museum, which tries to avoid universalisation as much as closure and instead emphasises the impossibility of stitching the images of history into one coherent narrative. In this sense, the potential for thinking and curating museum spaces and history differently that is apparent in both Benjamin's and White's observations can be related back to the aforementioned gaps, in particular to the gap between image and language. If we lay open this gap, make it visible, the Museum of Doubt might actually become a space in which histories are allowed, even encouraged to disintegrate.

Struggles for memory and the irritation of time

Even though the prominent position which Holocaust memory holds today might suggest otherwise, it took decades of labour to establish memorial sites, museums, educational programmes and days of remembrance to commemorate the victims of the Holocaust, let alone the commitment to restitution or the payment of so-called "reparations" (Diner 1996; Gallas 2013; Wüstenberg 2017). The first instances of Holocaust memory were assembled under the most adverse circumstance: during the genocide itself, for example, in the Warsaw Ghetto by Emanuel Ringelblum and the activist of Oneg Shabt, with artefacts of Jewish life the ghetto and evidence of the horrific crimes smuggled all the way to Palestine by Zionist youth (Shalev 2002); or even in the killing centres, by prisoners who risked their lives to collect and hide evidence of their existence and experiences (Didi-Huberman 2012). In the immediate postwar years, when the first survivors began to give testimony (Roth and Maxwell 2001) and soldiers from the Allied forces were reporting about what they had seen as they liberated Europe from the Nazis and their many collaborators (Abzug 1994), the struggle for the dignified memorialisation of the Holocaust continued despite these accounts. Instead of listening to the voices of the survivors, Holocaust memory was considered dangerous and potentially harmful to peace processes, nation-building and the reestablishment of an international order (Linenthal 2001; Diner 2007b; Sznaider 2008). To many survivors and descendants of the victims of the Shoah, the scale of its horror forbade any integration of its events into a historical narrative (Postone 2005). For philosopher and political theorist Hannah Arendt (1972), for example, the Shoah was unforgivable and not something that could ever be atoned for because, for her, it had destroyed any future possibility of "plurality", by which she meant a world in which every human being could live regardless of difference or similarity, a world that cherishes the plurality of all humans. The murderous practices of the Nazis had ultimately denied Jews, Sinti, Roma and all others who were deemed "unworthy of living" the opportunity to become part of humanity and therefore part of this world. Thus, for Arendt and for the philosopher Vladimir Jankélévitch (2004), for example, it would be impossible to ever peacefully share a world with the Nazi perpetrators again, despite any utterances of remorse or even apologies. Their calls for the right to resentment (Améry 1970) stand proxy for all the claims voiced in regard to the Shoah that demand rupture.

Author Jean Améry, who was persecuted as a Jew and for being a member of the Belgian Résistance, for which he was eventually deported to camps like Auschwitz, published a series of essays in the 1960s. One of these is his essay "Ressentiment", written in 1966 in response to a journey through Germany which Améry had made shortly before. On this trip, he had been forced to realise that, in Germany, about twenty years after its defeat, life was flourishing once again and no one seemed to want to know anything about the war anymore, let alone the Shoah (Améry 1970, 77). This made him aware of how deep a resentment he was harbouring, which was explicitly directed at the perpetrators of the Nazi regime but also more generally at the Germans of the present, who were striving for normality and seemed to face their past with relative indifference (Améry 1980, 62–65; Heyd 2004, 189). In particular, the feeling that Germany was acting as if it had already done enough penance for its crimes of the National Socialist era caused Améry the greatest unease: "I feel uncomfortable in this peaceful, lovely land, inhabited by hardworking, efficient, and modern people." (Améry 1980, 63). Germany had moved on, was once again stable in the centre of Europe, and only "we, the victims, will appear as the truly incorrigible, irreconcilable one" (1980, 80). Drawing explicitly on his own experiences, Améry writes from a subjective position and adopts a personal tone which makes it difficult to proceed from his individual moral stance towards the Germans towards a more universal "ethics of resentment" (Heyd 2004).

Nevertheless, Améry's concept of resentment does not conform to what people usually seem to think about the value of forgiveness in the name of progress, namely, the expectation that the perpetrators are absolved of their guilt in order to re-establish them as respectable members of society, to exert a supposedly therapeutic, healing influence on the victims and to make reconciliation possible for society as a whole (Zolkos 2007, 26). However, for Améry, and with him many other survivors of the Holocaust, forgiveness is something that cannot be granted. Forgiveness against the background of the Shoah is an impossibility for him, something which he claims is "hostile to history" (Améry 1980, 78). It was unbearable to him that the traces of defeat in the Germany he later experienced had been erased, and he would rather have seen Germany still in ruins. Too quickly, Germany had stopped being the "potato field of Europe" (1980, 65) that Améry would have liked it to remain for much longer, and so, it is not surprising that he reaches the verdict that looking towards the future helps perpetrators above all. The resentment that Améry continues to harbour against these forward-looking Germans fulfils the task of making "the crime [...] a moral reality for the criminal, so that he is pulled into the reality of his misdeed", and in this sense, resentment "blocks the exit to [...] the future" (Améry 1980, 68). This is a seldom-heard perspective, which instantly reminds us of the effect of the historical operation that denies any ongoing impact of the past in the present. Améry's disobedient views have special pertinence for the Museum of Doubt and serve as a contrast to the memory politics I have focused on in the previous chapters, because, as Magdalena Zolkos puts it in regard to transitional justice mechanisms as a manifestation of the historical operation:

> Amery's resentment "upsets time" and the neat division into the past, present and future that the "transitional justice" project strives to achieve. The performative force of resentment disallows the experience of victimhood to be grasped and contained in the distant narratives of the past and insists on invoking the experience in the political now. (Zolkos 2007, 29)

Therefore, blocking "the exit into the future", which means interrupting history's presumably progressive flow, can be understood as an antidote to the politics of the historical operation in general and of the human rights project's utilisation of historic lessons from the Holocaust in particular. Consequently, another key aspect of the Museum of Doubt is that it confounds the clear-cut distinction between past, present and future, and hence foregrounds narratives that "upset time".

Harbouring "self-mistrust": Disruptive memory in a (post-) human rights era

The mirror-image to Améry's notion of resentment is what he called "self-mistrust" (1980, 77). In his view, harbouring a reflexive self-mistrust could lead to the constant, critical reflection on personal involvement in the violence of National Socialism that he demanded from every German, no matter the generation. This self-mistrust, as Améry claims, is necessary in order to resist the logic of progress and its promise of redemption. Thus, it will only be when self-mistrust is internalised by all Germans and their collaborators that resentment will become obsolete. In this sense, memory, which includes even the most disturbing and least digestible aspects of the Holocaust should be evoked as such, not merely to shock those who learn about this difficult knowledge (Failler et al. 2015, 100) but precisely to keep intact the self-mistrust which each beneficiary of histories and realities of violence should maintain. In this way, mistrusting oneself also becomes a means to *not* simply move on, something that forbids any easy exit towards the future and instead remains as an acknowledgement of the past's presence.

What I find particularly fascinating about these two concepts, resentment and self-mistrust, is how they speak to the different positionalities of victims and perpetrators (and also bystanders) of violence and, specifically, of the Holocaust. Améry grasps the distinct responsibly of the perpetrators and their descendants in contrast to that of the victims – not only concerning memory but also as an ongoing, unevenly held duty to improve our nonetheless shared world. Taking this thoughtful differentiation into account, the Museum of Doubt will emphasise two additional interrelated issues: how to engage with the past in all its messiness and encourage people to dare to question everything, including ourselves and the principles on which our self-image and our societies are built. In this way, memory might actually contribute to more pluriversal utopian thinking, which cannot do without the notion of uncertainty and the courage to doubt, and thereby relates to three main characteristics which make up the definition of the "utopia": the utopia is something unknown or even impossible; it should include everyone and serve everyone (though this does not necessarily mean that it has to be universal); and, lastly, it implies the thorough criticism of the society of which it desires to take leave (Mannheim 1936).[2] It has, in other words, a critical energy that politically evaluates the society of which it sees itself as a counter-project. In this sense, the human rights project cannot be utopian, even if it were "as shared as the sky", simply because it lacks the notion of insufficiency and self-criticism. As Michele Tedeschini writes,

> [W]hile it may be true that a world in which everyone enjoys the whole set of recognised human rights is, in a very general and colloquial sense, utopian; it does not seem to be accurate, even in that general sense (and despite their alleged universal character), to depict human-rights discourse as a utopia – be it the last utopia, a realistic one, or otherwise. Utopianism is more appropriately described as a critically informed imaginative exercise. (Tedeschini 2019, 14)

The human rights project, however, is very much about policies and interventions, and not so much a critical endeavour, let alone an "informed imaginative exercise". What is more, human rights are closely tied to ventures for reconciliation, which are far too seldom about critically assessing political conditions and instead about superficially harmonising potential conflicts. Taking this into consideration, can claims for peace and reconciliation be at all legitimate in our time, which some are already characterising as the post-human rights age? If

2 This is of course only one of many definitions of "utopia" and does not make the often-heard distinction between "concrete" and "abstract" utopias that, e.g., Ernst Bloch suggests.

we view "the demand for peace and reconciliation against a background of continuing injustice and inequality", these issues become even more pressing, as Bevernage cautions (2019, 82).

The Museum of Doubt therefore tries to do without affirming harmony or a sense of "righting wrongs", because

> [a]ll that seems possible to surmise is that the redressing work of Human Rights must be supplemented by an education that can continue to make unstable the presupposition that the reasonable righting of wrongs is inevitably the manifest destiny of groups – unevenly class-divided, embracing North and South – that remain poised to right them; and that, among the receiving groups, wrongs will inevitably proliferate with unsurprising regularity. (Spivak 2004, 530)

On the contrary, the Museum of Doubt is premised on the conviction that morality should never be normative. Moreover, difference it not approached for the conflict it is supposedly prone to cause but rather envisaged in the way Nigerian novelist and thinker Chimamanda Ngozi Adichi suggests, serving the purpose of making "difference ordinary" and "normal", attempting "not to attach value to difference", because "difference is the reality of our world" (2017, 56). Accordingly, the Museum of Doubt will refrain from evoking the sense that anyone is better, more knowing or morally superior to anyone else, or for any other reason the one who will right wrongs and is therefore "the end product of history" (Spivak 2004, 532). Quite the contrary: in the context of self-mistrust and doubt, normalising difference means destabilising hierarchies of identity and knowing, and instead favouring a multitude of identities and voices with equal value. On the practical side, this entails the explicit inclusion of disruptive voices who, like Améry, Arendt, Sholem, Jankélévitch and many other Holocaust survivors and Jewish thinkers, simply do not subscribe to the idea that their singular experiences of the Holocaust can or should be transcended and transformed into a universal human rights paradigm. Speaking more generally, efforts made to realise equality will ask that everyone "engage in the systematic and critical study of indigenous forms of knowledge" (Serequeberhan 2009, 4), which might make the criticism expressed by someone like Améry even more complicated and, furthermore, open up room for discussions that go beyond the limits of liberal democracy and its single story (Gilroy 2010).

The Museum of Doubt is therefore about posing questions as much as it is about learning from an inexhaustible pool of possible answers, not in order to eventually single out the best and most comfortable answer but with the aim of fostering constant dialogue. In this way, the Museum of Doubt will serve as a reminder that there are many ways towards equality, even though some might cause feelings of discomfort for those who are still benefitting from the hierarchies that structure our worlds. While being deeply inclined towards liberatory ideas, the museum will nonetheless never be able to know about all of the struggles taking place for a more just present, nor about all of the existing visions for better futures, and it thus nourishes the notion of incompleteness, of being a never-ending project with many changing horizons of hope. So, is the Museum of Doubt a place of memory education? In my view, yes. However, it is one that is aware that "the only possible way in which education can live up to the promises of democracy is through becoming hospitable in its openness to the other [...]. The other is that which is outside our *logos*, it is that which cannot be grasped, and is therefore incalculable" (Friedrich 2014, 121). For this reason, education should not be prescriptive, which means that it should not insist on being able to grasp everything, especially what is not our own experience, let alone on being able to translate it into a greater narrative of universal meaning. At the same time, we need to be cautious about attaching too much value to experiences, as these are the result of having attached too much meaning to difference earlier on, of having created, for instance, "races" in the plural for the purpose of differentiating between different degrees of humanness on the basis of a scientifically untenable logic of biology and culture (Dladla 2017). It is only through this differentiation that certain experiences are brought into being; hence, the Museum of Doubt will be careful to listen to and learn from experiences without naturalising them in any sense (Scott 1992).

Not upholding fixed identities or human categories, not subscribing to a single morality, nor one supposedly best vision for the future is therefore, in a way, the most frightening part of the Museum of Doubt, because it invites not just uncertainty about the lessons of the Holocaust to take the stage but also a much more general sense of not-knowing. Despite this anxiety about being unsure, "it is a quest from the known to the patently unknown, which raises epistemological questions and their relationship to ontological ones [sic!]. In short, the contingent elements of human existence mean building a world of possibility, which means what we know also offers a path to many things we at this point cannot know" (Bragato and Gordon 2018, 3). On that account, embracing the unknown is exactly how the Museum of Doubt, with its focus on the "terrible gift" of Holocaust memory, might contribute to imagining different, maybe better horizons of hope, and in this sense to letting the future be governed a little less. It might, by emphasising gaps and inconsistencies, also help to decolonise the imaginary in the sense that it wishes to contribute to the project of articulating and disseminating a "non-colonial worldview" (Allen-Paisant 2020, 3) which casts doubt on the pillars of Western epistemology. One of the focuses central to this counter-hegemonial philosophy is "a more liquid conception of time, place/space, things, and persons that would transcend the epistemological paradigms of Western modernity" (Allen-Paisant 2020, 3).

The impossibilities of a Museum of Doubt

At the outset of this book, I suggested that the increase in visitors numbers at Holocaust-related memorial sites can be explained by the way they promise reassurance and that visitors will find themselves on the "right side" of history. This leads me to infer that many people do not want or like to be unsettled, not by history nor by our current realities either. The Museum of Doubt will thus most probably attract only very few visitors, will not receive much, if any, funding and, aside from these practical issues, will not ever realise its claim to incompleteness and dedication to the unknown within the institutional setting of a museum. And maybe that is for the best, at least for now. However, there are visionary ideas for the museum to be found that go beyond the usual institutional framework, that attempt to leave behind the colonial gaze and avoid luring visitors towards defined ends. In this regard, critical museum scholars are discussing "the very idea of a museum, its political sense, the outbreak of its function [...] as a space for the accumulation of heritage and the construction of an official account of history" and thereby envisioning "[a] museum beyond itself, overflowing, capable of harboring rituals, inhabited by improper uses and festive modes" (Longoni 2020, qtd. in Dàvila-Freire 2020, 106).

At this point, I am not sure how a museum can actually go "beyond itself", though the motif of something that is "overflowing" is very appealing, and I imagine it in relation to the many histories that will come together in the Museum of Doubt and truly make it a "contact zone" (Clifford 1997) ready for quarrels and continuous negotiations of meaning. If, however, the Museum of Doubt were to become a reality, I would like it to be a place that not only exceeds itself but also continuously undermines its own essence as a commanding institution for civic education. Instead, it should become a transparent, porous, self-reflective and self-mistrusting space from which not one but many, maybe even contradictory lessons of history may be learned. But do we really want to realise the Museum of Doubt? Could it keep its promise to *not* foster closure if it were to become its own entity, which, after all, would still need to play by the rules of global capitalism and could always only partially (if at all) free itself from neoliberal rationale? Maybe it could function as an intervention into existing museum spaces that is constantly reworked and tweaked like the Museum of Canadian Human Rights Violations.

In this way, the Museum of Doubt might maintain its potential to unsettle long-held beliefs in the norms of liberal democracy precisely because it remains, at least partially, an impossibility. As such, by building on incompleteness, the Museum of Doubt might, at least for a moment, undo what Fanon identified as a core feature of "the oppressor's culture", which secures the colonial status, because it makes "[...] even dreams of liberty impossible for the native" (2001, 73). The Museum of Doubt wants to open up possibilities for new and old aspirations to become imaginable again, for dreams of liberation. The more I think about it, the more I see the potential of an incomplete museum, because only in its non-realisation will it add to forms of memorialisation that contribute to a democracy still to come. For, as Roger Simon beautifully puts it,

> "democracy" is the name given to a social order which declares its historicity and its perfectibility while carrying an understanding of its never-ending inadequacy and thus the recognition that its full realization is always still to come. Understood as such, democracy requires forms of remembrance that help open up existing relations to continual critique and the difficult (and often conflicted) work of repair, renewal and re-invention of desirable institutions. This work can be supported by taking on the pedagogical possibilities and risks inherent in the recognition of and response to the incommensurable character of the historical experience of others. (Simon 2006, 188)

This passage could be used to describe a memory and museum practice that challenge visitors to accept the loss of what is familiar and recognisably reassuring in order to make them consider the prospect of remembering and living differently. This vision is similar to the way that Torodorov thinks about the different possibilities of remembering in the quotation with which I began this chapter. After all, it is exactly this "still to come", with its open ends and constant demand for new relations, to which I believe Holocaust memory has the ability to contribute if it can be disentangled from the human rights project and its morally charged narrative devices.

However, the imaginative experiment of the Museum of Doubt has, for now, already achieved its purpose if readers, during their next visit to a conventional memorial museum, find themselves searching for the unsettling, the unknown; if they actively dare to doubt and thereby confirm the constructively disruptive potential of Holocaust memory (and the memory of violence more generally) – a memory that, with less emplotment, opens up new ways of understanding and envisioning the world(s) we live in and can thus foster "politics of anticipation" (Dhawan 2018), rather than projects of knowing.

10 Towards Pluriversal Memory: A Conclusion

After imagining the Museum of Doubt and its purpose of resisting closure, it now seems almost wrong to conclude this research project, which of course has many findings to offer and has also given rise to a number of new questions that have yet to be answered. I originally set out on my investigation with the intention of probing the assumption that exhibitions and global educational programmes dedicated to the Holocaust are increasingly being designed to foster the core values of liberal democracy and aim to create a sense of widely shared responsibility for one's own society as well as for humanity as a whole. In order to grasp the global dimensions of this trend, I chose to study sites of memory – more precisely, museums – which are located on different continents and which build on a historical conscience in order to advocate for a more just world. The museums I examined all see themselves as human rights museums and, at the same time, focus on representations of the Holocaust, though each to a different extent. I was unfortunately only able to conduct research at three museums, one in Nuremberg, Germany, one in Winnipeg, Canada, and one in Johannesburg, South Africa. As well as their specific museological approach, what all three museums also have in common is their location in countries that have a history of systematised racial segregation (either because of different variations of settler colonialism or because of National Socialism), even leading to distinct forms of genocide in Germany and Canada. My case-study-based investigation sought to determine the extent to which and the manner in which the Holocaust-human rights nexus takes shape within the particular space of these human rights museums. I paid special attention to a new global citizenship ideal that posits historical literacy, looking at difficult pasts, as the best foundation for active participation in society. This focal point raised the questions of if and how this ideal is brought into being where Holocaust memory and human rights discourse intersect and how the narratives that have produced this ideal turn these museums into conveyers of a specific behavioural norm. Inspired by Mieke Bal and Hayden White, I looked at the *narratives* of exhibitions and paid special attention to the narrative strategies they employ as well as any emotions they evoke in order to extract how the Holocaust is "emplotted" within each of the museum's overarching storylines. The next step was to discuss whether the production and dissemination of a normative idea of the citizen-subject turns the mnemonic practices found in and around the museums into techniques of government (in the Foucauldian sense).

What this study was, unfortunately, unable to examine was visitors' points of view, which would have been a valuable addition to the material I collected

https://doi.org/10.1515/9783110788044-012

and analysed. By this I mean that I did not engage with the visitors to the respective museums or with any other participants in global Holocaust memory education, though this side of the "coin" should not be neglected in any more comprehensive attempts to grasp the forms and functions of Holocaust memorialisation in human rights museums – including their effects on the individual. Nevertheless, in order to learn as much as possible from my empirical material, I concentrated on understanding the specifics of each museum in its societal context. My comparative analysis of the case studies then served to draw out larger underlying themes that helped to illuminate memory's functions in light of governmentality and the global colonial matrix of power.

Thus, in the course of my investigation, I demonstrated how the Holocaust-human rights nexus has the capacity to influence the conduct of citizens, their desires for themselves and others, as well as the ways in which they engage in society. By approaching this aspect of the nexus from the analytical perspective of governmentality, I was able to emphasise that this specific constellation of memory must be understood as part of what Foucault and others have called technologies of the self and therefore as an integral part of governmental rationale and the ways in which it is promulgated. Consequently, I argued that all public memory can, in this broader context of governmental rationalities, be understood as a means of government itself. In this way, I simultaneously showed the potential that an analysis of memory undertaken from the perspective of governmentality has for providing an important diagnosis of our time(s) and political conditions, and for illuminating how these are derived from narratives about the past. As maintained so persuasively by Foucault and many of the scholars who have followed him, power can best be grasped in terms of specific practices, and I suggest that one such practice is memory (conceived of as something you do rather than simply have).

Present-day neoliberal subjects are controlled through their freedom, and the reason I claim that the constellation of memory discussed here is an important feature of this specific mechanism of power is because of its "moralization of the consequences of this freedom" (Brown 2003, 44). By this I mean that the turn to Holocaust memory has become a tool to moralise the consequences of "ill-handled" freedoms, of "wrong" choices, and to urge every subject and citizen to instead consider these consequences and make conscious decisions in accordance with society's norms. Herein lies the highly political nature of this form of memorialisation that I have been tracing throughout this book. And while it might have sounded paradoxical at first to critically examine modes of empowerment and moral education in the name of tolerance when we are moving towards a post-human rights age, it should by now have become clear that even emphasising the need for active global citizenship in the name of human rights is a form of government that is deeply entangled with current neoliberal rationality, a specific form that, though it proclaims otherwise, does not intend to fundamentally change the worlds we live in but instead functions to keep us in line so that we do not, one day, turn to "rebellion" – as it was put in the Universal Declaration of Human Rights.

The paradox of Holocaust memory education

Overall, what I have discussed in this book is the result of a line of thought closely entwined with the paradox of universality, with globalised lessons for humanity and the specific role they allocate to the past – a past thought of as the natural product of the linear flow of time. Part of this episteme is the universalisation of one single time frame and the influence its coloniality has on the imaginary, meaning on "modes of signification" and more generally, on aspirations in the present and for the future (Quijano 2007, 169). Today, liberal democracy – towards which supposedly underdeveloped nations can progress in the same manner as the subject can progress towards becoming a rational and hence responsible citizen – is identified as the most universal aspiration in politics. The link between these two aspects and the analysis that I have pursued here is twofold: first of all, forms of memorialisation and performances of public memory do not work without the "historical operation", meaning the way in which history is represented to make the present appear "better", i.e., more progressive, than the past that we look back to (de Certeau 1988; Scott 2020). Secondly, what makes public memory a highly political endeavour is not only the questions of representation it implies but also its entanglements with modes of prescriptive visions for the future, and thus the imaginary.

Public memory and the upsurge of "moral remembrance" (David 2020, 41) in museums is part and parcel of a globally imposed "European culture" and its liberal democratic governmentality. As such, this governmentality is understood as a discourse composed of various institutions, from so-called civil society to the implementation of laws as tactics (Foucault 1971), with the more recent governmental rationale aimed at transforming highly disruptive economic conflicts and political forms of disorder into quasi-technical or moral problems for social administration. What is more, political rationality conditions our socio-political contexts and constitutes the subjects of which a population comprises. If certain societies or parts of their populations are not conceived of as democratic, there is always the familiar "yet" at the end of the sentence, i.e., if they work hard enough and free themselves from older (undemocratic) allegiances, they might *yet* reach the desired state of liberal democracy and democratic citizenship.

While this logic had already been productive of different forms of colonialism, culminating in the proclaimed "white man's burden" to bring law and order as well as morality to the colonies (Narain 2020), new forms of indirect rule, or more precisely, of impinging upon the aspirations of supposedly less democratic subjects and states, are now being exercised through practices of memorialisation (and by other means). In this vein, pedagogy was, and as my study shows, often still is employed with the purpose of "enlighten[ing]" and "empower[ing]" the "othered" subject in line with "the norm" of Euro-modernity that has claimed the universal position of humanity for itself (Chatterjee 2012). As Ayça Çubukçu notes about these practices of education, "Here, as elsewhere, pedagogical violence was to be received by insufficiently proper humans – who lacked Christianity, civilization, culture, rationality or the correct ideology – as a gift of love, a violent yet redemptive and liberatory love for the development of (their) humanity" (Çubukçu 2017, 263). Therefore, if one seeks to understand the implications of techniques of governmentality such as memory that target future horizons of hope, it is key to look at the coloniality of dominant imaginaries that strengthen "the single story" (Andreotti 2016) and reject pluriversality. By relating the decolonial critique of the Euro-modern conception of the "human being" back to the research conducted for this book, the position of "the citizen" comes to mind once again. Like the rationale described by Çubukçu (2017), which inevitably entails "pedagogical violence" in order to bring potential humans closer to realising their prospects, "citizen" status, too, is still reserved for supposedly mature and morally credible people (Gordon 2008).

This analytical viewpoint therefore further illuminates how the colonial past and some of its practices are still alive in the present, as popular politics remain fractured by the issues of who is a citizen, who can rightfully belong and hence how to govern the citizen-subject. It was in this field of tension that I found Holocaust memory education to be a subfield of human rights education, which is itself a contested area for the dissemination and articulation of different forms of knowledge (Keet 2017), and ultimately an exercise of power. Therefore, as my research shows, even though the linkage between public Holocaust memory and the human rights project is presented as neutral in terms of ideology and, what is more, even as highly beneficial for the members of the "global community", it also functions as a technique of government. On this note, I argued that, in a specific constellation and most vividly when the Holocaust is memorialised for the tolerance and respect for human rights that its memory is expected to engender, we find a storyline that makes no reference to any kind of (global) power relations at work in our current worlds, including the actual perpetrators, beneficiaries and victims of the conflicts that still characterise our age.

Interestingly, in the museums which I examined, this seems to hold true even when the exhibitions are nuanced, rich in content and historically accurate. The reason that this general impression of an oversimplified narrative nonetheless remains is the morally charged closure that all three museums attempt to facilitate, pointing us in the direction of universal human rights instead of leaving us unsettled and full of the resulting questions in the way that the Museum of Doubt does. That museums as institutions of authority are prone to providing us with answers, not questions, adds even more weight to the lessons we are expected to learn from the Holocaust in human rights museums. Even sites such as the JHGC, which intend to foster dialogue and not simply provide predefined, "correct" responses to the past, cannot keep their promises, as the narrative of human rights only has one possible ending, which is liberal democracy.

This lack stimulates the future-oriented memorialisation of both the Holocaust and universal human rights, which takes the experience of the Holocaust, conceptualised as the worst genocide in history, as the point of departure for a better future in which human rights are fully respected. In this way, the dominant narrative about human rights that I have outlined in this book not only determines how those rights are articulated and understood but also consequently shapes the choices people make and the actions they take. Here, the rather new format of human rights museology only potentiates the traditional role of museums as devices of 'civilisation' established to educate the populace (Bennett 1995). This is because the development of supranational bodies and agencies such as the ICOM and the Federation of International Human Rights Museums, together with UNESCO and the IHRA, have shifted this mechanics onto a global level. In other words, if national museums were once established for the purpose of "representing national values and realities" (Knell and Aronsson 2010, 68), new, socially active "idea" museums are displaying (supposedly) universal values and realities to global publics and, moreover, telling them how to act on them, meaning that human rights museums serve even more explicitly to influence visitors' behaviour than museums with a weaker focus on the norms and values of society. The same can be said about the global educational programmes on citizenship that I analysed along with the museums. In most of these programmes, as in the museums themselves, the aim is "soft reform", which is underpinned by a hope for continuity. Only the JHGC gestures towards what Vanessa Andreotti (2014) calls "radical reform" – reform that does intend to change social conditions but nevertheless still hopes to fix the system from the inside, meaning without any intention of going beyond the notion of reform or looking for new possible interhuman relations, let alone utopian political ideas.

Thus, as has become apparent throughout this project, the Holocaust-human rights nexus nurtures certain norms and values, and consequently motivates citizens to behave in accordance with them, thereby ensuring their voluntary compliance to not go "beyond reform". I was therefore able to flesh out how the "urgency of memory" (Derrida 2001, 28) provides legitimacy to a particular form of government and, furthermore, to show how it narrates and hence authorises ideas about the future, thereby making memory as a technique of the self even more influential. In this sense, instead of acknowledging the many entanglements of Euro-modernity and liberal democracy with epistemic and ontological violence, and the many injustices caused by those who now claim a position at the forefront of peacekeeping and democratising missions, the interpretation of our worlds underlying the memory endeavours outlined here is far too simple and therefore tends to serve the purpose of securing the status quo instead of working towards real equity.

In this context, it is essential to pay close attention to memory education as a mechanism for conveying certain truths about the world (which it conceptualises in the singular) and for understanding that it does in fact matter who is educating whom, on the basis of what knowledge, and to what end. Accordingly, as said above, it has been another key aim of this book to raise awareness of how memory politics might uphold racial and colonial power structures, and how it contributes to the project of colonising the political imagination, even where its proclaimed goal is to help realise a more just world.

Broader political implications of the nexus

Relying on the memory of past atrocities as a point of reference from which to define a better world has become a common trope in both national and international politics. As a result, public memory of the Holocaust has gained a future-setting capacity that is especially pertinent in the largely uncontroversial lessons to be learned from the history of the Holocaust. These lessons, which I have discussed extensively throughout my case studies as well as in the eighth chapter, are often utilised to evoke moral sentiment in order to ensure more humane conduct. Thus, making long detours through historical disasters paves the way for emotionally charged future politics. What is more, in its linkage to human rights discourse, looking at the history of the Holocaust relegates atrocities and injustices to the past and therefore banishes them from the present. By following this logic, we run the risk of maintaining the structural oppression (re)produced in a still unjust age. This might be due to a complacency which is legitimised by the morally superior position of the human rights advocate, which makes it possible, for instance, that the descendants of the colonisers and settlers, and similarly the German descendants of Nazi perpetrators, can now give lessons in tolerance.

In other words, those who are in a position to claim that they are on the "right side of history" can once again act as teachers of both history and moral conduct, with consequences such as, to give but one example, refugees in Germany being accused of antisemitism – even though many studies show how antisemitic many Germans are themselves (Öztürk and Pickel 2021) – and not being accepted as new members of German society because they supposedly do not value democracy enough. In this example, the memory of the Holocaust, at the juncture with human rights discourse, has become a means of governing not only German citizens but also Germany's "others" – ignoring the fact that wherever there are conceptual "others", there is always domination and perceived supremacy, which should be rejected as alien to the memory of genocide and not disguised within it. Another reason that this specific form of memory might perpetuate injustices rather than resolve them is its fixation on the individual and, correspondingly, on the idea that "conflicting identities" are at the root of genocide. This oversimplification of conflict – which gives credence to the idea that historical narratives have the potential to harmonise as they supposedly have the power to form identity and serve as a bridge or unifier for difficult or even hostile relationships – contributes to the risk of singling out those individuals or even entire communities that are accused of holding on to undesired attitudes (such as the resentment of which Jean Améry speaks).

Thus, this book has not only drawn attention to the ways in which public memory runs the risk of becoming a mechanism of exclusion but has also shown that, in contrast to the Museum of Doubt, the memory politics produced at the crossroads with human rights advocacy have little in common with the once proclaimed ability of Holocaust memory (and the memory of violence in general) to deeply unsettle and call into question every core assumption of our contemporary political order. It does not pay attention to the rupture that philosophers such as Hannah Arendt, Jean Améry and Theodor W. Adorno emphasised in response to the Shoah. Moreover, the clear distinction made between the Nazi regime and European liberal democracies is challenged by the colonial history of those countries, with the decolonial critique of Western epistemology and its neocolonial practices also leading to a more sceptical attitude towards the legitimacy of the liberal democratic order and its demarcation of grievable and less grievable lives. For this reason, I would like to emphasise one last time that the production of knowledge about the past and therefore about visions for a better future is a way to exercise power, even though it is one that presents itself as a moral and not a political project.

In this regard, it would be very interesting to conduct further research into other mechanisms of power inherent in this specific constellation of memory, for example, with a stronger focus on security technologies. I am thinking of global NGOs that work in the field of genocide prevention and local initiatives like some actors in German civil society that engage in memory work as one way to prevent crime – primarily in connection with discourses on migration. Such issues relate to some of my deliberations in chapter 8 and would enrich them immensely, as I was, in the limited context of this book, only partly able to grasp the broader political implications of the Holocaust-human rights nexus. Similarly, though with a very different focus that does not primarily look at governmental means but at their contestation, a very interesting field of related research could turn out to be social justice movements and how they make sense of the history of genocides, how they include memory in their struggles: What narratives are employed in such explicitly political settings? Do they involve forms of moralisation? And what lessons, if any, are they trying to teach? Another possible direction in this regard would be investigating anti-democratic movements and how they make use of, for example, symbols from the Holocaust such as the yellow star in order to add weight to their claims of victimhood (most recently as the "victims" of anti-Covid measures and related vaccination campaigns). Various scholarly methodologies could be applied to approach some of these issues, from ethnographic studies based on interviews and participatory research to theory-based conceptual work such as discourse analysis. The field is far from exhausted.

I could go on and on suggesting follow-up questions for further investigation that could take my findings as a starting point, but in order to draw to a close, I would like to reiterate the hopeful notion to which this conclusion owes its title and which gestures towards a pluriversal memory. Despite the rather pessimistic assessment of dominant memory politics that I have focused on, the potential of memory that I have envisioned in relation to the Museum of Doubt should not be neglected in this conclusion. Rich in perspectives and stories, memory can lead in many different directions. Accordingly, as said above, I do not want to end by judging one form of memory to be better or more legitimate than another, or one lesson more relevant than the other, but would like to instead suggest that, while Holocaust memory politics risk contributing to the project of governing the future even where they aim to contribute to a more just world, they nonetheless still have the power to, as it was put so beautifully in the opening quote to chapter nine, lead us *astray* in the most positive, most critical and thus utopian sense.

11 Bibliography

Abzug, Robert H. *GIs Remember: Liberating the Concentration Camps.* Washington D.C.: National Museum of American Jewish Military History, 1994.

Achebe, Chinua. *Things Fall Apart.* London: Penguin Books, 1994.

Adorno, Theodor W. "Was Bedeutet Aufarbeitung Der Vergangenheit?" *Gesammelte Schriften. 10.2: Kulturkritik Und Gesellschaft II: Eingriffe, Stichworte, Anhang.* Frankfurt am Main: Suhrkamp, 1997. 555–572.

Agamben, Giorgio. *Sovereign Power and Bare Life.* Stanford, CA: Stanford University Press, 1995.

Agamben, Giorgio. *Remnants of Auschwitz: The Witness and the Archive.* Brooklyn, NY: Zone Books, 2002.

Ahmed, Sara. 'Black Feminism as Life-Line'. *Feministkilljoys*, 27 August 2013 https://feministkilljoys.com/2013/08/27/black-feminism-as-life-line/ (20 October 2021).

Aksenova, Marina. 'The Role of International Criminal Tribunals in Shaping the Historical Account of Genocide'. In *Law and Memory: Towards Legal Governance of History.* Ed. Uladzislau Belavusau and Aleksandra Gliszczyńska-Grabias. Cambridge: Cambridge University Press, 2017.

Alba, Avril. "'Here There Is No Why' – so Why Do We Come Here? Is a Pedagogy of Atrocity Possible?" *Holocaust Studies* 21.3 (2015): 121–138.

Alba, Avril. 'Lessons from History? The Future of Holocaust Education'. *A Companion to the Holocaust.* Ed. Simone Gigliotti and Hilary Earl. New York: Wiley, 2020. 599–617.

Alba, Avril, Jessica Barrett, and A. Dirk Moses. "The Holocaust and Human Rights: An Inclusive Critical Field for Museums." *Museum Galleries Australia Magazine* 27.1 (2018).

Aldrich, Robert. "Colonial Museums in a Postcolonial Europe". *African and Black Diaspora: An International Journal* 2.2 (2009): 137–156.

Alexander, Edward P., and Mary Alexander. *Museums in Motion. An Introduction to the History and Functions of Museums.* Lanham, MD: Rowman & Littlefield, 1979.

Allen-Paisant, Jason. "Unthinking Philosophy: Aimé Césaire, Poetry, and the Politics of Western Knowledge". *Atlantic Studies* 18.2 (2020): 193–216.

Allwork, Larissa. *Holocaust Remembrance between the National and the Transnational: The Stockholm International Forum and the First Decade of the International Task Force.* London; New York: Bloomsbury Academic, 2015.

Améry, Jean. *At the Mind's Limits.* Translated by Sidney Rosenfeld and Stella P. Rosenfeld. Bloomington: Indiana University Press, 1980.

Anderson, Benedict. *Imagined Communities.* 3rd edition. London; New York: Verso, 2006.

Anderson, Stephanie Blair. "The Stories Nations Tell: Historical Consciousness and the Construction of National Identity at the Canadian Museum for Human Rights." PhD Thesis, University of British Columbia, 2017.

Andreotti, Vanessa De Oliveira. "Postcolonial and Post-Critical 'Global Citizenship Education.'" *Education and Social Change: Connecting Local and Global Perspectives.* London: Bloomsbury, 2010.

Andreotti, Vanessa De Oliveira. *The Political Economy of Global Citizenship Education.* London; New York: Routledge, Taylor & Francis Group, 2014.

https://doi.org/10.1515/9783110788044-013

Andreotti, Vanessa De Oliveira. "The Educational Challenges of Imagining the World Differently". *Canadian Journal of Development Studies / Revue Canadienne d'études Du Développement* 37.1 (2016): 101–112.

Andreotti, Vanessa De Oliveira. "Education, Knowledge and the Righting of Wrongs." *Towards a Just Curriculum Theory: The Epistemicide.* Ed. João M. Paraskeva. New York: Routledge, 2017.

Andreotti, Vanessa De Oliveira, and Lynn Mario T. M. de Souza. *Postcolonial Perspectives on Global Citizenship Education.* Milton Park: Routledge, 2012.

Annan, Kofi. Action Plan to Prevent Genocide. UN Press Release, 07/04/2004. http://www.preventgenocide.org/prevent/UNdocs/KofiAnnansActionPlantoPreventGenocide7Apr2004.htm (21. November 2021).

Antweiler, Katrin. "Unlearning Prejudice Through Memory? Contemporary German Memory Politics and Human Rights Education." *Studia Territorialia* 19.2 (2019): 55–79.

Apsel, Joyce, and Amy Sodaro. *Museums and Sites of Persuasion: Politics, Memory and Human Rights.* New York: Routledge, 2019.

Arendt, Hannah. *The Origins of Totalitarianism.* New York: Harcourt, Brace and Co., 1951.

Arendt, Hannah. *The Human Condition.* Chicago: The University of Chicago Press, 1958.

Arendt, Hannah, *Nach Auschwitz.* Ed. Eike Geisel, and Klaus Bittermann. Berlin: Edition Tiamat, 1989.

Arendt, Hannah. *Men in Dark Times.* San Diego, CA: Harcourt, Brace & Company, 1995.

Arnold-de Simine, Silke. *Mediating Memory in the Museum: Trauma, Empathy, Nostalgia.* Houndmills, Basingstoke, Hampshire; New York, NY: Palgrave Macmillan, 2013.

Asad, Talal. Reflections of Violence, Law and Humanitarianism. *Critical Inquiry.* https://criticalinquiry.uchicago.edu/reflections_on_violence_law_and_humanitarianism/. 2015 (19 November 2021).

Asper Foundation. "Canadian Museum for Human Rights". https://asperfoundation.com/canadian-museum-for-human-rights/ (25. November 2021).

Assmann, Aleida. *Der lange Schatten der Vergangenheit: Erinnerungskultur und Geschichtspolitik.* Munich: C.H. Beck, 2006.

Assmann, Aleida. "The Holocaust – a Global Memory? Extensions and Limits of a New Memory Community". *Memory in a Global Age: Discourses, Practices and Trajectories.* Ed. Sebastian Conrad and Aleida Assmann. Basingstoke: Palgrave Macmillan, 2010. 97–119.

Assmann, Aleida. *Auf dem Weg zu einer europäischen Gedächtniskultur? Wiener Vorlesungen im Rathaus.* Vol. 161. Wiener Vorlesungen im Rathaus. Vienna: Picus, 2012.

Assmann, Aleida, and Peter Novick. "Europe: A Community of Memory?" *Bulletin of the German Historical Institute* 40 (2007): 11–38.

Assmann, Jan. *Das kulturelle Gedächtnis: Schrift, Erinnerung und politische Identität in frühen Hochkulturen.* Beck'sche Reihe 1307. Munich: Beck, 1992.

Assmann, Jan. "Zum Geleit". *Kontexte und Kulturen des Erinnerns: Maurice Halbwachs und das Paradigma des kollektiven Gedächtnisses.* Ed. Gerald Echterhoff, Martin Saar, and Jan Assmann. Theorie und Methode. Konstanz: UVK Verlagsgesellschaft, 2002. 7–11.

Assmann, Jan, and John Czaplicka. "Collective Memory and Cultural Identity". *New German Critique.* 65 (1995): 125–133.

Atkinson-Phillips, Alison. "Remembering Experience: Public Memorials Are Not Just about the Dead Anymore". *Memory Studies*, 27 May 2020.

Bajaj, Monisha. “Human Rights Education: Ideology, Location, and Approaches”. *Human Rights Quarterly* 33.2 (2011): 481–508.

Bajohr, Frank, and Michael Wildt. *Volksgemeinschaft. Neue Forschungen zur Gesellschaft des Nationalsozialismus.* Frankfurt am Main: S. Fischer, 2009.

Bajohr, Frank, Axel Drecoll, and John Lennon. *Dark Tourism: Reisen zu Stätten von Krieg, Massengewalt und NS-Verfolgung.* Berlin: Metropol, 2020.

Baker, Carrie N. “Making Missing and Murdered Indigenous Women and Girls Visible”. *Ms. Magazine.* https://msmagazine.com/2019/12/02/making-missing-and-murdered-indigenous-women-and-girls-visible/. 2 December 2019 (21 October 2021).

Bal, Mieke. “Telling, Showing, Showing Off”. *Critical Inquiry* 18.3 (1992): 556–594.

Bal, Mieke. *On Meaning-Making: Essays in Semiotics.* Salem: Polebridge Press, 1994.

Bal, Mieke. *Double Exposures: The Subject of Cultural Analysis.* Milton Park: Routledge, 1996.

Barkan, Elazar. *The Guilt of Nations: Resitituion and Negotiating Histories Injustices.* New York, NY: W. W. Norton & Company, 2000.

Barkan, Elazar, and Alexander Karn. *Taking Wrongs Seriously: Apologies and Reconciliation.* Stanford, CA: Stanford University Press, 2006.

Bauman, Zygmunt. *Modernity and the Holocaust.* Cambridge: Polity, 1989.

Baur, Joachim. *Museumsanalyse: Methoden und Konturen eines neuen Forschungsfeldes.* Bielefeld: Transcript, 2010.

Beevor, Antony. *The Second World War.* New York: Little, Brown and Co, 2012.

Bekerman, Zvi, and Michalinos Zembylas. “Some Reflections on the Links between Teacher Education and Peace Education: Interrogating the Ontology of Normative Epistemological Premises”. *Teaching and Teacher Education* 41 (2014): 52–59.

Belavusau, Uladzislau. “The Rise of Memory Laws in Poland: An Adequate Tool to Counter Historical Disinformation?” *Security and Human Rights* 29.1–4 (2018): 36–54.

Belavusau, Uladzislau, and Aleksandra Gliszczyńska-Grabias. *Law and Memory: Towards Legal Governance of History.* Cambridge: Cambridge University Press, 2017.

Bender, Jim. “400,000 Artifacts Dug up from Human Rights Museum Site”. *Winnipeg* Sun, 28 August 2013. https://winnipegsun.com/2013/08/28/400000-artifacts-dug-up-from-human-rights-museum-site (22 October 2021).

Benjamin, Walter. *The Arcades Project.* Edited by Howard Eiland and Kevin MacLaughlin. Cambridge, MA; London: Harvard University Press, 2002.

Bennett, Tony. *The Birth of the Museum: History, Theory, Politics.* London; New York, NY: Routledge, 1995.

Bennett, Tony. *Pasts beyond Memory: Evolution Museums Colonialism.* Museum Meanings. London; New York: Routledge, 2004.

Bennett, Tony. “MUSEUM, FIELD, COLONY: Colonial Governmentality and the Circulation of Reference”. *Journal of Cultural Economy* 2.1–2 (2009): 99–116.

Bennett, Tony. “Thinking (with) Museums: From Exhibitionary Complex to Governmental Assemblage”. *The International Handbooks of Museum Studies*, Volume I: Museum Theory. Ed. Sharon Macdonald and H. Rees Leahy. New York: John Wiley & Sons, 2015. 3–20.

Bennett, Tony. *Museums, Power, Knowledge: Selected Essays.* London; New York: Routledge, 2018.

Berek, Mathias. *Kollektives Gedächtnis und die gesellschaftliche Konstruktion der Wirklichkeit: Eine Theorie der Erinnerungskulturen.* Wiesbaden: Harrassowitz, 2009.

Bernhardt, Darren. “Winnipeg's 100-Year-Old Aqueduct Has Brought a Century of Hardship to Shoal Lake First Nation”. *CBC News*, 2 June 2019. https://www.cbc.ca/news/canada/manitoba/winnipeg-aqueduct-shoal-lake-100-years-1.5152678 (21 October 2021).

Bernstorff, Jochen von, and Philipp Dann. *The Battle for International Law: South-North Perspectives on the Decolonization Era*. Oxford: Oxford University Press, 2019.

Bevernage, Berber. “The Past Is Evil/Evil Is Past: On Retrospective Politics, Philosophy of History, and Temporal Manichaeism”. *History and Theory* 54.3 (2015): 333–352.

Bevernage, Berber. “Tales of Pastness and Contemporaneity: On the Politics of Time in History and Anthropology”. *Rethinking History* 20.3 (2016): 352–374.

Bevernage, Berber. “Narrating Pasts for Peace? A Critical Analysis of Some Recent Initiatives of Historical Reconciliation through ‘Historical Dialogue’ and ‘Shared History’”. *The Ethos of History*. Ed. Stefan Helgesson and Jayne Svenungsson. New York: Berghahn Books, 2018. 70–93.

Bhambra, Gurminder K. *Rethinking Modernity: Postcolonialism and the Sociological Imagination*. London: Palgrave Macmillan, 2007.

Bhambra, Gurminder K. *Connected Sociologies*. London: Bloomsbury Academic, 2014.

Biko, Steve. *I Write What I Like: A Selection of His Writings*. Johannesburg: Picador, 2017.

Blank, Melanie, and Julia Debelts. “Was Ist Ein Museum? Eine Metaphorische Complication.” *Museum zum Quadrat*, No. 9. Vienna: Turia + Kant, 2002.

Bloxham, Donald. *Genocide on Trial: War Crimes Trials and the Formation of Holocaust History and Memory*. Oxford; New York: Oxford University Press, 2001.

Bokova, Irina. “Foreword”. *Holocaust Education in a Global Context*. Ed. Karel Fracapane and Matthias Haß. Paris: UNESCO, 2014. 5–6.

Bond, Lucy, and Jessica Rapson. *The Transcultural Turn: Interrogating Memory between and beyond Borders*. Berlin, Boston: De Gruyter, 2014.

Bonilla-Silva, Eduardo. *Racism without Racists: Color-Blind Racism and the Persistence of Racial Inequality in America*. Lanham: Rowman & Littlefield Publishers, Inc, 2014.

Bose, Friedrich, et al. *Museum X: zur Neuvermessung eines mehrdimensionalen Raumes*. Berlin: Panama, 2011.

Bragato, Fernanda Frizzo, and Lewis R. Gordon. *Geopolitics and Decolonization: Perspectives from the Global South*. London; New York: Rowman & Littlefield International, 2018.

Breckenridge, Carol A., and Arjun Appadurai. “Museums Are Good to Think. Heritage on View in India”. *No Touching, No Spitting, No Praying: The Museum in South Asia*. Ed. Kavita Singh and Saloni Mathur, 2017. http://www.vlebooks.com/vleweb/product/openreader?id=none&isbn=9781351556248.

Bröckling, Ulrich. *Das Unternehmerische Selbst: Soziologie einer Subjektivierungsform*. Frankfurt am Main: Suhrkamp, 2007.

Bröckling, Ulrich, Susanne Krasmann, and Thomas Lemke. “From Foucault's Lectures at the Collège des France to Studies of Governmentality. An Introduction”. *Governmentality Current Issues and Future Challenges*. Ed. Ulrich Bröckling et al. London; New York, NY: Routledge, 2010. 1–33.

Brown, Karen, and François Mairesse. “The Definition of the Museum through Its Social Role”. *Curator: The Museum Journal* 61.4 (2018): 525–539.

Brown, Wendy. *Politics Out of History*. Princeton: Princeton University Press, 2001.

Brown, Wendy. “Neo-Liberalism and the End of Liberal Democracy”. *Theory & Event* 7.1 (2003).

Brown, Wendy. "'The Most We Can Hope For…': Human Rights and the Politics of Fatalism". *South Atlantic Quarterly* 103.2–3 (2004): 451–463.

Brown, Wendy. *Regulating Aversion: Tolerance in the Age of Identity and Empire.* Princeton; Oxford: Princeton University Press, 2006.

Brown, Wendy. *Power After Foucault.* Vol. 1. Oxford: Oxford University Press, 2009.

Brown, Wendy. *Undoing the Demos: Neoliberalism's Stealth Revolution.* New York: Zone Books, 2015.

Brumlik, Micha, Hajo Funke, and Lars Rensmann. *Umkämpftes Vergessen: Walser-Debatte, Holocaust-Mahnmal und neuere deutsche Geschichtspolitik.* Berlin: Hans Schiler & Mücke, 2000.

Brumlik, Micha. *Postkolonialer Antisemitismus? Achille Mbembe, die palästinensische BDS-Bewegung und andere Aufreger. Bestandsaufnahme einer Diskussion.* Hamburg: VSA, 2021.

Brunner, José, and Daniel Stahl. *Recht auf Wahrheit. Zur Genese eines neuen Menschenrechts.* Göttingen: Wallstein, 2016.

Budrytė, Dovile. "Memory and World Politics". *International Relations.* Oxford: Oxford University Press, 2020.

Burchell, Graham. "Peculiar Interests: Civil Society and Governing 'the System of Natural Liberty'". *The Foucault Effect: Studies in Governmentality: With Two Lectures by and an Interview with Michel Foucault.* Ed. Michel Foucault, Graham Burchell, Colin Gordon, and Peter Miller. Chicago: University of Chicago Press, 1991. 119–151.

Busby, Karen, Adam Muller, and Andrew Woolford. *The Idea of a Human Rights Museum.* Winnipeg: University of Manitoba Press, 2015.

Butler, Judith. *Frames of War: When Is Life Grievable?* London; New York: Verso, 2009.

CBC News. "Human Rights Museum Criticized at Public Meeting." *cbc.ca*, 7 December 2011 https://www.cbc.ca/news/canada/manitoba/human-rights-museum-criticized-at-public-meeting-1.1037046. (21 October 2021).

Carter, Jennifer. *The Rise of Human Rights Museology: The Evolving Relationship of Historical Memory and Rights Discourses in Holocaust and Human Rights Museums.* Unpublished Conference Paper. 2017.

Carter, Jennifer. "Museums and Justice". *Museum Management and Curatorship* 34.6 (2 November 2019): 541–543.

Carter, Jennifer, and Jennifer Orange. "The Work of Museums: The Implications of a Human Rights Museology". *FIHRM – Federation of International Human Rights Museums.* Liverpool, 2011. https://www.fihrm.org/wp-content/uploads/2017/07/JCarterJOrange-Paper-2011.pdf (19. November 2021).

Castro Varela, María do Mar. "Europa – Ein Gespenst geht um". *Europa: Entgrenzungen.* Ed. Gregor Maria Hoff. Innsbruck; Vienna: Tyrolia, 2015a. 49–82.

Castro Varela, María do Mar. "Integrationsregime und Gouvernementalität. Herausforderungen an interkulturelle/internationale soziale Arbeit". *Bildung, Pluralität und Demokratie Vol. 2.* Ed. Mechtild Gomolla et al. Hamburg: Helmut-Schmidt-Univ, 2015b. 66–83.

Castro Varela, María do Mar, and Barış Ülker. *Doing Tolerance: Urban Interventions and Forms of Participation.* Opladen; Berlin; Toronto: Barbara Budrich, 2020.

Castro Varela, María do Mar, and Nikita Dhawan. *Postkoloniale Theorie: Eine kritische Einführung.* Bielefeld: Transcript, 2014.

Cave, Alfred A. "Genocide in the Americas". *The Historiography of Genocide.* Ed. Dan Stone. Basingstoke; New York: Palgrave Macmillan, 2011. 273–296.

Césaire, Aimé, and Robin D. G. Kelley. *Discourse on Colonialism.* New York: Monthly Review Press, 2000.

Chakrabarty, Dipesh. *Provincializing Europe: Postcolonial Thought and Historical Difference.* Princeton, NJ: Princeton University Press, 2000.

Chatterjee, Partha. *The Black Hole of Empire: History of a Global Practice of Power.* Princeton, NJ: Princeton University Press, 2012.

Christensen, Amber. *Canadian Museum for Human Rights: Building a Historical Consciousness Through Omission.* York University, 2015. https://www.academia.edu/12306014/Canadian_Museum_for_Human_Rights_building_a_historical_consciousness_through_omission (19 November 2021).

Clifford, James. *Routes: Travel and Translation in the Late Twentieth Century.* Cambridge, MA: Harvard University Press, 1997.

Canadian Museum for Human Rights. *CMHR Releases Important Archaeology Findings: New Light Cast on Historic Role of The Forks*, 28 August 2013. https://humanrights.ca/news/cmhr-releases-important-archaeology-findings-new-light-cast-on-historic-role-of-the-forks (22 October 2021).

Canadian Museum for Human Rights. *News Release: CMHR works with Canadian War Museum to present "Peace" as first temporary exhibit*, 7 August 2014. https://humanrights.ca/news/cmhr-works-canadian-war-museum-present-peace-first-temporary-exhibit (19 November 2021).

Canadian Museum for Human Rights. *Teacher Guide* (2017). https://humanrights.ca/education.resources/search?collections=Human%20rights%20in%20times%20of%20conflict&languages=English&formats=Text ((19 November 2021).

Canadian Museum for Human Rights. "Public Service Announcement 4" (commercial), *YouTube*, uploaded by The Asper Foundation, 17 January 2017, https://www.youtube.com/watch?v=rc4WyDctiRo (19 November 2021).

Canadian Museum for Human Rights. *Our History.* https://humanrights.ca/about/our-history (19 November 2021).

Canadian Museum for Human Rights. *Galleries, https://humanrights.ca/exhibition/galleries* (19 November 2021).

Canadian Museum for Human Rights. *Be an Upstander.* https://humanrights.ca/virtual-field-trip/be-an-upstander (19 November 2021).

Content Advisory Committee. *Content Advisory Committee final report to the Canadian Museum for Human Rights*, 25 May 2010 [electronic resource]. https://publications.gc.ca/collections/collection_2011/mcdp-cmhr/NM104-1-2010-eng.pdf (19 November 2021).

Cook, Deborah. *Adorno, Foucault and the Critique of the West.* London; New York: Verso, 2018.

Coombes, Annie E. *Reinventing Africa: Museums, Material Culture, and Popular Imagination in Late Victorian and Edwardian England.* New Haven, CN; London: Yale University Press, 1994.

Coombes, Annie E. *Rethinking Settler Colonialism: History and Memory in Australia, Canada, Aotearoa New Zealand and South Africa.* Manchester: Manchester University Press, 2017.

Coulthard, Glen Sean. *Red Skin, White Masks: Rejecting the Colonial Politics of Recognition.* Minneapolis, MN: University of Minnesota Press, 2014.

Cox, Alicia. "Settler Colonialism". *obo in Literary and Critical Theory*, Jul. 26. 2017. https://www.oxfordbibliographies.com/view/document/obo-9780190221911/obo-9780190221911-0029.xml. (24 June 2022).

Coysh, Joanne. *Human Rights Education and the Politics of Knowledge*. London: Routledge, 2017.

Coysh, Joanne. "Exploring Power and Discourse in Human Rights Education". *Critical Human Rights, Citizenship, and Democracy Education. Entanglements and Regenerations*. Ed. Michalinos Zembylas and André Keet. London; New York: Bloomsbury Academic, 2018. 51–66.

Cruikshank, Barbara. *The Will to Empower: Democratic Citizens and Other Subjects*. Ithaca, NY: Cornell University Press, 1999.

Çubukçu, Ayça. "Thinking Against Humanity". *London Review of International Law* 5.2 (2017): 251–267.

Dallas Holocaust and Human Rights Museum. *Human Rights Wing*. https://www.dhhrm.org/exhibitions/human-rights-wing/. (21 October 2021).

David, Lea. "Against Standardization of Memory". *Human Rights Quarterly* 39.2 (2017): 296–318.

David, Lea. "Human Rights as an Ideology? Obstacles and Benefits". *Critical Sociology* 46.1 (2018): 37–50.

David, Lea. "The Emergence of the 'Dealing With the Past' Agenda: Sociological Thoughts on Its Negative Impact on the Ground". *Modern Languages Open* 1 (2020): 19.

David, Lea. *The Past Can't Heal Us: The Dangers of Mandating Memory in the Name of Human Rights*. Cambridge: Cambridge University Press, 2020.

Dàvila-Freire, Mela. "Museums of the Future: Between Promise and Damnation". *Das Museum der Zukunft: 43 neue Beiträge zur Diskussion über die Zukunft des Museums*. Ed. Joachim Baur and schnittpunkt. Bielefeld: Transcript, 2020. 105–108.

De Cesari, Chiara, and Ann Rigney. *Transnational Memory: Circulation, Articulation, Scales*. Berlin; Boston: De Gruyter, 2014.

de Certeau, Michel. *Heterologies: Discourse on the Other*. Minneapolis, MN: University of Minnesota Press (1986): 199–221.

de Certeau, Michel. *The Writing of History*. New York: Columbia Univ. Press, 1988.

DeGooyer, Stephanie, et al. *The Right to Have Rights*. London; Brooklyn, NY: Verso, 2017.

de Larrinaga, Miguel, and Marc G. Doucet. *Security and Global Governmentality. Globalization, Governance and the State*. Milton Park: Routledge, 2011.

Dean, Amber. "The CMHR and the Ongoing Crisis of Murdered or Missing Indigenous Women: Do Museums Have a Responsibility to Care?" *Review of Education, Pedagogy, and Cultural Studies* 37.2–3 (2015): 147–165.

Dean, Amber, and Angela Failler. "'An Amazing Gift'? Memory Entrepreneurship, Settler Colonialism and the Canadian Museum for Human Rights". *Memory Studies* 14. 2 (2019): 451–465.

Dean, Mitchell. *Governmentality: Power and Rule in Modern Society*. London; Thousand Oaks, CA: SAGE, 1999.

Dean, Mitchell *Governmentality. Power and Rule in Modern Society*. London: Sage, 2006.

Dean, Mitchell. *Governmentality. Power and Rule in Modern Society*. 2nd ed. Los Angeles; London; New Delhi; Singapore; Washington DC: Sage, 2010.

Department of Basic Education, Republic of South Africa. *Curriculum and Assessment Policy Statement – Grades 7–9: Social Sciences.* Pretoria: Department of Basic Education, 2011.

Department of Basic Education, Republic of South Africa. *National Curriculum Statements Grade R – 12.* Pretoria: Department of Basic Education, 2012. https://www.education.gov.za/Curriculum/NationalCurriculumStatementsGradesR-12.aspx. (22 October 2021).

Derrida, Jacques. *On Cosmopolitanism and Forgiveness.* London; New York: Routledge, 2001.

Derrida, Jacques. *Rogues: Two Essays on Reason.* Stanford, CA: Stanford University Press, 2005.

Dhawan, Nikita. *Decolonizing Enlightenment. Transnational Justice, Human Rights and Democracy in a Postcolonial World.* Opladen: Barbara Budrich, 2014.

Dhawan, Nikita. "Colonial Repercussions / Koloniales Erbe. Welcome Address" (2018). *YouTube*, uploaded by Akademie der Künste, https://www.youtube.com/playlist?list=PLfJugoeO9YFervitRNBaD8GJes9tiZhla.

Didi-Huberman, Georges, and Shane B Lillis. *Images in Spite of All: Four Photographs from Auschwitz.* Chicago: University of Chicago Press, 2012.

Didi-Huberman, Georges. *Bark.* Cambridge; London: The MIT Press, 2017.

Diner, Dan. "Ereignis und Erinnerung. Über Variationen historischen Gedächtnisses". *Shoah. Formen Der Erinnerung: Geschichte, Philosophie, Literatur, Kunst.* Ed. Nicolas Berg, Jess Jochimsen, and Bernd Stiegler. Munich: Fink, 1996. 13–31.

Diner, Dan. "Restitution and Memory: The Holocaust in European Political Cultures". *New German Critique.* 90 (2003): 36.

Diner, Dan. *Cataclysms: A History of the Twentieth Century from Europe's Edge.* Madison, WI: The University of Wisconsin Press, 2007a.

Diner, Dan. *Gegenläufige Gedächtnisse: Über Geltung und Wirkung des Holocaust.* Göttingen: Vandenhoeck & Ruprecht, 2007b.

Dladla, Ndumiso. "Blacks Could Be Racist: A Note on Historical Power". *HuffPost UK*, 3 April 2017. https://www.huffingtonpost.co.uk/ndumiso-dladla/blacks-could-be-racist-a-note-on-historical-power_a_22022517/ (22 October 2021).

Dladla, Ndumiso. "The Liberation of History and the End of South Africa: Some Notes towards an Azanian Historiography in Africa, South". *South African Journal on Human Rights* 34.3 (2018): 415–440.

Douzinas, Costas. *The End of Human Rights: Critical Legal Thought at the Turn of the Century.* Oxford; Portland, OR: Hart Pub., 2000.

Douzinas, Costas. *Human Rights and Empire: The Political Philosophy of Cosmopolitanism.* London; New York: Routledge, 2007.

Douzinas, Costas. "The Paradoxes of Human Rights". *Constellations* 19.2 (2013): 51–67.

Douzinas, Costas. "What Are Human Rights?". *The Guardian*, 18 March 2009. https://www.theguardian.com/commentisfree/libertycentral/2009/mar/18/human-rights-asylum (19 November 2021).

Douzinas, Costas, and Conor A. Gearty. *The Meanings of Rights. The Philosophy and Social Theory of Human Rights.* Cambridge: Cambridge University Press, 2014.

Du Bois, W. E. B. *The Oxford W.E.B. Du Bois.* Ed. H. L. Gates. New York: Oxford University Press, 2007.

Eccleshall, Robert. *English Conservatism Since the Restoration.* London: Routledge, 2002.

Echterhoff, Gerald, and Martin Saar. *Kontexte und Kulturen des Erinnerns: Maurice Halbwachs und das Paradigma des kollektiven Gedächtnisses.* Konstanz: UVK, 2002.

Eckel, Jan. *Die Ambivalenz des Guten: Menschenrechte in der internationalen Politik seit den 1940ern.* Göttingen; Bristol, CT: Vandenhoeck & Ruprecht, 2014.

Eid, Haitham. *Museum Innovation and Social Entrepreneurship: A New Model for a Challenging Era.* Milton Park: Routledge, 2019.

Elkana, Yehuda. The Need to Forget. *Ha'aretz*, 2 March 1988.

Ellis, David C. "On the Possibility of 'International Community'". *International Studies Review* 11. 1 (2009): 1–26.

Erll, Astrid. *Kollektives Gedächtnis und Erinnerungskulturen: Eine Einführung.* Stuttgart: Metzler, 2005.

Erll, Astrid. *Memory in Culture.* Basingstoke: Palgrave Macmillan, 2011.

Erll, Astrid, Ansgar Nünning, and Sara B. Young. *Cultural Memory Studies: An International and Interdisciplinary Handbook.* Berlin; New York: De Gruyter, 2008.

Eser, Patrick. "State of the Art in Memory Studies: An Interview with Andreas Huyssen". *Politika* (2018). https://www.politika.io/en/notice/state-of-the-art-in-memory-studies-an-interview-with-andreas-huyssen (21 October 2021).

Eslava, Luis. "The Moving Location of Empire: Indirect Rule, International Law, and the Bantu Educational Kinema Experiment". *Leiden Journal of International Law* 31.3 (2018): 539–567.

Eslava, Luis, and Sundhya Pahuja. "The State and International Law: A Reading from the Global South". *Humanity: An International Journal of Human Rights, Humanitarianism, and Development* 11.1 (2020): 118–138.

Europe-wide Global Education Congress. *Maastricht Declaration on Global Education* (2002). https://rm.coe.int/168070e540 (22 October 2021).

Failler, Angela. "Hope Without Consolation: Prospects for Critical Learning at the Canadian Museum for Human Rights". *Review of Education, Pedagogy, and Cultural Studies* 37.2–3 (2015): 227–250.

Failler, Angela, Peter Ives, and Heather Milne. "Introduction: Caring for Difficult Knowledge – Prospects for the Canadian Museum for Human Rights". *Review of Education, Pedagogy, and Cultural Studies* 37. 2–3 (2015): 100–105.

Fairweather, Ian S. "Colonialism and the Museum". *The International Encyclopedia of Anthropology.* Ed. Hilary Callan. New York: Wiley, 2018.

Falk, John H., and Lynn D. Dierking. *Learning from Museums: Visitor Experiences and the Making of Meaning.* Walnut Creek, CA: AltaMira Press, 2000.

Fanon, Frantz. *The Wretched of the Earth.* New York: Grove Press, Inc., 2001 [1963].

Fanon, Frantz. *Black Skin, White Masks.* Sidmouth: Pluto Press, 2008 [1952].

Fassin, Didier. *Humanitarian Reason. A Moral History of the Present.* Berkeley: University of California Press, 2012.

Fassin, Didier, and Richard Rechtman. *The Empire of Trauma: An Inquiry into the Condition of Victimhood.* Princeton; Oxford: Princeton University Press, 2009.

Federal Foreign Office. *Inaugural speech by Federal Foreign Minister Heiko Maas on 14 March 2018.* https://www.auswaertiges-amt.de/en/newsroom/news/bm-maas-amtsantritt/1792452. 2018 (25 October 2021).

Feldman, Ilana, and Miriam Ticktin, eds. *In the Name of Humanity: The Government of Threat and Care.* Durham: Duke University Press, 2010.

Ferencz, Benjamin. “Nuremberg Einsatzgruppen Case #9 Opening”. *YouTube*, uploaded by RobertHJacksCenter, 07 May 2018, https://www.youtube.com/watch?v=b67B-MoKG_o (25 November 2021).

Ferencz, Benjamin. “The 75th Anniversary of the Beginning of the Nuremberg Trials”. *YouTube*, uploaded by phoenix, 20. November 2020, https://www.youtube.com/watch?v=EWSqZAF5i-M (25 November 2021).

Findlen, Paula. “The Museum: Its Classical Etymology and Renaissance Genealogy”. *Grasping the World. The Idea of the Museum*. Ed. Donald Preziosi and Claire J. Farago. London New York: Routledge, Taylor & Francis Group, 2004.

Fine, Robert. “Crimes Against Humanity: Hannah Arendt and the Nuremberg Debates”. *European Journal of Social Theory* 3.3 (2000): 293 – 311.

Fischer, Torben, and Matthias N. Lorenz. *Lexikon Der ‘Vergangenheitsbewältigung’ in Deutschland: Debatten- Und Diskursgeschichte des Nationalsozialismus Nach 1945*. Bielefeld: Transcript, 2009.

Foucault, Michel. “The Archaeology of Knowledge”. *Social Science Information* 9.1 (1970): 175 – 185.

Foucault, Michel. “Orders of Discourse”. *Social Science Information* 10.2 (1971): 7 – 30.

Foucault, Michel, and Sherry Simon. “Nietzsche, Genealogy, History”. *Language, Counter-Memory, Practice: Selected Essays and Interviews*. Ed. Donald F. Bouchard. Ithaca, NY: Cornell Univ. Press, 1977.

Foucault, Michel. *The History of Sexuality. Volume 3: The Care of the Self*. New York: Pantheon Books, 1986.

Foucault, Michel. *The History of Sexuality*. New York: Vintage Books, 1990.

Foucault, Michel. “Interview with Michel Foucault”. *Power: The Essential Works of Michel Foucault 1954 – 1984*. Ed. J. Faubion, 239 – 240. New York: New Press, 2000.

Foucault, Michel. *Security, Territory, Population: Lectures at the Collège de France 1977 – 78*. Ed. Michel Senellart. Basingstoke: Palgrave Macmillan, 2007.

Foucault, Michel. *The Birth of Biopolitics: Lectures at the Collège de France, 1978 – 79*. Ed. Michel Senellart. Basingstoke: Palgrave Macmillan, 2010.

Fracapane, Karel, and Matthias Haß. *Holocaust Education in a Global Context*. Paris: United Nations Educational, Scientific and Cultural Organization, 2014.

Fraser, Nancy. “Foucault on Modern Power: Empirical Insights and Normative Confusions. *Praxis International*, Vol. 1, No. 3 (1981): 272 – 287.

Freedman, Richard. “Engaging with Holocaust Education in Post-Apartheid South Africa”. *Kaplan Center Occasional Paper Series*. 10 (2012).

Freedom House. Freedom in the World 2019. Highlights from Freedom House’s annual report on political rights and civil liberties. https://freedomhouse.org/sites/default/files/Feb2019_FH_FITW_2019_Report_ForWeb-compressed.pdf (25 November 2021).

Frehse, Lea. “Heiko Maas: Eine Reise mit vielen Botschaften”. *Die Zeit*, 27 March 2018, https://www.zeit.de/politik/ausland/2018-03/heiko-maas-israel-analyse-botschaften. (25 November 2021).

Fremuth, Michael Lysander. *Menschenrechte: Grundlagen und Rechtsdokumente*. Bonn: Bundeszentrale für politische Bildung, 2015.

Frevert, Ute. “Der jüngste Erinnerungsboom in der Kritik”. *Aus Politk und Zeitgeschichte*. https://www.bpb.de/apuz/27381/der-juengste-erinnerungsboom-in-der-kritik. 2003 (22 October 2021).

Friedländer, Saul. *Nazi Germany and the Jews, 1933–1945.* Abridged edition, New York: HarperCollins Publishers, 2009.

Friedman, Lawrence M. "Legal Culture and the Welfare State". *Dilemmas of Law in the Welfare State.* Ed. by Gunther Teubner. Berlin; New York: De Gruyter, 2011: 13–27.

Friedrich, Daniel. *Democratic Education as a Curricular Problem: Historical Consciousness and the Moralizing Limits of the Present.* London: Routledge, 2014.

Frieze, Donna-Lee. "New Approaches to Raphael Lemkin". *Journal of Genocide Research* 15.3 (2013): 247–252.

Gallas, Elisabeth. *"Das Leichenhaus der Bücher": Kulturrestitution und jüdisches Geschichtsdenken nach 1945.* Göttingen: Vandenhoeck & Ruprecht, 2013.

Gensburger, Sarah, and Sandrine Lefranc. *Beyond Memory: Can We Really Learn from the Past?* London: Palgrave Macmillan, 2020.

Gilbert, Shirli. "Nazism and Racism in South African Textbooks". *Holocaust Memory and Racism in the Postwar World.* Ed. Shirli Gilbert and Avril Alba. Detroit, MI: Wayne State University Press, 2019. 350–385.

Gilbert, Shirli, and Avril Alba. *Holocaust Memory and Racism in the Postwar World.* Detroit, MI: Wayne State University Press, 2019.

Gilroy, Paul. "Fanon and Améry". *Theory, Culture & Society* 27.7–8 (2010): 16–32.

Glowacka, Dorota. "'Never Forget'. Intersecting Memories of the Holocaust and the Settler Colonial Genocide in Canada". *Holocaust Memory and Racism in the Postwar World.* Ed. Shirli Gilbert and Avril Alba. Detroit, MI: Wayne State University Press, 2019.

Goldberg, Amos. "Ethics, Identity and Anti-Fundamental Fundamentalism: Holocaust Memory in the Global Age". *Marking Evil: Holocaust Memory in the Global Age.* Ed. Amos Goldberg and Haim Hazan. New York: Berghahn Books, 2015.

Gordon, Lewis R. *An Introduction to Africana Philosophy.* Cambridge, UK; New York: Cambridge University Press, 2008.

Gordon, Lewis R. "Shifting the Geography of Reason in an Age of Disciplinary Decadence". *TRANSMODERNITY: Journal of Peripheral Cultural Production of the Luso-Hispanic World* 1.2 (2011): 95–103.

Gordon, Lewis R. "Four Kinds of Invisibility from Euromodernity". TEDxUConn. YouTube, uploaded by TEDx Talks, 3 January 2019, https://www.youtube.com/watch?v=bW_G3-DwtQw (25 November 2021).

Gouws, Brenda. "Emotions in Holocaust Education – the Narrative of a History Teacher" *Yesterday and Today,* 2019: 47–79.

Gray, Mandi, and Karl Gardner. "(In) Visible Histories: Colonialism, Space and the Canadian Museum for Human Rights". *Annual Review of Interdisciplinary Justice Research, Visualizing Justice (IJR),* Volume 5 (2016). https://www.cijs.ca/volume-5.

Guterres, António. "The Highest Aspiration: A Call to Action for Human Rights". Secretary-General's remarks to the UN Human Rights Council, 24 February 2020. https://www.un.org/sg/en/content/sg/statement/2020-02-24/secretary-generals-remarks-the-un-human-rights-council-"the-highest-aspiration-call-action-for-human-rights-delivered-scroll-down-for-all-english (21. November 2021).

Gurney, Christabel. "'A Great Cause': The Origins of the Anti-Apartheid Movement, June 1959–March 1960". *Journal of Southern African Studies* 26.1 (2000): 123–144.

Güven, Ferit. *Decolonizing Democracy. Intersections of Philosophy and Postcolonial Theory.* Lanham: Lexington Books, 2015.

Haardt, Oliver F. R. "Das Grundgesetz im Strom der Zeit. Entstehung und zeitliche Verortung der deutschen Verfassungen von 1949". *Aus Politik und Zeitgeschichte* 16 – 17.67 (2019): 10 – 17.

Habermas, Jürgen. *The Postnational Constellation: Political Essays.* Translated by M. Pensky, Cambridge, NJ: The MIT Press, 2001.

Halbwachs, Maurice. *Das kollektive Gedächnis.* Stuttgart: Enke, 1991 [1967].

Halbwachs, Maurice. *Das Gedächnis und seine sozialen Bedingungen.* Berlin: Luchterhand, 1992 [1966].

Hall, Stuart. "The Neo-Liberal Revolution". *Cultural Studies* 25.6 (2011a): 705 – 728.

Hall, Stuart, and Paul du Gay. *Questions of Cultural Identity.* London: SAGE Publications Ltd, 2011b.

Hamm, Margot, et al. Haus der Bayerischen Geschichte, and Kloster Ettal. *Wald, Gebirg und Königstraum: Mythos Bayern: Katalog zur Bayerischen Landesausstellung 2018 in der Benediktinerabtei Ettal.* Lizenzausgabe. Regensburg: Friedrich Pustet, 2018.

Haraway, Donna. "Situated Knowledges: The Science Question in Feminism and the Privilege of Partial Perspective". *Feminist Studies* 14.3 (1988): 575 – 599.

Hankivsky, Olena, and Rita Kaur Dhamoon. "Which Genocide Matters the Most? An Intersectionality Analysis of the Canadian Museum of Human Rights." *Canadian Journal of Political Science / Revue Canadienne de Science Politique*, vol. 46, no. 4, 2013, pp. 899 – 920.

Hasselbach, Christoph. "Sophie Scholl und Anne Frank: Was haben NS-Opfer mit Corona zu tun?" *Deutsche Welle*, 25 November 2020, https://www.dw.com/de/sophie-scholl-und-anne-frank-was-haben-ns-opfer-mit-corona-zu-tun/a-55723380. (21 October 2021).

Henare, Amiria J. M. *Museums, Anthropology and Imperial Exchange.* New York: Cambridge University Press, 2005.

Hess, Sabine, et al. *Der lange Sommer der Migration.* Grenzregime III. Hamburg, Berlin: Assoziation A, 2017.

Heyd, David. "Ressentiment and Reconciliation. Alternative Responses to Historical Evil". *Justice in Time. Responding to Historical Injustice.* Ed. Lukas H. Meyer. Baden-Baden: Nomos, 2004.

Hirsch, Francine. "The Soviets at Nuremberg: International Law, Propaganda, and the Making of the Postwar Order." *The American Historical Review*, vol. 113, no. 3 (2008): 701 – 30.

Hirsch, Marianne. *The Generation of Postmemory: Writing and Visual Culture after the Holocaust.* New York: Columbia University Press, 2012.

Hodgkin, Katharine, and Susannah Radstone, eds. *Contested Pasts: The Politics of Memory.* London; New York: Routledge, 2003.

Holodomor Research and Education Consortium. *Holodomor Monuments in Canada. HREC Research.* https://education.holodomor.ca/introduction/holodomor-monuments/ (21 October 2021).

Hopgood, Stephan. *The Endtimes of Human Rights.* Ithaca, NY: Cornell University Press, 2013.

Horkheimer, Max, and Theodor Adorno. *Dialectic of Enlightenment: Philosophical Fragments.* Translated by Edmund Jephcott. Stanford, CA: Stanfort University Press, 2002.

Hunt, Lynn. *Inventing Human Rights: A His*tory. New York: Norton, 2007.

Huyssen, Andreas. "Present Pasts: Media, Politics, Amnesia". *Public Culture* 12.1 (2000): 21 – 38.

Huyssen, Andreas. “Natural Rights, Cultural Rights, and the Politics of Memory”. *E-Misférica* 6.2 (2010).

Huyssen, Andreas. “International Human Rights and the Politics of Memory. Limits and Challenges”. *Criticism* 53.4 (2011): 607–624.

Huyssen, Andreas. “Memory Culture and Human Rights. A New Constellation”. *Historical Justice and Memory.* Ed. Klaus Neumann and Janna Thompson. Madison, WI: The University of Wisconsin Press, 2015.

International Council of Museums. *History of ICOM.* https://icom.museum/fr/a-propos-de-licom/history-of-icom/ (21 October 2021).

International Council of Museums. *Museum Definition,* 24 August 2007. https://icom.museum/en/resources/standards-guidelines/museum-definition/ (21 October 2021).

International Council of Museums. *News: ICOM Announces the Alternative Museum Definition That Will Be Subject to a Vote,* 25 July 2019. https://icom.museum/en/news/icom-announces-the-alternative-museum-definition-that-will-be-subject-to-a-vote/ (21 October 2021).

International Holocaust Remembrance Alliance. *Our Structure.* https://www.holocaustremembrance.com/about-us/our-structure (21 October 2021).

International Holocaust Remembrance Alliance. *Why Teach About the Holocaust. https://www.holocaustremembrance.com/resources/educational-materials/why-teach-about-holocaust* (21 October 2021).

International Holocaust Remembrance Alliance. *Working Definitions and Charters. https://www.holocaustremembrance.com/resources/ihra-working-definitions-and-charters* (21 October 2021).

International Holocaust Remembrance Alliance. *International Memorial Museum Charter* (2016). https://www.holocaustremembrance.com/resources/working-definitions-charters/international-memorial-museums-charter (21 October 2021).

International Holocaust Remembrance Alliance. *One Year of Implementing the IHRA's Recommendations for Teaching and Learning about the Holocaust,* 9 December 2020. https://www.holocaustremembrance.com/news-archive/one-year-implementing-ihras-recommendations-teaching-and-learning-about-holocaust (10 December 2020).

Ishay, Micheline. *The History of Human Rights: From Ancient Times to the Globalization Era.* Berkeley, CA: Univ. of California Press, 2008.

Jaeger, Stephan. *The Second World War in the Twenty-First-Century Museum: From Narrative, Memory, and Experience to Experientiality.* Berlin; Boston: De Gruyter, 2020.

Janes, Robert R. “The Mindful Museum”. *Curator: The Museum Journal* 53.3 (2010): 325–338.

Jankélévitch, Vladimir. *Das Verzeihen: Essays Zur Moral Und Kulturphilosophie.* Ed. Ralf Konersmann. Frankfurt am Main: Suhrkamp, 2004.

Joas, Hans. *Die Sakralität der Person: Eine neue Genealogie der Menschenrechte.* Frankfurt am Main: Suhrkamp, 2011.

Joas, Hans. *Sind die Menschenrechte westlich?* Munich: Kösel, 2015.

Johannesburg Holocaust and Genocide Centre. *Learner Groups,* https://www.jhbholocaust.co.za/education/learner-groups/ (20 November 2021).

Johannesburg Holocaust and Genocide Centre. *Programme Menu,* https://jhbholocaust.co.za/wp-content/uploads/2018/06/Programme-menu-new2.pdf (20 November 2021).

Joseph, Jonathan. “Governmentality of What? Populations, States and International Organisations”. *Global Society* 23.4 (2009): 413–427.

Joseph, Jonathan. *The Social in the Global: Social Theory, Governmentality and Global Politics*. Cambridge, NJ: Cambridge University Press, 2012.

Judt, Tony. *Postwar: A History of Europe Since 1945*. New York: Penguin Books, 2006.

Jureit, Ulrike, and Christian Schneider. *Gefühlte Opfer: Illusionen der Vergangenheitsbewältigung*. Stuttgart: Klett-Cotta, 2010.

Kaiser, Wolfram, and Anette Homlong Storeide. “International Organizations and Holocaust Remembrance: From Europe to the World”. *International Journal of Cultural Policy* 24.6 (2018): 798–810.

Kalpagam, U. “Colonial Governmentality and the ‘Economy’”. *Economy and Society* 29.3 (2000): 418–438.

Karlsson, Klas-Göran. “Lessons at the Limits. On Learning Holocaust History in Historical Culture”. *Remembering the Holocaust in Educational Settings*. Ed. Andy Pearce. London; New York: Routledge Taylor & Francis Group, 2018.

Karn, Alexander. “Toward a Philosophy of Holocaust Education: Teaching Values without Imposing Agendas”. *The History Teacher* 45.2 (2012): 221–240.

Karn, Alexander. *Amending the Past: Europe’s Holocaust Commissions and the Right to History*. Madison, WI: The University of Wisconsin Press, 2015.

Karp, Ivan, and Corinne A. Kratz. *Museum Frictions: Public Cultures/Global Transformations*. Durham: Duke University Press, 2006.

Kazeem, Belinda. “Die Zukunft der Besitzenden. Oder fortwährende Verstrickungen in neokoloniale Argumentationsmuster”. *Das Unbehagen im Museum: Postkoloniale Museologien*. Ed. Belinda Kazeem, Charlotte Martinz-Turek, and Nora Sternfeld. Vienna: Turia + Kant, 2009. 43–60.

Kazeem, Belinda, Nicola Lauré Al-Samarai, and Peggy Piesche. “Museum. Raum. Geschichte: Neue Orte politischer Tektonik”. *Das Unbehagen im Museum: Postkoloniale Museologien*. Ed. Belinda Kazeem, Charlotte Martinz-Turek, and Nora Sternfeld. Vienna: Turia + Kant, 2009. 167–184.

Keet, Andre, and Nazir Carrim. “Human Rights and Curriculum Transformation-A Critical Reflection.” *Quarterly Review of Education and Training in South Africa*, 9.4 (2002): 28–36.

Keet, André. “Does Human Rights Education Exist?” *International Journal of Human Rights Education* 1.1 (2017).

Keet, André. “Crisis and Critique: Critical Theories and the Renewal of Citizenship, Democracy and Human Rights Education”. *Critical Human Rights, Citizenship and Democracy Education, Entanglements and Regenerations*. Ed. Michalinos Zembylas and André Keet. London; New York: Bloomsbury Academic, 2018.

Kerr, David. “The Council of Europe Charter on Education for Democratic Citizenship and Human Rights Education (EDC/HRE): And Its Implementation”. *Council of Europe*, 2013. https://ec.europa.eu/jrc/sites/default/files/cce2013rome_s2_the-council-of-europe-charter-on-edc-and-hre.pdf (22 October 2021).

Khatib, Sami. “Where the Past Was, There History Shall Be: Benjamin, Marx, and the ‘Tradition of the Oppressed’”. *Anthropology & Materialism*. Special Issue I (2017).

Kiersey, Nicholas J. “World State or Global Governmentality? Constitutive Power and Resistance in a Post-Imperial World”. *Global Change, Peace & Security* 20.3 (2008): 357–374.

Klüger, Ruth. *Still Alive. A Holocaust Girlhood Remembered.* New York: Feminist Press at CUNY, 2001.

Knell, Simon J., and Peter Aronsson. *National Museums. Studies from around the World.* London: Routledge, 2010.

Kranjc, Gregor. Memory Politics: "Ottawa's Monument to the Victims of Communism". *Active History*, 14 March 2015. http://activehistory.ca/papers/papershistory-papers-19/ (21 October 2021).

Kroh, Jens. *Transnationale Erinnerung: Der Holocaust im Fokus geschichtspolitischer Initiativen.* Frankfurt am Main: Campus, 2008.

Landwehr, Achim. "Die Kunst, sich nicht allzu sicher zu sein: Möglichkeiten kritischer Geschichtsschreibung". *Werkstatt Geschichte* 61 (2012): 7–14.

Landwehr, Achim. *Historische Diskursanalyse.* Frankfurt am Main: Campus, 2009.

Larner, Wendy, and William Walters (Eds.). *Global Governmentality: Governing International Spaces.* London: Routledge, 2004.

Lauren, Paul Gordon. *The Evolution of International Human Rights: Visions Seen.* Philadelphia, PA: University of Pennsylvania Press, 2011.

Lehrer, Erica. "Thinking through the Canadian Museum for Human Rights". *American Quarterly* 67.4 (2015): 1195–1216.

Lehrer, Erica T., Cynthia E. Milton, and Monica Eileen Patterson. *Curating Difficult Knowledge. Violent Pasts in Public Spaces.* Basingstoke; New York: Palgrave Macmillan, 2011.

Levy, Daniel, and Natan Sznaider. "Memory Unbound: The Holocaust and the Formation of Cosmopolitan Memory". *European Journal of Social Theory* 5.1 (2002): 87–106.

Levy, Daniel, and Natan Sznaider. *The Holocaust and Memory in the Global Age.* Philadelphia: Temple University Press, 2006.

Levy, Daniel, and Natan Sznaider. *Human Rights and Memory.* University Park, Pa: Pennsylvania State University Press, 2010.

Levi, Primo. *If This is a Man.* New YorK: Vintage, 1996.

Linenthal, Edward Tabor. *Preserving Memory: The Struggle to Create America's Holocaust Museum.* New York: Columbia University Press, 2001.

Logan, Tricia. "National Memory and Museums: Remembering Settler Colonial Genocide of Indigenous Peoples in Canada". *Remembering Genocide.* Ed. Nigel Eltringham. Remembering the Modern World. London: Routledge, 2014. 112–130.

Loomba, Ania. *Colonialism/Postcolonialism.* 3rd Edition, London: Routledge, 2015.

Lorde, Audre. "The Master's Tools Will Never Dismantle the Master's House." *Sister Outsider: Essays and Speeches.* Berkeley, CA: Crossing Press, 2007. 110–114.

Maas, Heiko. "Wer "Tod den Juden" ruft, gehört vor Gericht". *Der Spiegel*, 15 December 2017. https://www.spiegel.de/politik/deutschland/heiko-maas-will-holocaust-in-integrationskursen-abfragen-lassen-a-1183363.html (22 October 2021).

Macdonald, Sharon. *A Companion to Museum Studies.* Malden, MA: Blackwell Pub, 2010.

Macdonald, Sharon, and Helen Rees Leahy. *The International Handbooks of Museum Studies.* New York: John Wiley & Sons, 2015.

Macdonald, Sharon. "Is 'Difficult Heritage' Still 'Difficult'?: Why Public Acknowledgment of Past Perpetration May No Longer Be So Unsettling to Collective Identities". *Museum International* 67.14 (2016): 6–22.

McHoul, Alec, and Wendy Grace. *A Foucault Primer: Discourse, Power and the Subject.* London: Routledge, 1993.

MacNabb, Lauren. "Canadian Museum for Human Rights: A decade of building". *Global News*, 12 September 2014, https://globalnews.ca/news/785095/canadian-museum-for-human-rights-a-decade-of-building/. (21 October 2021).

Madlingozi, Tshepo. "Social Justice in a Time of Neo Apartheid Constitutionalism: Critiquing the Anti-Black Economy of Recognition, Incorporation and Distribution". *Stellenbosch Law Review* 28.1 (2017): 123–147.

Madlingozi, Tshepo. "Taking Stock of the South African Truth and Reconciliation Commission 20 Years Later: No Truth, No Reconciliation and No Justice". 3rd International Colloquium of the Instituto Humanitas at UNISINOS, Brazil, 2015.

Mamdani, Mahmood. *Citizen and Subject: Contemporary Africa and the Legacy of Late Colonialism.* Princeton, NJ: Princeton University Press, 1996.

Mannheim, Karl. *Ideology and Utopia: An Introduction to the Sociology of Knowledge.* London: Routledge & Kegan Paul Ltd, 1936.

Margalit, Avishai. *The Ethics of Memory.* Cambridge, MA; London: Harvard University Press, 2002.

Maron, Jeremy, and Clint Curle. "Balancing the Particular and the Universal: Examining the Holocaust in the Canadian Museum for Human Rights". *Holocaust Studies* 24. 4 (2018): 418–444.

Martini, Annaclaudia, and Dorina Maria Buda. "Dark Tourism and Affect: Framing Places of Death and Disaster." *Current Issues in Tourism*, vol. 23, no. 6, Routledge (2020): 679–692.

Mason, Rhiannon. "Cultural Theory and Museum Studies". *A Companion to Museum Studies.* Ed. Sharon Macdonald. Malden, MA: Blackwell Pub, 2010. 17–32.

May, Jackie. "Architect of Change 5: Lewis Levin on the Johannesburg Holocaust and Genocide Centre." *Twyg,* 26 October 2018. https://twyg.co.za/architect-of-change-5-lewis-levin-on-the-johannesburg-holocaust-and-genocide-centre/. (22 October 2021).

Mbembe, Achille. *Critique of Black Reason.* Durham: Duke University Press, 2017a.

Mbembe, Achille. *Politik der Feindschaft.* Berlin: Suhrkamp, 2017b.

McGhie, Henry A. "Museums and the Sustainable Development Goals: A How-to Guide for Museums, Galleries, the Cultural Sector and Their Partners". *Curating Tomorrow.* https://curatingtomorrow236646048.files.wordpress.com/2019/12/museums-and-the-sustainable-development-goals-2019.pdf. 2019 (21 October 2021).

McQuaid, Sara Dybris, and Sarah Gensburger. "Administrations of Memory: Transcending the Nation and Bringing Back the State in Memory Studies". *International Journal of Politics, Culture, and Society* 32.2 (2019): 125–143.

Mendel, Meron, and Astrid Messerschmidt. *Fragiler Konsens: Antisemitismuskritische Bildung in der Migrationsgesellschaft.* Frankfurt am Main; New York: Campus, 2017.

Meral, Ziya. "A Duty to Remember? Politcs and Morality of Remembering Past Atrocities". *International Political Anthropology* 5.1 (2012).

Messerschmidt, Astrid, and Karim Fereidooni. "Zwischen Feindschaft und Missachtung. emotionale Aufladungen im Umgang mit Rassismus und Antisemitismus in der Migrationsgesellschaft". *Politische Bildung mit Gefühl.* Ed. Anja Besand. Bonn: Bundeszentrale für politische Bildung, 2019. 352–365.

Mignolo, Walter D. "Citizenship, Knowledge, and the Limits of Humanity". *American Literary History* 18.2 (2006): 312–331.

Mignolo, Walter D. “Introduction: Coloniality of Power and de-Colonial Thinking”. *Cultural Studies* 21. 2–3 (2007): 155–167.

Mignolo, Walter D. “Epistemic Disobedience, Independent Thought and Decolonial Freedom”. *Theory, Culture & Society* 26.7–8 (2009): 159–181.

Mihr, Anja. “Why Holocaust Education Is Not Always Human Rights Education”. *Journal of Human Rights* 14.4 (2015): 525–544.

Mikel-Arieli, Roni. “Ahmed Kathrada in Post-War Europe: Holocaust Memory and Apartheid South Africa (1951–1952)”. *African Identities* 17. 1 (2019): 1–17.

Miller, Peter, and Nikolas Rose. “Political Power beyond the State. Problematics of Government”. *Governing the Present: Administering Economic, Social and Personal Life.* Cambridge Malden: Polity Press, 2009. 55–83.

Mills, Charles W. *The Racial Contract.* Ithaca, NY: Cornell Univ. Press, 1997.

Mills, Sara. *Discourse.* New Critical Idiom. London; New York: Routledge, 1997.

Miloševic, Ana, and Tamara Trošt. *Europeanisation and Memory Politics in the Western Balkans.* Cham: Palgrave Macmillan, 2021.

Modiri, Joel M. *Conquest, Constitutionalism and Democratic Contestations: South African Perspectives.* London New York: Routledge, Taylor & Francis Group, 2019.

Moses, A. Dirk. “The Canadian Museum for Human Rights: The ‘Uniqueness of the Holocaust’ and the Question of Genocide”. *Journal of Genocide Research* 14. 2 (2012): 215–238.

Moses, A. Dirk. *Empire, Colony, Genocide: Conquest, Occupation, and Subaltern Resistance in World History.* New York: Berghahn Books, 2008.

Moses, A. Dirk. “The German Catechism”. *Geschichte der Gegenwart* (23 May 2021a). https://geschichtedergegenwart.ch/the-german-catechism/ (22 October 2021).

Moses, A. Dirk. “The Pantomime Drama of Victims and Villains Conceals the Real Horrors of War”. *Aeon* (2021b). https://aeon.co/essays/the-pantomime-drama-of-victims-and-villains-conceals-the-real-horrors-of-war (22 October 2021).

Motshekga, Angie. “A country that does not know its History has no future”. Keynote Address by the Minister of Basic Education, Mrs Angie Motshekga, MP, at the 1st History RoundTable Discussion held at the DBE Conference Centre, Pretoria, 3 December 2015. https://www.gov.za/af/speeches/minister-angie-motshekga-1st-history-roundtable-discussion-3-dec-2015-0000 (21 November 2021).

Moyn, Samuel. *The Last Utopia: Human Rights in History.* Cambridge, MA: Belknap Press of Harvard Univ. Press, 2010.

Moyn, Samuel. *Human Rights and the Uses of History.* London; New York: Verso, 2014.

Moyn, Samuel. *Not Enough: Human Rights in an Unequal World.* Cambridge, MA: The Belknap Press of Harvard University Press, 2018.

Museen der Stadt Nürnberg. *From the Nuremberg Trials to the Memorial Nuremberg Trials – press release.* 21 November 2010 (25 November 2021).

Museum of Canadian Human Rights Violations. Facebook, https://de-de.facebook.com/MuseumofCanadianHumanRightsViolations/ (25 November 2021).

Mutua, Makau. *Human Rights NGOs in East Africa: Political and Normative Tensions.* Philadelphia, PA: University of Pennsylvania Press, 2009.

Mutua, Makau. *Human Rights Standards. Hegemony, Law and Politics.* Albany: State University of New York Press, 2016.

Nancy, Jean-Luc. “On Human Rights. Two Simple Remarks.” *The Meanings of Rights: The Philosophy and Social Theory of Human Rights.* Ed. Costas Douzinas and C. A. Gearty. Cambridge: Cambridge University Press, 2014. 15–20.

Narain, Seema. “International Relations Theory: Still a White Man’s Burden”. *E-International Relations.* https://www.e-ir.info/2020/05/29/international-relations-theory-still-a-white-mans-burden/. 29 May 2020 (22 November 2021).

Nates, Tali. “‘But, apartheid was also genocide … What about our suffering?’ Teaching the Holocaust in South Africa – opportunities and challenges.” *Intercultural Education* 21 (2010): 17–26.

Nates, Tali. “The Presence of the Past: Creating a New Holocaust & Genocide Centre of Educa-Tion and Memory in Post-Apartheid South Africa.” *Remembering the Holocaust in Educational Settings.* Ed. Andy Pearce. London; New York: Routledge Taylor & Francis Group, 2018.

Nates, Tali, “Holocaust Remembrance and Public Memorials: The Complexities and Challenges of Facing the Past” (Roundtable discussion), 10 October 2020, United Nations, Zoom event.

National Commission on Terrorist Attacks upon the United States. *The 9/11 Commission Report: Final Report of the National Commission on Terrorist Attacks Upon the United States (9/11 Report).* https://www.govinfo.gov/app/details/GPO-911REPORT/. 22 July 2004 (23 November 2021).

Neumann, Iver B., and Ole Jacob Sending. “‘The International’ as Governmentality”. *Millennium: Journal of International Studies* 35.3 (2007): 677–701.

Ngcaweni, Wandile, and Busani Ngobeni. *We Are No Longer at Ease: The Struggle for #FeesMustFall.* Auckland Park, South Africa: Jacana, 2018.

Nora, Pierre. *Zwischen Geschichte Und Gedächtnis.* Frankfurt/Main: Fischer, 2001.

Olick, Jeffrey K. “Collective Memory: The Two Cultures”. *Sociological Theory* 17.3 (1999): 333–348.

Olick, Jeffrey K. *The Politics of Regret: On Collective Memory and Historical Responsibility.* New York: Routledge, 2007.

Olick, Jeffrey K. “From Collective Memory to the Sociology of Mnemonic Practices and Products”. *Cultural Memory Studies.* Ed. Astrid Erll and Ansgar Nünning. Berlin: De Gruyter, 2008. 151–162.

Olick, Jeffrey K. “Sites of Memory Studies (Lieux Des Études de Mémoire)”. *International Handbook of Memory Studies.* Ed. Anna Lisa Tota and Trever Hagen. London; New York: Routledge, 2015. 41–52.

Ong, Aihwa. “Experiments with Freedom: Milieus of the Human”. *American Literary History* 18. 2 (2006): 229–244.

Overy, Richard. “Total War II: The Second World War”. *The Oxford History of Modern War.* Ed. Charles Townshend. Oxford; New York: Oxford University Press, 2005.

Öztürk, Cemal, and Gert Pickel. “Der Antisemitismus Der Anderen: Für Eine Differenzierte Betrachtung Antisemitischer Einstellungen Unter Muslim:Innen in Deutschland.” *Zeitschrift Für Religion, Gesellschaft Und Politik*, 2021.

Pabst, Kathrin. “From the ICOM Code of Ethics towards a New Museum Ethics?” *Towards New Relations between the Museum and Society.* Ed. Kathrin Pabst, Eva D. Johansen, and Merete Ipsen. Oslo: Vest-Agder Museum, 2016.

Palmater, Pamela. *Indigenous Nationhood: Empowering Grassroots Citizens.* Halifax: Fernwood, 2015.

Paul, Herman. *Hayden White: The Historical Imagination.* Cambridge, UK; Malden, MA: Polity, 2011.

Pearce, Andy, and Arthur Chapman. "Holocaust Education 25 Years on: Challenges, Issues, Opportunities". *Holocaust Studies* 23.3 (2017): 223–230.

Pearce, Susan M. *Interpreting Objects and Collections.* London; New York: Routledge, 1994.

Pedwell, Carolyn. *Affective Relations: The Transnational Politics of Empathy.* Basingstoke; New York: Palgrave Macmillan, 2014.

Perla, Armando. "Centering the Human in Human Rights Museology". *International Committee on Collecting (COMCOL) Newsletter.* 36. https://www.academia.edu/48761391/Centering_the_Human_in_Human_Rights_Museology. (22 October 2021).

Perugini, Nicola, and Neve Gordon. *The Human Right to Dominate.* New York: Oxford University Press, 2015.

Petersen, Tracey. *Teaching Humanity: Placing the Cape Town Holocaust Centre in a Post-Apartheid State.* Unpublished, University of the Western Cape, 2015.

Pethes, Nicolas. *Kulturwissenschaftliche Gedächtnistheorien.* Zur Einführung. Hamburg: Junius, 2013.

Petrunina, Liubov. "Museums: Towards the Social Institution". *The Future of Tradition in Museology Materials for a Discussion. Papers from the ICOFOM 42nd Symposium Held in Kyoto (Japan), 1–7 September 2019.* Ed. Kerstin Smeds. 2019, 133–137.

Phillips Casteel, Sarah. "Caribbean Literature and Global Holocaust Memory". *Holocaust Memory and Racism in the Postwar World.* Ed. Shirli Gilbert. Detroit, MI: Wayne State University Press, 2019. 240–272.

Porter, Catherine and Ian Austen. "'Racism Is Pervasive and Systemic'at Canada's Museum of Human Rights', Report Says". *The New York Times*, 6 August 2020, https://www.nytimes.com/2020/08/06/world/canada/museum-of-human-rights-discrimination.html. (22 October 2021).

Postone, Moishe. *Deutschland, die Linke und der Holocaust politische Interventionen.* Freiburg: Ca Ira, 2005.

Prottas, Nathaniel. "Interview with Nora Sternfeld, Author of Das Radikaldemokratische Museum". *Journal of Museum Education* 45.2 (2020): 210–220.

Przybilla, Olaf. "Von Schuld und Sühne". *Süddeutsche.de.* https://www.sueddeutsche.de/kultur/memorium-nuernberger-prozesse-von-schuld-und-suehne-1.1026660. 22 November 2020 (22 October 2021).

Puckett, Dan J. "The Jim Crow of All the Ages": The Impact of Hitler, World War II, and the Holocaust on Black Civil Rights in Alabama. *Holocaust Memory and Racism in the Postwar World.* Ed. Shirli Gilbert and Avril Alba. Detroit, MI: Wayne State University Press, 2019. 41–71.

Quaternary Consultants Ltd. *Final Report on Archeological Mitigation for the Canadian Museum for Human Rights at The Forks, Winnipeg, Manitoba. Submitted to PCL Constructors Canada Inc. On Behalf of Friends of the Canadian Museum for Human Rights.* https://www.theforks.com/about/history/bibliography/307/Archaeological-Mitigation-For-The-Canadian-Museum-For-Human-Rights-At-The-Forks-Winnipeg-Manitoba. July 2013 (22 October 2021).

Quijano, Aníbal. "Coloniality and Modernity/Rationality". *Cultural Studies* 21.2 – 3 (2007): 168 – 178.

Rabinow, Paul. *French Modern: Norms and Forms of the Social Environment.* Cambridge, MA.: MIT Press, 1989.

Radonić, Ljiljana. "Der Kampf um das Gedächtnis im Museum". *Gedächtnis im 21. Jahrhundert. Zur Neuverhandlung eines kulturwissenschaftlichen Leitbegriffs.* Bielefeld: Transcript, 2016. 137 – 158.

Radonić, Ljiljana, and Heidemarie Uhl. *Gedächtnis im 21. Jahrhundert. Zur Neuverhandlung eines kulturwissenschaftlichen Leitbegriffs.* Bielefeld: Transcript, 2016.

Rai, Shirin M. "(Re)defining empowerment, measuring survival" (Paper prepared for Workshop on Empowerment: Obstacles, Flaws, Achievements, Carleton University, Ottawa, May 2007), http://www.ethicsofempowerment.org/papers/RaiEmpowerment.pdf (22 October 2021).

Ramose, Mogobe B. "In Memoriam: Sovereignty and the 'New' South Africa". *Griffith Law Review* 16. 2 (2007): 310 – 329.

Ramose, Mogobe B. "An African Perspective on Justice and Race". *polylog.* https://them.polylog.org/3/frm-en.htm . 2001 (26 November 2020).

Rausch, Sahra. "'We'Re Equal to the Jews Who Were Destroyed. [...] Compensate Us, Too'. An Affective (Un)Remembering of Germany's Colonial Past?" *Memory Studies*, vol. 15, no. (2022): 418 – 435.

Reichel, Peter. *Politik mit der Erinnerung: Gedächtnisorte im Streit um die nationalsozialistische Vergangenheit.* Munich: Hanser, 1995.

Ricoeur, Paul. *Gedächtnis, Geschichte, Vergessen.* Munich: Fink, 2004.

Rieff, David. *In Praise of Forgetting: Historical Memory and Its Ironies.* New Haven: Yale University Press, 2016.

Rigney, Ann. "Cultural Memory Studies: Mediation, Narrative, and the Aesthetic". *Routledge International Handbook of Memory Studies.* Ed. Anna Lisa Tota and Trever Hagen. London; New York: Routledge, Taylor & Francis Group, 2015. 65 – 76.

Robinson, Helena. "Curating Good Participants? Audiences, Democracy and Authority in the Contemporary Museum". *Museum Management and Curatorship* 35. 5 (2020): 470 – 487.

Rose, Nikolas. "Government, Authority and Expertise in Advanced Liberalism". *Economy and Society* 22.3 (1993): 283 – 299.

Rose, Nikolas. *Powers of Freedom. Reframing Political Thought.* Cambridge: Cambridge Univ. Press, 2005.

Rose, Nikolas. "Still 'like Birds on the Wire'? Freedom after Neoliberalism". *Economy and Society* 46. 3 – 4 (2017): 303 – 323.

Rose, Nikolas, and Peter Miller. "Political Power beyond the State: Problematics of Government". *The British Journal of Sociology* 43.2 (1992): 173.

Rosenfeld, Alvin H. *The End of the Holocaust.* Bloomington: Indiana University Press, 2011.

Roth, John K., and Elisabeth Maxwell. *Remembering for the Future: The Holocaust in an Age of Genocide.* Basingstoke; New York: Palgrave, 2001.

Rothberg, Michael. *Multidirectional Memory. Remembering the Holocaust in the Age of Decolonization.* Stanford, CA: Stanford University Press, 2009.

Rothberg, Michael. "Remembering Back: Cultural Memory, Colonial Legacies, and Postcolonial Studies". *The Oxford Handbook of Postcolonial Studies.* Ed. Graham Huggan, Oxford: Oxford University Press, 2013. 359 – 379.

Rothberg, Michael, and Yasemin Yildiz. "Memory Citizenship: Migrant Archives of Holocaust Remembrance in Contemporary Germany". *Parallax* 17.4 (2011): 32–48.

Rushdie, Salman. *Midnight's Children.* New York: Random House Children's Books, 2006.

Rutazibwa, Olivia U. "Understanding Epistemic Diversity: Decoloniality as Research Strategy". *Bliss.* http://issblog.nl/2018/07/04/epistemic-diversity-understanding-epistemic-diversity-decoloniality-as-research-strategy/. 4 July 2018 (23 November 2021).

Rutazibwa, Olivia U. "What's There to Mourn? Decolonial Reflections on (the End of) Liberal Humanitarianism". *Journal of Humanitarian Affairs* 1.1 (2019): 65–67.

Said, Edward W. "Invention, Memory, and Place." *Critical Inquiry*, vol. 26, no. 2 (2000): 175–92. JSTOR, http://www.jstor.org/stable/1344120.

Said, Edward W. *Culture and Imperialism.* London: Vintage, 1994.

Sandell, Richard. *Museums, Moralities and Human Rights.* London: Routledge, 2016.

Sassen, Robyn. "'Dark Choreography' of the Johannesburg Holocaust and Genocide Centre". *Performance Research*, 25:2 (2020): 87–94.

Sayın, Yiğit, et al. "Land Law and Limits on the Right to Property: Historical, Comparative and International Analysis". *European Property Law Journal* 6.1 (2017): 4–52.

Schabas, William A. "Origins of the Genocide Convention: From Nuremberg to Paris". *Case Western Reserve Journal of International Law* 40. 1 (2007–2008): 35–55.

Schabas, William A. *Genocide in International Law: The Crime of Crimes* (2nd ed.). Cambridge: Cambridge University Press, 2009.

Schmid, Harald. "Europäisierung des Auschwitzgedenkens? Zum Aufstieg des 27. Januar 1945 als 'Holocaustgedenktag' in Europa." *Universalisierung des Holocaust? Erinnerungskultur und Geschichtspolitik in internationaler Perspektive.* Ed. Jan Eckel and Claudia Moisel Göttingen: Wallstein, 2008. 174–202.

Schoder, Angelika. *Die Globalisierung des Holocaust-Gedenkens. Die UN-Resolution 60/7 (2005). Themenportal Europäische Geschichte.* http://www.europa.clio-online.de/essay/id/fdae-1571. 2012 (22 October 2021).

Schoor, Kerstin, and Stefanie Schüler-Springorum (Eds.). *Gedächtnis und Gewalt: Nationale und transnationale Erinnerungsräume im östlichen Europa.* Göttingen: Wallstein, 2016.

Schwarzer, Marjorie. "Museum Studies at a Crossroads", *Museum*, January/February (2012).

Sciurba, Alessandra, and Filippo Furri. "Human Rights Beyond Humanitarianism: The Radical Challenge to the Right to Asylum in the Mediterranean Zone: Human Rights Beyond Humanitarianism". *Antipode* 50.3 (2017): 763–782.

Scott, David. "Colonial Governmentality". *Social Text.* 43 (1995): 191.

Scott, Joan W. *Feminism and History.* Oxford; New York: Oxford University Press, 1996.

Scott, Joan W. "Experience". *Feminists Theorize the Political.* Ed. Judith Butler and Joan W. Scott. New York: Routledge, 2013. 22–40.

Scott, Joan W. *In the Name of History.* Budapest; New York: Central European University Press, 2020.

Serequeberhan, Tsenay. "African Philosophy as the Practice of Resistance". *Journal of Philosophy: A Cross-Disciplinary Inquiry* 4. 9 (2009): 44–52.

Shalev, Avner. "Yad Vashem. The Holocaust Martyrs' and Heroes' Remembrance Authority." *Holocaust. Der nationalsozialistische Völkermord und die Motive seiner Erinnerung.* Ed. Burkhard Assmus. Berlin; Wolfratshausen: Edition Minerva, 2002.

Sharma, Ananya. Review – Routledge Handbook of Postcolonial Politics. *E-International Relations.* https://www.e-ir.info/2019/06/18/review-routledge-handbook-of-postcolonial-politics/. 18 June 2019 (23 November 2021).

Shubin, Vladimir. *The Hot 'Cold War': The USSR in Southern Africa.* London: Pluto Press, 2015.

Simon, Roger I. "The Terrible Gift: Museums and the Possibility of Hope without Consolation". *Museum Management and Curatorship* 21.3 (2006): 187–204.

Singh, Jyotsna G., and David D. Kim. "'Always on Top'? The 'Responsibility to Protect' and the Persistence of Colonialism". *The Postcolonial World.* London; New York, NY: Routledge, 2017. 308–324.

Slaughter, Joseph R. *Human Rights, Inc: The World Novel, Narrative Form, and International Law.* New York: Fordham University Press, 2007.

Small, Zachary. "A New Definition of "Museum" Sparks International Debate". *Hyperallergic.* http://hyperallergic.com/513858/icom-museum-definition/. 19 August 2019 (21 October 2021).

Smith, Laurajane, and Gary Campbell. "The Elephant in the Room: Heritage, Affect, and Emotion". *A Companion to Heritage Studies.* Ed. William Logan, Mairead Nic Craith, and Ullrich Kockel. Oxford: Wiley-Blackwell, 2015. 443–460.

Sodaro, Amy. *Exhibiting Atrocity: Memorial Museums and the Politics of Past Violence.* New Brunswick, NJ: Rutgers University Press, 2018.

Sommer, Gert, and Jost Stellmacher. *Menschenrechte Und Menschenrechtsbildung: Eine Psychologische Bestandsaufnahme.* Wiesbaden: VS Verlag für Sozialwissenschaften, 2009.

South African Government. *Human Rights Month 2019,* https://www.gov.za/Human RightsMonth2019 (22 October 2021).

South African History Online. "Sharpeville Massacre, 21 March 1960". https://www.sahistory.org.za/article/sharpeville-massacre-21-march-1960. (22 October 2021).

South African Holocaust and Genocide Foundation. *Annual Review 2013,* https://ctholocaust.co.za/wp-content/uploads/2021/09/SAHGFAnnualReview2013.pdf (22 October 2021).

Spivak, Gayatri C. "Righting Wrongs". *South Atlantic Quarterly* 103.2–3 (2004): 523–581.

Stein, Sharon, and Vanessa Andreotti. "Global Citizenship Otherwise". *Conversations on Global Citizenship Education. Perspectives on Research, Teaching, and Learning in Higher Education.* Ed. Emiliano Bosio. New York, NY: Routledge/Taylor & Francis Group, 2021. 13–36.

Sternfeld, Nora. *Kontaktzonen Der Geschichtsvermittlung: Transnationales Lernen über den Holocaust in der postnazistischen Migrationsgesellschaft.* Vienna: Zaglossus, 2013.

Sternfeld, Nora. "Das Museum deprovinzialisieren." *Body luggage: migration of gestures = migration von Gesten* [exhibition, Kunsthaus Graz, 24/09/2016–08/01/2017]. Ed. Steirischer Herbst et al. Graz; Berlin: Archive Books, 2016.

Stevick, Doyle. *How Does Education about the Holocaust Advance Global Citizenship Education?* UNESCO, 2018. https://unesdoc.unesco.org/ark:/48223/pf0000261969. 2018 (25 October 2021).

The Stockholm International Forum on the Holocaust. *Declaration of the Stockholm International Forum on the Holocaust.* 2000, https://www.holocaustremembrance.com/about-us/stockholm-declaration (25. November 2021)

Sznaider, Natan. *Gedächtnisraum Europa: Die Visionen des europäischen Kosmopolitismus. Eine jüdische Perspektive.* Bielefeld: Transcript, 2008.

Tagesschau. *@tagesschau. Twitter.* https://twitter.com/tagesschau/status/977919565681307648. 25 March 2018 (22 October 2021).

Tedeschini, Michele. "Human Rights as a Limit to Utopian Thinking?" *MenschenRechtsMagazin* 24.1/2 (2019): 12–23.

Teitel, Ruti G. *Transitional Justice.* Oxford: Oxford Univ. Press, 2000.

Teitel, Ruti G. *Humanity's Law.* New York, NY: Oxford University Press, 2011.

Teitel, Ruti G. *Globalizing Transitional Justice.* Oxford; New York, NY: Oxford University Press, 2016.

Terri-Anne, Teo, and Elisa Wynne-Hughes. *Postcolonial Governmentalities: Rationalities, Violences and Contestations.* London; New York: Rowman & Littlefield International, 2020.

Thorsteinson, Arni. *Report to the Minister of Canadian Heritage on the Canadian Museum for Human Rights,* 31 March 2008, https://publications.gc.ca/collections/collection_2008/ch-pc/CH4-133-2008E.pdf (25 November 2021).

Tibbitts, Felisa, and André Keet. "Curriculum Reform in Transitional Justice Environments: The South African Human Rights Commission, Human Rights Education and the Schooling Sector". *Globalisation, Human Rights Education and Reforms.* Ed. Sev Ozdowski and Joseph Zajda. 2017. Dordrecht: Springer Netherlands, 2017. 87–110.

Todorov, Cvetan. *Hope and Memory: Lessons from the Twentieth Century.* Princeton, NJ: Princeton Univ. Press, 2003.

Traverso, Enzo. *Geschichte als Schlachtfeld: Zur Interpretation der Gewalt im 20. Jahrhundert.* Nuremberg: Neuer ISP Verlag, 2014.

Truth and Reconciliation Commission of Canada. *Honouring the Truth, Reconciling for the Future: Summary of the Final Report of the Truth and Reconciliation Commission of Canada. http://epe.lac-bac.gc.ca/100/201/301/weekly_acquisition_lists/2015/w15-24-F-E.html/collections/collection_2015/trc/IR4-7-2015-eng.pdf.* 2015 (21 October 2021).

Tuck, Eve, and K. Wayne Yang. "Decolonization Is Not a Metaphor." *Decolonization: Indigeneity, Education & Society* 1.1 (2012): 1–40.

Tusa, Ann, and John Tusa. *The Nuremberg Trial.* London: Macmillan, 1984.

Uhl, Heidemarie. *Neuer EU-Gedenktag: Verfälschung der Geschichte? ORF.at.* https://sciencev1.orf.at/sciencev1.orf.at/science/uhl/156602.html. 21 August 2009 (21 October 2021).

Ukrainian Canadian Congress. *Historic Holodomor Bill Fast Tracked*, 27 May 2008, https://www.ucc.ca/2008/05/27/historic-holodomor-bill-fast-tracked/ (22 October 2021).

UNESCO. *Citizenship Education for the 21st Century.* Paris: United Nations Educational, Scientific and Cultural Organization, 1998.

UNSECO. *Education 2030: Incheon Declaration and Framework for Action for the implementation of Sustainable Development Goal 4: Ensure inclusive and equitable quality education and promote lifelong learning opportunities for all.* https://unesdoc.unesco.org/ark:/48223/pf0000245656. 2016 (22 October 2021).

UNESCO. *Education About the Holocaust and Preventing Genocide: A Policy Guide.* Paris: United Nations Educational, Scientific and Cultural Organization, 2017.

UNESCO. *International Holocaust Remembrance Day. UNESCO.* https://en.unesco.org/commemorations/holocaustremembranceday. 3 February 2021 (22 October 2021).

UNESCO press release. *UNESCO Brings Museums of the World Together to Reflect on Their Future'. UNESCO.* https://en.unesco.org/news/unesco-brings-museums-world-together-reflect-their-future. 15 March 2021 (22 October 2021).

United Nations Treaty Series. Constitution of the United Nations Educational, Scientific and Cultural Organisation. https://treaties.un.org/doc/Publication/UNTS/Volume%204/volume-4-I-52-English.pdf. 12 June 1947 (22 October 2021).

United Nations. *Agreement for the prosecution and punishment of the major war criminals of the European Axis. Signed at London, on 8 August 1945. United Nations Treaty Series.* https://www.un.org/en/genocideprevention/documents/atrocity-crimes/Doc.2_Charter%20of%20IMT%201945.pdf. 15 March 1951 (22 October 2021).

United Nations. *Address by Secretary-General Kofi Annan to the Stockholm International Forum in Stockholm, Sweden, on 26 January 2004 United Nations Secretary-General.* https://www.un.org/sg/en/content/sg/speeches/2004-01-26/address-secretary-general-kofi-annan-stockholm-international-forum. 26 January 2004 (21 October 2021).

United Nations. Resolution 60/7. Holocaust Remembrance. https://documents-dds-ny.un.org/doc/UNDOC/GEN/N05/487/96/PDF/N0548796.pdf?OpenElement. 1 Novemeber 2005 (21 October 2021).

United Nations. “General Assembly decides to designate 27 January as annual International Day of Commemoration to honour Holocaust victims”. *Meetings Coverage and Press Releases.* https://www.un.org/press/en/2005/ga10413.doc.htm. 11 January 2005 (25 October 2021).

United Nations. *Museums, Memorials and Memorialization after Atrocity – Communicating a Form of Ongoing Justice? https://media.un.org/asset/k1g/k1gjegp5zq.* 8 July 2020 (23 November 2021).

Van Rompuy, Herman. “Nobel Lecture by Herman Van Rompuy”. *NobelPrize.org.* https://www.nobelprize.org/prizes/peace/2012/eu/26124-european-union-eu-nobel-lecture-2012/. 2012 (25 October 2021).

Veracini, Lorenzo. *Settler Colonialism: A Theoretical Overview.* Houndmills, Basingstoke; New York: Palgrave Macmillan, 2011.

Vergo, Peter. *The New Museology.* London: Reaktion Books, 1989.

Villadsen, Kaspar. “Michel Foucault and the Forces of Civil Society”. *Theory, Culture & Society* 33.3 (2016): 3–26.

Walters, William. *Governmentality: Critical Encounters.* New York: Routledge, 2012.

Weeks, Eric. “Forging an Identity in Bronze: Nation-Building Through Ottawa's Memorial Landscape”. *Études Canadiennes / Canadian Studies.* 78 (2015): 49–75.

Weinberg, Teddy. *Baldwin's Understanding of the Holocaust'. Jewish Herald-Voice* (2012). https://jhvonline.com/baldwins-understanding-of-the-holocaust-p12358-157.htm. (22 November 2021).

Weitz, Eric D. *A World Divided: The Global Struggle for Human Rights in the Age of Nation-States.* Princeton, NJ: Princeton University Press, 2019.

Welsh, Jennifer. “The Responsibility to Protect: Dilemmas of a New Norm”. *Current History* 111.748 (2012): 291–298.

Welzer, Harald, Sabine Moller, and Karoline Tschuggnall. *Opa war kein Nazi: Nationalsozialismus und Holocaust im Familiengedächtnis.* Frankfurt am Main: Fischer Taschenbuch, 2002.

Werker, Bünyamin. *Gedenkstättenpädagogik im Zeitalter der Globalisierung. Forschung, Konzepte, Angebote.* Münster: Waxmann, 2016.

Werle, Gerhard. "Von der Ablehnung zur Mitgestaltung: Deutschland und das Völkerstrafrecht". *Völkerrecht als Wertordnung. Common Values in International Law: Festschrift für Christian Tomuschat.* Ed. Pierre-Marie Dupuy and Christian Tomuschat. Kehl am Rhein: N.P. Engel, 2006. 655–669.

White, Hayden. *The Content of the Form: Narrative Discourse and Historical Representation.* Baltimore: Johns Hopkins University Press, 1990.

White, Hayden. *Tropics of Discourse: Essays in Cultural Criticism.* Baltimore: Johns Hopkins Univ. Pr, 2003.

White, Hayden. "Reflections on 'Gendre' in the Discourses of History". *New Literary History: A Journal of Theory & Interpretation* 40.4 (2009).

White, Hayden. "The Stakes of Narrative. Historical Truth, Estrangement and Disbelief." *Probing the Ethics of Holocaust Culture.* Ed. Claudio Fogu, Wulf Kansteiner, and Todd Samuel Presner. Cambridge, Massachusetts: Harvard University Press, 2016.

Whyte, Jessica. "Human Rights: Confronting Governments? Michel Foucault and the Right to Intervene". *New Critical Legal Thinking. Law and the Political.* Ed. Matthew Stone, Illan Rua Wall, and Costas Douzinas. Abingdon; New York, NY: Routledge, 2012. 11–31.

Whyte, Jessica. "Human Rights after October". *Overland* 228 (2017).

Whyte, Jessica. *The Morals of the Market: Human Rights and the Rise of Neoliberalism.* Brooklyn: Verso Books, 2019.

Willaert, Thijs. "Postcolonial Studies after Foucault: Discourse, Discipline, Biopower, and Governmentality as Travelling Concepts". PhD Thesis, Justus-Liebig-Universität Giessen, 2013.

Williams, Peter. *Memorial Museums. The Global Rush to Commemorate Atrocities.* London; New York: Bloomsbury Publishing, 2007.

Witcomb, Andrea. "Understanding the Role of Affect in Producing a Critical Pedagogy for History Museums". *Museum Management and Curatorship* 28.3 (2013): 255–271.

Wüstenberg, Jenny. *Civil Society and Memory in Postwar Germany.* Cambridge: Cambridge University Press, 2017.

Wynter, Sylvia. "The Ceremony Must Be Found: After Humanism". *Boundary 2* 12. 3 (1984): 19.

Wynter, Sylvia. *Do Not Call Us Negroes: How Multicultural Textbooks Perpetuate Racism.* San Francisco, CA: Aspire, 1992.

Wynter, Sylvia. "No Humans Involved: An Open Letter to My Colleagues." *Forum H.H.I. Knowledge for the 21st Century* 1.1 (1994): 42–73.

Young, James Edward. *The Texture of Memory: Holocaust Memorials and Meaning.* New Haven, CT: Yale Univ. Press, 1993.

Young, James Edward. *At Memory's Edge. After-Images of the Holocaust in Contemporary Art and Architecture.* New Haven, CT: Yale Univ. Press, 2000.

Zabalueva, Olga. "Museology and Museum-making: Cultural Policies and Cultural Demands", *ICOFOM Study Series*, 46 (2018): 231–247.

Zembylas, Michalinos, and André Keet. *Critical Human Rights, Citizenship and Democracy Education, Entanglements and Regenerations.* London; New York: Bloomsbury Academic, 2018.

Zentgraf, Henrike. "'Nürnberg' in Vergangenheit und Gegenwart". *Aus Politik und Zeitgeschichte* 63.25–26 (17 June 2013): 8–14.

Zerubavel, Evitar. *Time Maps. Collective Memory and the Social Shape of the Past.* Chicago: Univ. of Chicago Press, 2004.

Zolkos, Magdalena. "Jean Améry's Concept of Resentment at the Crossroads of Ethics and Politics". *The European Legacy* 12.1 (2007): 23–38.

Index of Names

https://doi.org/10.1515/9783110788044-014

www.ingramcontent.com/pod-product-compliance
Lightning Source LLC
LaVergne TN
LVHW050955080826
845145LV00006B/1507

* 9 7 8 3 1 1 1 6 2 7 1 1 3 *